The Coming Jesus and the Anthropocene

The Coming Jesus
and the Anthropocene

RYAN LAMOTHE

CASCADE *Books* • Eugene, Oregon

THE COMING JESUS AND THE ANTHROPOCENE

Copyright © 2024 Ryan LaMothe. All rights reserved. Except for brief quotations in critical publications or reviews, no part of this book may be reproduced in any manner without prior written permission from the publisher. Write: Permissions, Wipf and Stock Publishers, 199 W. 8th Ave., Suite 3, Eugene, OR 97401.

Cascade Books
An Imprint of Wipf and Stock Publishers
199 W. 8th Ave., Suite 3
Eugene, OR 97401

www.wipfandstock.com

PAPERBACK ISBN: 978-1-6667-5885-6
HARDCOVER ISBN: 978-1-6667-5886-3
EBOOK ISBN: 978-1-6667-5887-0

Cataloguing-in-Publication data:

Names: LaMothe, Ryan, author.

Title: The coming Jesus and the Anthropocene / Ryan LaMothe.

Description: Eugene, OR: Cascade Books, 2024. | Includes bibliographical references and indexes.

Identifiers: ISBN 978-1-6667-5885-6 (paperback). | ISBN 978-1-6667-5886-3 (hardcover). | ISBN 978-1-6667-5887-0 (ebook).

Subjects: LCSH: Sovereignty. | Alienation (Philosophy). | Global Warming—Political aspects. | Global Warming—Philosophy. | Theology. | Jesus Christ.

Classification: BT695.5 L35 2024 (print). | BT695.5 (epub).

VERSION NUMBER 02/16/24

Scripture quotations are taken from the New Revised Standard Version Bible, copyright © 1989 National Council of the Churches of Christ in the United States of America. Used by permission. All rights reserved worldwide.

Always for Cyn
and
Marcos McPeek Villatoro and Robert Dykstra

Contents

Acknowledgments | ix

   Introduction | 1

1 Civilization, Scripture, and the Rise and Artifice of Sovereignty | 11

2 Climate Calamities: Iterations and Consequences of Western Sovereignty | 48

3 Sovereignty's Ontological Chasm and Its Psychosocial Dynamics | 86

4 The Emergence of a Philosophical/Theological Explanation and "Remedy" for the Ontological Rift/Alienation: Sin and Salvation | 111

5 A Coming Radical Jesus for the Anthropocene | 140

Bibliography | 181
Subject Index | 197
Names Index | 207

Acknowledgments

Books written by AI machines will no longer need to include acknowledgments, except perhaps to their anonymous creators. Human authors, however, are indebted to numerous people, often too many to acknowledge. For those whom I have overlooked, my sincerest apologies. Over the last few years, I have had opportunities to test out some of the ideas in these chapters in varied venues, such as Princeton Seminary's Jacob Neumann Lecture, a series of three lectures on climate change at Fordham University, three lectures at the National Psychological Association for Psychoanalysis and Appalachian Psychoanalytic Society, and a keynote address at the International Conference of Practical Theologians in Seoul. Since I straddle more than one discipline, I have benefited from face-to-face and virtual conversations with and support from Robert Dykstra, Nancy Ramsay, Bruce Rogers-Vaughn, Carrie Doehring, Panu Pihkala, Pamela McCarroll, Phil Helsel, Heidi Park, Jaco Hamman, Kirk Bingaman, Phil Zylla, as well as psychoanalysts Claire Steinberger, Tony Pipolo, Hattie Myers, Susan Kassouf, Kurt Jacobsen, and David Morgan. Many thanks for their interest in my ideas and for their comments about them. A special thanks to Lewis Rambo who served as editor of *Pastoral Psychology* for over three decades. Lewis was an active supporter of my work. I also offer deep-felt thanks to K. C. Hanson. Since my first book with Cascade Books, he has enthusiastically supported my multidisciplinary forays into political theology, philosophy, and psychoanalysis. I recall sending him a proposal for this book late Friday afternoon months ago. Since it was late, I was hoping to hear within a week or two that he had received the proposal. Instead, I noticed an email from him within the hour, indicating that he wanted me to write this book for Cascade Books with the proviso that the board agreed, which they later did. I am grateful for his support and for the opportunity to share my ideas with others. Editors have copyeditors, who painstakingly scour the manuscript, offering corrections and alterations. Jeremy Funk deserves my thanks for his attention to detail and his editorial suggestions, and I recognize that any remaining errors are mine. Heartfelt thanks also go to Mary Jeanne Schumacher and Cindy Geisen for their editorial corrections and comments on this and other works. Cindy, over the months, frequently offered relevant sources for my consideration, which I gratefully included. Let me also mention my gratitude for Cindy's patience during times when I am preoccupied with research and writing. This book, in my view, represents past and present voices of people concerned about the well-being of a biodiverse Earth and its inhabitants. These voices provide solace and encouragement to care in the midst of facing a direr future.

Introduction

> Only through sustained thought, or attention, to the world and others can we locate the sources of oppression and how they ripple across our lives.[1]
>
> The future of humanity depends on the existence today of the critical attitude.[2]
>
> The present period is one of those when everything that seems normally to constitute a reason for living dwindles away, when one must, on pain of sinking into confusion or apathy, call everything in question again... We are living through a period bereft of a future. Waiting for that which is to come is no longer a matter of hope, but of anguish.[3]
>
> Whether we are prepared to embark on a painful intellectual journey to discover the parameters of reconciling history and nature is the question of this generation.[4]

I have an hour commute to work that takes me through the rolling hills of southern Indiana—hills that have their origin in the last Ice Age. In the spring, there are mornings when the sweat of the Earth clings stubbornly to the hillsides as the sun rises, and herds of deer or an

---

1. Zaretsky, *Subversive Simone Weil*, 80.
2. Wolin, *Politics and Vision*, 231.
3. Simone Weil in Zaretsky, *Subversive Simone Weil*, 80.
4. Deloria, *God Is Red*, 59.

occasional fox, coyote, or hawk appear in the fields. In the winter, at times, mists freeze and turn the trees white and the dawn reveals a magical world of glistening trees. During an afternoon last October, the fall leaves were surprisingly vivid, providing a rich tableau of varied hues of yellow, red, and green. Experiencing these beautiful landscapes cannot be captured but only approached in prose and poetry. Even paintings or pictures, however good, must concede their limitations.

Thirty years ago, these experiences would have included a sense of gratitude, awe, and pleasure. This is true today, except in the last ten years, I am also aware of eco-sorrow and a pang of eco-guilt.[5] The sorrow emerges from the realization that the trajectory of climate change is dire,[6] not only for human beings, but for millions of other species.[7] And the remorse rises in the recognition that I, despite my attempts to recycle, drive a hybrid, plant trees, and so forth, contribute to this trajectory—a trajectory that seems unstoppable. There is, in other words, a sense of anguish intertwined with experiences of beauty—an anguish that comes from the realization that we face a bleak future.

As many readers know, we are in the midst of what Paul Crutzen and Edward Stoermer[8] called the "Anthropocene Age."[9] While there is some

---

5. There has been a great deal written about eco-emotions. See Comtesse et al., "Ecological Grief as a Response"; Cunsolo and Landman, eds., *Mourning Nature*; Cunsolo and Ellis, "Ecological Grief as a Mental Health Response"; Cunsolo et al., "Ecological Grief and Anxiety"; Macy, "Working through Environmental Despair"; Pihkala, "Eco-Anxiety"; Pihkala, "Toward a Taxonomy"; Pihkala, "Religious Communities"; Taylor, "Anxiety Disorders."

6. For a summary of the research on climate change see LaMothe, *Pastoral Care*. For those interested in more scientific data regarding global warming, I suggest the following websites: *Intergovernmental Panel on Climate Change 2023* (https://www.ipcc.ch/?__cf_chl_tk=B6kJ9fhVaHc4ZD_Jky3zL1c8Hpry3Iboqelkltm_Lho-1679382216-0-gaNycGzNCWU); NASA, *Global Climate Change 2023* (https://climate.nasa.gov). There are also United Nations reports that are compiled by climate scientists from around the world. I add here that Pentagon and CIA reports indicate that there will be more political upheaval and violence within and between nations as resources become scarce as a result of climate change (see Davenport, "Pentagon Signals Security Risks"). While the reports do not take into consideration the sufferings of other species, we can safely predict that other species will be negatively impacted by climate change and human violence.

7. Klein, *This Changes Everything*; Kolbert, *Sixth Extinction*; LaMothe, *Radical Political Theology*; Wilson, *Future of Life*.

8. Crutzen and Stoermer, "Anthropocene.'"

9. Jason Moore (see Moore, "Name the System!") prefers the term "Capitalocene Era" because, he argues, capitalism is the primary culprit in global warming. While there is much to be said for this term, I will use the more common Anthropocene Era, in part because it is more inclusive of the many human factors causing climate change

controversy over this term, it does alert us to the specter of mass extinctions as a result of an uninhabitable Earth. The growing public recognition of ecological crises over the last forty years has led scientists of varied persuasions to seek solutions,[10] however fantastical, or to imagine and work toward escaping a degraded planet and residing on other orbs.[11] In the meantime, researchers in the human sciences have noted the significant rise of eco-anxiety, eco-despair, eco-sorrow, and the like among young people, who will face the brunt of climate disasters.[12] Some political philosophers, psychoanalysts, and theologians, recognizing the dangers and sufferings associated with climate change, have turned their critical attention to the varied social-political, economic, and religious sources of our troubled and destructive relation to other species and the Earth with the aim of finding ways of living that are ecologically sustainable.[13] As Clayton Crockett argues, "we need to experiment radically with new ways of thinking and living, because the current [Western] paradigm is in a state of exhaustion, depletion, and death."[14] This book is also a step in that direction.

While concerned theologians and philosophers have offered varied critiques of the sources of climate change and offered constructive responses,[15]

---

and species extinctions. I also recognize that this term carries its own controversies, especially considering that not all human beings are implicated in the rise of the climate emergency. Nevertheless, human activity is the source of the current rise in global warming.

10. John Bellamy Foster, *Return of Nature*, explores the historical roots of socialism and ecological concerns in the late nineteenth century. Activists like William Morris recognized that capitalism was degrading the environment. Unfortunately, Morris's (and others') concerns went unheeded by the media, politicians, and public for decades.

11. See Elon Musk aiming for Mars so humanity is not a single planet species (https://www.cnbc.com/2020/03/09/spacex-plans-how-elon-musk-see-life-on-mars.html).

12. See Ágoston et al., "Identifying Types of Eco-Anxiety"; Crandon et al., "Social-Ecological Perspective"; Barnett, *Mourning in the Anthropocene*.

13. Clinebell, *Ecotherapy*; Graham, *Care of Persons, Care of Worlds*; Helsel, "Loving the World"; McCarroll, "Listening"; Hoggett, "Governance"; Hoggett, ed., *Climate Psychology*; Keller, *Political Theology of the Earth*; Miller-McLemore, "Climate Violence"; Orange, *Climate Crisis*; Weintrobe, ed., *Engaging with Climate Change*; Weintrobe, *Psychological Roots*.

14. Crockett, *Radical Political Theology*, 165.

15. In this book I will not be delving into the literature associated with what I would call nihilistic or antihumanist responses to the climate emergency. Many of the proponents of these responses or forms of living believe that the extinction of human beings will be better for the survival and flourishing of other species. This may be the case, but there are some significant problems with these views. There is the tendency to lump all human beings into a category of being destructive to the Earth and other species. There have been indigenous peoples who have lived sustainably for thousands of years.

they "have not gone far enough in challenging doctrines of God that situate God outside or above creation and humans over animals and nature."[16] Moreover, as Pamela McCarroll points out, philosophical and theological renditions of human flourishing are not "uncontested" ends: these ends often exclude other species.[17] Moreover, human exceptionalism and anthropocentrism lies at the core of much of the scientific, philosophical, and theological discourse regarding climate change.[18] This, I believe, bolsters Crockett's argument that we must find new ways of thinking and living. This is why I consider the Western paradigm to include Abrahamic traditions and their apparatuses,[19] which are imbricated in Western political philosophies and theologies. As political theorist Carl Schmitt recognized, "all significant concepts of the modern theory of the state are secularized theological concepts."[20] To my mind, this insight means we cannot separate dominant Western religious traditions from political or economic theories, which is not to overlook distinctions between them. Rather, we must acknowledge that the current paradigm, which is in a state of exhaustion, depletion, and death, requires a critical and constructive examination of the Abrahamic traditions as a necessary step for moving toward new ways of thinking about and relating to other species and the Earth. The first four chapters of this book are aimed at a critical exploration of the problems within Western Abrahamic traditions and philosophies, while the last chapter offers a way of reimagining forms of living that renders Western political and religious apparatuses inoperative.

Before saying more about the coming chapters, I offer a few comments about the climate emergency, as well as some caveats and clarifications. Over

---

Many human beings alive today grew up in "civilizations" built on market societies largely responsible for our global climate woes, but even within these societies some human beings live sustainably. Instead of antihumanism as a response, perhaps it would be better to be anti-capitalist, anti-imperialist, and anti-nationalist. See Benatar, *Better Never to Have Been*; Kirsch, *Revolt against Humanity*; McCormack, *Ahuman Manifesto*.

16. Miller-McLemore, "Climate Violence," 361.
17. McCarroll, "Listening," 37.
18. Miller-McLemore, "Climate Violence."

19. For Giorgi Agamben, the term "apparatus" refers to "a set of practices, bodies of knowledge, measures and institutions that aim to manage, govern, control, and orient—in a way that purports to be useful—the behaviors, gestures, and thoughts of human beings." Referencing Foucault, Agamben writes that "in a disciplinary society, apparatuses aim to create—through a series of practices, discourses, and bodies of knowledge—docile, yet free, bodies that assume their identity and their 'freedom' as subjects" (Agamben, *Potentialities*, 13, 19). The apparatuses associated with Christianity include its attending theologies, narratives, and rituals.

20. Brown, *Walled States*, 59.

the last few years, the discourse regarding climate change has increasingly shifted to climate emergency, as the window closes for keeping the climate from exceeding a rise of 1.5 degrees Celsius. Another shift in climate discourse is the move from attempting to stop this rise to finding ways to adapt to and become more resilient in the face of current and inevitable climate disasters (rising seas, desertification, increasingly powerful and destructive weather events, and so forth). I am more inclined to ascribe to the idea of a climate emergency. As with any emergency, we not only need to consider how to stop or drastically slow our current trajectory, but also to reimagine our ways of relating to other-than-human species and the Earth. To do this, we must identify the apparatuses that have contributed to our ecologically destructive forms of living (mainly in market societies). And while I do think climate resiliency is important, it can lull people into thinking that this strategy is going to work in the long term—even as we continue our harmful relations to other species and the Earth. Only so much resiliency is possible in the face of global extinctions. The collapse of insect populations and fish populations, for instance, will make Earth uninhabitable for human beings.[21]

What has also been interesting in the shifts in discourse around climate change is the decline in the mention of climate deniers. To be sure, some people continue to deny climate change or to deny that human beings have a role in it, yet these individuals are becoming as common and as relevant as members of The Flat Earth Society. This said, there continues to be significant political-economic resistance in the US and elsewhere toward coordinated climate action, whether this is coordination and cooperation between political parties or between nations. For instance, the global north, especially the United States, China, and Russia, have placed and are creating substantial obstacles to reduce greenhouse gas emissions, while countries of the global south are already struggling with the effects of climate change. While many political leaders interfere with efforts to reduce greenhouse gas emissions, it is important to understand the macro systems that themselves serve as significant obstacles to climate action. So, while I am critical of Abrahamic traditions, I also include critiques of other related macro systems, such as capitalism, nationalism, and imperialism—systems that shape subjectivities and behaviors that are detrimental to living sustainably.

By focusing on systemic, intersecting apparatuses of sovereignty, capitalism, nationalism, and imperialism and their perpetuating the ontological rift between human beings and other-than-human species, I make a number of large generalizations. This view from one hundred thousand feet, if

---

21. See Wallace-Wells, *Uninhabitable Earth*.

you will, can help provide an overall picture, though it can also result in missing some details. Nevertheless, in thousands of ways, we consciously and unconsciously internalize the ideas, beliefs, and values, of the religious, cultural, political, and economic apparatuses at work around us. In short, our subjectivity, relations, and behaviors are shaped by these apparatuses. Given this premise, I will endeavor to provide particular illustrations of this in the coming chapters, especially in Chapter 3.

Let me add a few other clarifications. I am confident that readers will already be convinced that human beings and other-than-human species face a terrifying future as a result of climate change. And it is for this reason that I am not going to spend time addressing the data or depicting current and possible future disasters associated with climate change. My assumption is that readers will already have some knowledge of how dire the climate emergency is. I also wish to make clear that the critical analysis seen in the next four chapters does not connote the abject failure of the Abrahamic traditions and Western political philosophies vis-à-vis our relations to other species and the Earth. There is a great deal of wisdom in these traditions, though my focus is on their Achilles' heel. In addition, it is important to note that within these traditions there have been a few philosophers and theologians who have advocated for our caring for other species and the Earth, though these voices have largely been drowned out by the dominant, anthropocentric voices.[22] It is also important to mention, since the idea was broached in the previous sentence, that for decades I have been a political pastoral theologian and pastoral psychotherapist. A central concept that bridges these disciplines is "care." Given that "care" undergirds much of my work in general, and this book in particular, it is important to briefly discuss how I am using this term.

Care theorists from varied disciplines have written about the notion of care and its relation to politics over the last five decades.[23] It is not necessary

---

22. Plutarch, Porphyry, Bentham, Schopenhauer, Sedgewick, Singer, and Nussbaum are philosophers who demonstrate concern for the suffering of other species and human beings' unjust treatment of other species. From the religious side, we could include Saint Francis of Assisi and Pierre Teilhard de Chardin. This said, I think it is safe to say that the preponderance of Western philosophies and theologies simply omit other species from discussions regarding politics and justice.

23. See Bubeck, *Care, Gender, and Justice*; Engster, *Heart of Justice*; the Care Collective (Chatzidakis, et al.), *Care Manifesto*; Groys, *Philosophy of Care*; Hamington, *Embodied Care*; Held, *Ethics of Care*; Helsel, *Pastoral Power*; LaMothe, *Care of Souls, Care of Polis*; Oliner and Oliner, *Toward a Caring Society*; Ramsay, "Compassionate Resistance"; Robinson, *Globalizing Care*; Robinson, *Ethics of Care*; Rogers-Vaughn, *Caring for Souls*; Rumscheidt, *No Room for Grace*; Sevenhuijsen, *Citizenship*; Tronto, *Moral Boundaries*; Tronto, *Caring Democracy*; Zúñiga, *Pluralist Politics*.

to delve into these discussions, but it is essential to offer a definition of care, while recognizing that there are different scholarly definitions, and that care varies depending on one's cultural location and time period. Briefly, care is everything we do to help individuals, families, communities, and societies to (1) meet their vital biological, psychosocial, and existential or spiritual needs; (2) develop or maintain basic capabilities with the aim of human flourishing; (3) facilitate participation in the polis's space of appearances; and (4) maintain a habitable environment for human beings and other species. While this definition, on its face, appears to privilege human flourishing, our flourishing cannot be attained without a habitable environment. This means that we must consider the needs and capacities of other-than-human beings. Implicit here is the idea that care, as a political concept, must include the well-being of other species, because the polis depends on a viable Earth. While other-than-human species lack political agency, they are part of political life. In saying this, I am not simply saying that we must take care of other species because our survival depends on it. This is true, but I contend that there is a categorical command to care for the singularities of living beings and nonexistents,[24] whether they are human or otherwise. I want to move away from the proclivity of Western anthropocentrism and narcissism and closer to a kind of care that is not merely dependent on our survival.

I add to the definition of care by suggesting that care necessarily involves shared critical and constructive analyses of the ways religious, political, economic, and social structures (and their accompanying narratives and practices) and governing authorities meet or fail to meet the four features of the definition above. Ideally, as political philosopher Sheldon Wolin writes, "the state [and its leaders] . . . govern for the good of the entire community and not serve primarily the interests of a particular class or group."[25] "The political," he continues, "means the common well-being is the end and the definition of what is authentic political action."[26] Political ideals are needed, but Wolin knew well the necessity of maintaining a critical stance toward political, economic, religious, and social systems, and leaders, because, more often than not, the state's apparatuses and its leaders fail to govern for the good of all residents. Historically, they have overlooked or denied the needs of other species. Indeed, as Max Horkheimer presciently commented, "The

---

24. I am using the term "singularity" to refer to our capacity to recognize and respect the uniqueness of each living creature—human and other-than-human. An implication of this is plurality. Plurality is an essential feature of life, including political life. See Arendt, *Human Condition*; Zúñiga, *Pluralist Politics*.

25. Wolin, *Politics and Vision*, 247.

26. Wolin, *Politics and Vision*, 248.

future of humanity depends on the existence today of the critical attitude."[27] I have argued elsewhere that a critical stance is a spiritual practice, which in the midst of the Anthropocene Age is particularly needed.[28] This critical attitude, in my view, is for the sake of (1) examining systemic apparatuses that contribute to the sufferings of human beings and other species and (2) finding ways to foster structures, systems, and relations that promote care—care for other human beings, other-than-human species, and the Earth.

A final comment. I mentioned above two hats I wear, namely, political pastoral theologian and pastoral psychotherapist. Each embraces a similar approach, which is to begin with the question, What is going on? When encountering experiences of oppression and marginalization, political pastoral theologians seek to diagnose or grasp the experiences of suffering and their social, political, religious, and economic sources. Similarly, pastoral psychotherapists who encounter the suffering of individuals, couples, and families attempt to understand their experiences and what has contributed to them.[29] An accurate diagnosis, while not definitive, is necessary for the development of effective interventions. The first four chapters of this book are diagnostic, while the last chapter points in the direction of a remedy.

With this said, let me briefly outline the coming chapters. Chapter 1 tells the story of the marriage of civilization and sovereignty some six millennia ago. The chapter briefly depicts the origins of the rise of civilization and unpacks its meaning and its inherent proclivity to set itself against what is deemed to be uncivilized, primitive, or barbaric. Western civilization, it is then argued, developed in concert with religious and philosophical notions of sovereignty as essential to human political belonging. Sovereignty's attributes, dynamics, and contradictions are identified. The aim in this chapter is to begin a critique of civilization and sovereignty with the eventual aim, in the last chapter, of offering a theological reimaging of the nonsovereignty of God and human beings.

Chapter 2 furthers the diagnosis, contending that nationalism, imperialism, capitalism, and some forms and practices of science are all shoots of the same source, namely, the rhizome of sovereignty's epistemologies

---

27. Wolin, *Politics and Vision*, 231.

28. LaMothe, "Raising Amos."

29. I do see these two disciplines as distinct, yet interrelated. So, a pastoral psychotherapist is interested in understanding the social, political, and economic sources of persons' sufferings. This is evident in the work of psychiatrist Frantz Fanon, who argued that therapy aims (a) "to 'consciousnessize' [the patient's] unconscious, to no longer be tempted by a hallucinatory lactification," and (b) "to enable [the patient] to choose an action with respect to the real source of the conflict, i.e., the social structure" (Fanon, *Black Skin, White Masks*, 80).

and its accompanying apparatuses. They undergird civilization and forms of life that are wedded to power over Othered human beings, more-than-human species, and the Earth. I recognize that each of these iterations of sovereignty is distinct, but they are rooted in and depend on notions and apparatuses of sovereignty and its attending epistemologies. It is important to recognize the intersectionality of these systems because they are implicated in fostering forms of life that are, in the end, destructive to the planet[30] by undermining the dwelling and well-being of human beings and other species. If we focus on simply one or two systems, we will overlook the connectedness of these systems to many others and so will unwittingly collude in the overall continuance of environmental degradation. More positively, by acknowledging the connectivity and rootedness of most Western systems in sovereignty and its apparatuses, we might begin to imagine forms of life that eschew illusions of human superiority and the inferiority of other species. We could develop ways of living that reject relations of subordination and subjugation. We might foster forms of life rooted in epistemologies that recognize and respect the singularities of all species. These inoperative forms of life will be considered in the last chapter.

Sovereignty and its iterations give rise to the ontological rift between human beings and more-than-human beings. This rift is evident in and produced by Western political philosophies, which are themselves implicitly rooted in Abrahamic scriptures and political theologies. Chapter 3 explores this rift by depicting its psychosocial dynamics and functions. This discussion deepens our understanding of the destructiveness wrought by humanity in Western societies toward other species, and Western humanity's psychosocial resistances to change. In addition, this chapter sets the stage for the next chapter's discussion of the theologies that explain and offer an ontological remedy for alienation and destructiveness, while mystifying and unwittingly legitimating and producing the ontological rift and its illusions.

Chapter 4 argues that the rise of the ontological rift accompanied experiences of existential alienation. Religions of civilization provided theological explanations of and remedies for these experiences of alienation. I will argue that (Western) philosophical and theological explanations for experiences of alienation and attending remedies function to distract and mystify the real sources of alienation. In the meantime, they perpetuate, if not reproduce, sovereignty, the ontological rift between human beings and "Nature," and experiences of alienation. Put another way, Western philosophies and Israelite traditions (and later Christian and Islamic scriptures) emerged in the midst of the rise of civilization and the attending belief in

---

30. Gardner, *Perfect Moral Storm*.

the necessity of sovereignty for human dwelling, which accompanied the creation of the ontological rift and experiences of alienation. These traditions provided explanations for these experiences, which included varied remedies that obscured the real sources of our collective dis-ease.

The analysis of the first four chapters provides the foundation for a theological reimagining of the central figure of Christian thought and practice. In this final chapter, I discuss the radical coming Jesus for the Anthropocene. In this discussion I reconceptualize traditional theological concepts like sin and salvation, which are imbricated in theologies of sovereignty, and I reimagine religious practices/rituals. The coming Jesus, I argue, represents diverse ways of living that render inoperative the apparatuses of sovereignty and the ontological rift, and so generate relations wherein human beings: (1) accept existential insignificance and impermanence, (2) acknowledge and respect the singularities of other species, (3) reject the illusions of human superiority and nonhuman inferiority and attending relations of subordination and subjugation, and (4) embrace the categorical command to care for other human beings, other species, and the Earth despite the bleak future of the climate emergency.

Let me end with a return to my commute to work. My experiences of beauty of the southern Indiana landscape, which I and other inhabitants call home, carry with them my awareness of the fragility and impermanence of life on this tiny planet in the vastness of this one galaxy amid untold millions of other galaxies. Impermanence is foundational to the very experience of beauty (and love), as still-life artists have long recognized. Attending the experience of beauty and its underlying existential impermanence is our capacity to assign significance. The hills, trees, plants, and animals, while impermanent, are necessarily significant to me, for without that attribution there would be no experience of beauty. We have the capacity to designate significance, against the background of existential insignificance. In other words, attributing significance is fleeting, impermanent; yet attributing significance to this world is necessary for experiencing beauty. Experiences of beauty also attend our capacity to *care about* what we construct as significant. Truly, the challenge for the Anthropocene is caring *for* the Earth and its inhabitants, regardless of how bleak the future may be for life.

1

Civilization, Scripture, and the Rise and Artifice of Sovereignty

---

[T]he political body of the West hides a dangerous pathology.[1]

There are two forces in this world that propel our lives in opposite directions: the first is the power over life, and the second is the power of life.[2]

Most human beings are fascinated with origin stories, whether we are talking about a particular group of people or simply children wanting to know their own beginnings. We want to know how we came to be and where we come from. These stories secure our sense of individual and collective identity, as well as our diachronic and synchronic sense of significance. There are also origin stories about the beginning of civilization, and these stories often have varied uses or functions besides identity and significance. Thomas Hobbes's dystopic imaginative story of the origins of human life serves to explain the necessity of sovereignty for civilization, while also assuaging, in my view, his terror of the very idea of anarchy. For Hobbes, life would be nasty, brutish, and short

---

1. Kishik, *Power of Life*, 25.
2. Kishik, *Power of Life*, 100.

without a ruler, a leviathan who maintains social stability by the threat of political violence. Civilization, we have come to believe, depends on a ruler; otherwise, we would descend in violent chaos.[3] I suspect Hobbes wanted to strike fear into readers so that they, too, would accept a social contract that necessarily depends on a leviathan to enforce it.

By contrast, Jean-Jacques Rousseau had a decidedly different origin story vis-à-vis civilization.[4] He believed that in our "natural state" before civilization human beings lived in harmony with each other and Nature. Once civilization emerged, with its preoccupation with property and class, there was conflict, violence, and loss of freedom. Consider the last line of his *Discourse on the Origin of Inequality* wherein he observes that it seems to be a law of Nature "that the privileged few should gorge themselves with superfluities, while the starving multitude are in want of the bare necessities of life."[5] Turning Hobbes on his head, Rousseau asserts it is civilization's leviathans that we should fear.

In the twentieth century, Sigmund Freud told a different origin story regarding civilization, and he told it for different reasons. Freud argued that "the principal task of civilization . . . is to defend us against nature,"[6] which is a perennial task since he was under no illusion "that nature has already been vanquished."[7] It is "Nature" we should fear, because of its cruelty and indifference. Freud also had another story, not too dissimilar from Hobbes's. In Freud's *Totem and Taboo*, for example, it is obvious that patriarchal sovereignty is unquestioned and unquestionable. The origins of civilization emerge from the rule of the father, and when the father is killed by his sons, the sons end up ruling, which essentializes and universalizes both the origins of political violence vis-à-vis civilization and the necessity of a ruler for human belonging. Freud's story has other functions. This imaginary tale inscribes patriarchal sovereignty into Freud's formulation of psychosocial development, which is yet another way to universalize and essentialize patriarchal sovereignty as necessary for human belonging.

For Freud, Rousseau, Hobbes, and other political thinkers in the West, the issue of "sovereignty was reduced to the question of who within the political order was invested with certain powers, and the *very threshold of the political order was never called into question*."[8] For instance, in a monar-

3. Ryan, *On Politics*, 297.
4. Grayling, *History of Philosophy*, 250–59.
5. Rousseau, *Discourse on the Origin of Inequality*, 47.
6. Freud, *Future of an Illusion*, 15.
7. Freud, *Future of an Illusion*, 15.
8. Agamben, *Homo Sacer*, 12 (italics added).

chy the focus is on the king or queen rather than on critiquing the political system whose basis is the idea of sovereignty, which means political belonging cannot be reimagined. In short, origin stories vis-à-vis the political order have proclaimed the necessity of sovereignty for our being able to dwell together.

Origin stories, in one sense, reveal not the origins of human dwelling per se, but our anxieties related to existential vulnerability, precarity, uncertainty, insignificance, and impermanence.[9] Philosopher and novelist Iris Murdoch remarked that human beings "are anxiety-ridden animals. Our minds are continually active, fabricating an anxious, usually self-preoccupied, often falsifying veil which partially conceals the world."[10] Murdoch believed as well that it was fair to ask political philosophers (and, I would add, theologians) what they fear, because the elaborate constructions they concoct are birthed in the soil of anxiety and desire. Karl Popper, divining the texts of the *Republic* and other works, does a masterful job of bringing Plato's fears, anxieties, and desires out from the cave to the light of the day.[11] Plato's fears of democracy and its vicissitudes are at the base of his philosophical political constructions. Aristotle's preoccupation with hierarchical taxonomy screens, in my view, his anxiety about the existential insignificance of human animals. Similarly, I suspect Augustine, Aquinas, and many other theologians fear existential insignificance and impermanence, constructing complex theologies that keep these fears and anxieties hidden from view.

Our fears and anxieties propel our storytelling, whether we are theologians, philosophers, psychologists, or other storytellers. These fears and anxieties are kept at bay or hidden by our certainties regarding the stories we tell about our origins and the origins of our world. One of the dominant ideas embedded in the stories told by Western theologians and philosophers and lived out in our rituals is sovereignty, whether this sovereignty characterizes God or humanity. This idea, in the story I am telling, has become wedded to the notion of civilization. Indeed, sovereignty, as Hobbes, and inadvertently Freud, argued, is absolutely necessary, indeed essential, for the possibility of civilization. Whereas sovereignty is unquestionable, what can be incessantly questioned and bandied about is what type of sovereignty we ascribe to. This ceaseless discourse about the most effective kind of sovereignty functions as an apparatus or disciplinary regime that produces and

---

9. See Pulcini, "Global Vulnerability."
10. Murdoch, *Sovereignty of the Good*, 82.
11. Popper, *Open Society*.

maintains the belief (more accurately, the illusion) that sovereignty is necessary for the existence of civilization.

In this chapter, I begin with an origin story about the marriage of civilization and sovereignty. I make no claim as to its veracity but rather suggest that as the pairing relates to political belonging, it is not sacrosanct, and it is in fact accompanied by significant problems, which are revealed by the climate emergency. I begin by depicting what I mean by civilization and its tendency to stand against what is seen to be uncivilized, primitive, or barbaric. I then turn to the notion of sovereignty, identifying and describing its attributes and dynamics, as well as its inherent contradictions. The aim in this chapter is to begin a critique of civilization and sovereignty with the eventual aim, in the last chapter, of offering a theological reimaging of the nonsovereignty of God and human beings.

A few clarifications are offered before beginning. First, as mentioned in the Introduction, the current climate emergency can be seen as an existential crisis that, like a burning house, reveals "the fundamental architectural problem [that] becomes visible for the first time."[12] The architectural problem I am identifying and discussing in this and other chapters is sovereignty. This does not mean that sovereignty is the only structural issue, whether we are talking about Western Christianity, other Western political philosophies, capitalism,[13] or science. I am simply focusing on a major structural flaw in Western political philosophies and theologies. Second, if we become aware of an architectural problem and explore it, there is a possibility of repairing or rebuilding the structure without the structural flaw, though repairing or rebuilding is not the focus of this chapter. Rather, the focus in this and subsequent chapters is on diagnosing or understanding a central problem in Western philosophy and the Abrahamic traditions. Third, the metaphor "marriage" is meant to convey a choice and not an inevitability. In other words, I want to assert that civilization, as a form of human belonging, is not in and of itself dependent on or determined by sovereignty. We have a choice, albeit a difficult one. Fourth, since I brought up Iris Murdoch's question, I should probably say a word or two about my fear and anxiety in relation to the story I tell in this chapter.[14] My fear is

---

12. Agamben, *Potentialities*, 115.

13. Nancy Fraser, *Cannibal Capitalism*, argues persuasively that all forms of capitalism entail contradictions that are seen especially in the climate crisis. Her focus is on capitalism and its destructive contradictions, while I argue that a more foundational problem, which is evident in capitalism, is belief in human sovereignty vis-à-vis other species and Earth. See also Jason Moore's discussion on climate change and the role of capitalism (Moore, "Name the System!").

14. I no longer remember where I read that Hannah Arendt, when asked if she saw

not simply that humanity[15] is on a trajectory toward extinction or being unhoused vis-à-vis a biodiverse Earth; it is also that, in the process, we will cause the extinctions of millions of other species and destroy the beauty of this incredible, biodiverse planet. My fear is interwoven with anticipatory sorrow, both of which impel me to speak, to write about what is wrong with the way we dwell in the world and how we might, in our awakening, change. Lest one consider the last sentence a statement of hope, let me disabuse you. My fear is yoked to the absence of hope, though I do not despair. Instead, my fear is intertwined with the categorical imperative to care for other human beings, other species, and the Earth itself, regardless of an expected outcome. I do not need hope in order to care for and about the Earth and its innumerable diverse inhabitants.[16]

The Marriage of Civilization and Sovereignty: An Origin Story

In his translation of *The Epic of Gilgamesh*, Andrew George argues that a key theme in this ancient story is the "eternal conflict between nurture and nature—articulated as the benefits of civilization over savagery."[17] George's comment reflects a perennial feature when the notion of civilization emerges, and that is what it is defined against, namely, savagery/savages, barbarians, the primitive/uncivilized, and so forth. Civilization, in other words, is typically understood as the organization of human groups wherein occurs social and cultural development—advancement or progress versus so-called primitive peoples, who are constructed as lacking capability for either development or advancement. Developments that characterize rising civilizations can include the emergence of governments (and constitutions), art, architecture, written works, sciences, and more sophisticated technologies (e.g., guns and bombs as opposed to spears or arrows). Moreover, the notion of civilization has synonyms, such as progress, enlightenment, cultivation, refinement, etc.

---

herself as a political philosopher, replied that she was a storyteller. I think this is apt for political theologians as well.

15. To be fair, it is not all human beings, but many who are implicated in undermining Earth as the sole habitat for untold numbers of known and unknown species. There are some groups of people who live sustainably, as well as people who have little means in terms of being able to have a so-called carbon footprint.

16. LaMothe, *Radical Political Theology*, 263–94.

17. George, Introduction, xv.

Before moving to a story of the wedding of civilization and sovereignty, I spend a little time offering a view or story about the emergence of civilization, which will serve as a base for drawing out how "civilization" functions and has functioned for millennia, as well as how it became intertwined with the idea of sovereignty. It is commonly believed that millennia ago human beings were hunters and gatherers who operated in small groups. "People lived," Chris Harman, citing various scholars, writes, "in loose-knit groups of 40–50 which might periodically get together with other groups in bigger gatherings of up to 200."[18] The Neolithic revolution emerged as a result of human beings having developed tools and skills for cultivating crops, which, in time, gave rise to larger villages, towns, and cities. Harman indicates that civilization, which is the result of the Neolithic revolution, began around five thousand to ten thousand years ago and that the "first indications of it are the great edifices found in very different parts of the world—the pyramids of Egypt and Central America, the ziggurats (staged tower temples) of Iraq, the palace of Knossos in Crete, the fortress at Mycenae in mainland Greece, and the grid-planned 4,000-year-old cities of Harappa and Mohenjo-dero on the Indus."[19]

We can imagine that as civilization emerged, it did so in relation to people who continued to operate in small groups, outside of the city or town walls. While city walls denote physical boundaries designed for protection, it is not unreasonable to imagine that these walls, like the walls we construct today,[20] had psychosocial and political functions. For people within the walls, the boundary provided psychological distinctions (and barriers) between us and them, with "them," in this instance, being labeled as primitive people or barbarians—uncivilized, primitive, uncultured persons.[21] By juxtaposing the civilized and the uncivilized (primitive), those of the city would obtain a collective sense of self-esteem, self-respect, and self-confidence that attended categorical beliefs in their superiority and in "uncivilized" humans, if human at all, their inferiority. Uncivilized people occupy the lower end of the taxonomic scale, whereas civilized persons dwell on the higher end. These shared beliefs also shaped the motivation for the "civilized" members of the polis to stay together—shared identification/identity—while

---

18. Harman, *People's History of the World*, 6.

19. Harman, *People's History of the World*, 17. We can include in this list civilizations that emerged in the Americas.

20. See Brown, *Walled States*.

21. Montaigne wrote that "each man calls barbarism what is not his own practice" (quoted in Young-Bruehl, *Why Arendt Matters*, 183). This strikes me as true and when considered in light of the rise of civilization, we can see its psychosocial functions, as well as the consequences of exclusion and, in many cases, violence.

disidentifying and excluding those constructed as uncivilized. Who in the city could possibly be motivated to identify with the negative tropes associated with inferior, uncultured, primitive, or barbaric peoples? Freud, for instance, was incredulous at those (perhaps including Rousseau) who believed that "civilization is largely responsible for our misery, and that we should be happier if we gave it up and returned to primitive conditions."[22] Who would want to be associated with that which is constructed as inferior, lower, or base?

The juxtaposition of the civilized and uncivilized has roots in Western political philosophies. Aristotle's view of the polis included residents who were deemed to be barbarians—uncultured—or women, who were as a whole deemed to be closer to Nature than men and therefore incapable of reasoning to the degree necessary to establish and oversee flourishing civilization.[23] If we fast-forward to the nineteenth and twentieth centuries, Edward Said[24] and Stuart Hall[25] have demonstrated how literature in the West constructs "Oriental" peoples and their civilizations, as well as Caribbean peoples, as less civilized or uncivilized, which means they were and often are constructed as inferior, dependent, and in need of the help of civilized folk—help that justified exploitation. Indeed, the US has a long, sordid history of constructing African peoples and African Americans as primitive, less than human, and closer to Nature and to nonhuman animals than White Americans are. The terms "civilized" and "uncivilized" were also used, then, to justify the enslavement of African peoples by Western European "civilized" countries, and these discourses continued within the borders of the US. Enslaved persons born and raised in the US, while residents of the state, were deemed to be uncivilized, less than human. But the distinctions between the civilized and so-called primitive peoples operated not only within US borders. This dynamic can be seen elsewhere within and between civilizations and Othered peoples.

The vestiges of this binary thinking lie at the very foundation of the US. The very first colonizers in America constructed native peoples as uncivilized, which was a prelude to killing "uncivilized" peoples and expropriating their lands.[26] For instance, Puritans, fleeing religious oppression in Europe, turned to scripture to make sense of their experience, to prepare for

22. Freud, *Civilization and Its Discontents*, 33 (italics added).
23. Women, in political theologies and philosophies, have often been constructed as primitive or closer to nature and, therefore, inferior to men, who ostensibly possess greater reason (and distance from nature) to apprehend "the good."
24. Said, *Orientalism*; Said, *Culture and Imperialism*.
25. Hall, ed., *Representation*; Hall, *Cultural Studies 1983*.
26. Zinn, *People's History of the United States*.

the journey to a new land, and to justify dispossessing and killing native (so-called uncivilized or uncultured) peoples. John Winthrop and John Cotton, for example, preached to their congregations about being the new chosen people and identified America as the new promised land.[27] John Winthrop "created the excuse to take Indian land by declaring the area legally a 'vacuum.' The Indians, he said, had not 'subdued the land and therefore had only a 'natural' right to it, not a 'civil right.' A natural right did not have legal standing."[28] Roughly translated, uncivilized peoples do not have the rights of civilized Christians. In the nineteenth century, Catherine Beecher, a significant advocate of education for women, believed that the mission of the United States was to demonstrate "to the world the beneficent influences of Christianity, when carried into every social, civil, and political institution,"[29] which served as a rationalization to justify the brutal expropriation of land and wealth, as well as the exploitation of colonized peoples. On the political stage, this was echoed by Senator Albert J. Beveridge, of Indiana, who believed that the United States had a moral "duty to bring Christianity and civilization to 'savage and senile peoples.'"[30]

Senator Beveridge's comment may seem to be in the past, but this is not the case. To be sure, few if any politicians would use the term "savage" or "senile" when referring to people of other nations. However, these distinctions remain. The invasions of Vietnam, Haiti, Afghanistan, and Iraq were linked to discourses that implied that democracies, such as operated in US, were exceptional and something that the invaded people lacked.[31] Implied here are negative associations attributed to the Other, who must be forced into democracy—civilization. A more egregious illustration of this kind of binary thinking is the forty-fifth president's comment about "shithole" African nations and Haiti.[32] Racial animus is intermixed ideas of civilization.

Those who wipe their brows, being thankful that all this rot is in the past, are living an illusion—and a particularly deadly one at that, which seems to be wedded to the apparatuses of civilization. Consider the current political polarizing discourse in the US (and elsewhere). The term often associated with emotional political divisions between groups is "tribalism." If one googles "tribalism" and "politics," one discovers hundreds of thousands

27. Barry, *Roger Williams*, 120–26.
28. Zinn, *People's History of the United States*, 13–14.
29. Kaplan, *Anarchy of Empire*, 29.
30. Johnson, *Sorrows of Empire*, 43.
31. See Herring, *From Colony to Superpower*; Stone and Kuznick, *Untold History*.
32. Trump referred to Haiti and African nations as "shithole" countries (https://www.nbcnews.com/politics/white-house/trump-referred-haiti-african-countries-shithole-nations-n836946).

of references. I am less interested in what the meaning of "political tribalism" is, which is readily apparent, and I'm more interested in the use of "tribe" to ascribe a negative political reality to others. The term suggests a regression to less democratic or less civilized ways of living in society. We might ask, why use the term "tribe" to point out intense political conflict and affiliation? From my perspective, the term "tribe" is a coded reference to appellations like primitive or savage. It is a vestige of the civilization-barbarism binary. A cursory observation is that those who use the term are talking about people and groups other than themselves. A "civilized" pundit or scholar, for instance, hardly describes their own position as tribal or as a form of tribalism, which highlights the division between those who are constructed as tribal and those who are perceived to be members of a democratic-civilized population.

This psychosocial and physical division between civilized and uncivilized also occurred in relation to other species and the Earth. I mentioned Thomas Hobbes above. It is fair to suggest that Hobbes was desperately afraid of Nature, human and otherwise. Before civilization, in his telling of the story, human life was miserable, as human beings fought one another to survive the vicissitudes of Nature. This is also represented in Freud's myth of human life. For Freud, human beings are mostly helpless and vulnerable against the relentless, majestic, cruel, indifferent forces of Nature,[33] and, therefore, we need to band together (to create civilizations) in order to control, as much as possible, Nature for human benefit. If this is not quite sovereignty or dominion over Nature, Freud tacks close to it, recognizing that "the principal task of civilization . . . is to defend us against nature," which civilization does well.[34] He and others were under no illusion "that nature has already been vanquished,"[35] as if this is a reasonable goal. Nevertheless, Freud believed that civilization will always have the task of protecting

---

33. Freud, *Future of an Illusion*. Freud views human beings as animals, though he also differentiates human beings and nature, suggesting that human beings are somehow separate from nature even as they are part of nature. This is not simply an awkward formulation. It reveals, in part, what I will later address in Chapter 3 as the ontological rift between human beings and other species that is created and maintained by Western philosophies and Abrahamic theologies. I add two other points. First, Freud's appellations regarding nature reveal an antagonist relation marred by "nature's" cruelty and indifference. He obviously overlooked the long history of cruelty and indifference many human beings have exhibited toward Othered human beings, other species, and the Earth itself. Second and relatedly, nature is anthropomorphized. Nature is not and cannot be indifferent or cruel, only human beings, as far as I know, can manifest these attributes.

34. Freud, *Future of an Illusion*, 15.

35. Freud, *Future of an Illusion*, 15.

human beings from the primitivities of uncivilized nature, though, ironically and tragically, Western human beings have manifested immense brutality and indifference toward other species and the Earth, such that we are now a threat to "Nature."[36]

The idea that civilization entails the banding together of human beings to protect themselves from the cruelties or indifference of Nature not only represents an antagonistic division between human beings and Nature;[37] it also represents perennial human existential fear and anxiety related to human vulnerability and impermanence or insignificance.[38] In Freud's and Hobbes's stories of human origins, Nature threatens human beings, suggesting our vulnerability. These stories also reveal our ambivalence regarding our dependence on Nature. Civilization provides some protection against this vulnerability, even while we remain dependent on Nature. Part of this vulnerability, in my estimation, is anxiety about our existential insignificance and our impermanence vis-à-vis Nature. Nature, Hobbes, Freud, and their ilk believe, is indifferent, even cruel, ascribing no importance or permanence to human beings or other creatures. Civilization is founded on apparatuses human beings construct in order to provide ourselves, not simply with a sense of protection against Nature, but with a sense of our own significance vis-à-vis "lower" animals; this sense of our significance bolsters the illusion, if not of our permanence, at least of our continuity. Of course, we know we will die, but we tacitly believe that civilization will continue. Even better, for those of the Abrahamic religious traditions, human beings (meaning believers) retain ontological significance and a possibility of permanence, as noted in the belief in the kingdom of God—the theological pinnacle of civilization and a concept that does not encompass nonhuman species, since they are reputed to have no souls. The belief that other species have no souls means these species are ontologically impermanent

---

36. I have placed quotes here to indicate that there is a problem is constructing "Nature" in opposition to human beings, as if human beings and civilization are something different from nature. This is part of the problem of the ontological rift between human beings and other species, which will be addressed in greater detail in another chapter.

37. John Bellamy Foster notes that "For both Marx and Engels, the materialist conception of nature and the materialist conception of history were inextricably connected, just as alienation of nature and the alienation of labor were" (Foster, *Return of Nature*, 177). I agree, but I am arguing the sovereignty itself represents alienation from nature, as well as alienation between sovereign classes and those who submit to their rule.

38. Samuel Wells argues that in the West "the human project . . . has been to secure life against limitation in general and mortality in particular" (Wells, *Nazareth Manifesto*, 11). Core features of this project, I argue in this chapter, are social imaginaries associated with the ideas of civilization and sovereignty.

and insignificant. Their existence is derivative in the sense that their sole significance is to support human belonging.

Those constructed as uncivilized, primitive, or lower, in my telling of the story, are secretly or overtly feared and hated, whether they are other species or Othered human beings. That which is labeled primitive signifies the threat of human vulnerability, dependency, insignificance, and impermanence. Othered species (and Othered human beings) are constant conscious and unconscious reminders of our existential insignificance and impermanence. This helps explain why there is so much antipathy (and unconscious anxiety) toward those deemed to be uncivilized (and to "Nature," as evident in Hobbes and Freud). Why, for instance, did we not let native peoples continue to hold on to and practice their "primitive" beliefs? Why so much focus and effort at "civilizing" them? To be sure, the party line and justification were to bring native peoples within the walls of "civilization" where they might obtain protection from Nature and experience the advancements we knew. Yet, I am convinced that "primitive" peoples (and Nature) remain a source of anxiety and fear, and they can either be destroyed, as they often were and are, or be brutally assimilated into what we call civilization. This suggests that civilization and accompanying "civilized" religions do not, in fact, protect us from "Nature" but instead simply serve as a convenient screen to shield us from recognizing and accepting our existential insignificance and impermanence.

The tension between the binary opposition of civilized and primitive is not the only source of strain that attends civilization. Hobbes valued civilization for bringing human beings out of the brutish realities of primitive life, yet civilization inevitably has to deal with the inherent "primitivity" or aggression of human beings. This is accomplished by the construction of the leviathan, who uses political violence or threat of political violence to enforce the social contract.[39] Those who accede to the social contract are able to pursue, with some degree of freedom that our "primitive" ancestors lacked, their interests and desires—at least as long as they submit to the leviathan. Rousseau in many ways reverses Hobbes's perspective, believing there was greater freedom before civilization was founded. The emergence of civilization introduced a strain that had not existed before, and this strain, for Rousseau, was founded on apparatuses that produce the idea of property, which led to inequalities and, if you will, class conflict.[40] These inequalities did not, for Rousseau, exist in Nature or in so-called primitive gatherings of human beings. In the twentieth century, Freud, like Hobbes,

---

39. Grayling, *History of Philosophy*, 207–8.
40. Ryan, *On Politics*, 556–72.

recognized that civilization came with tension and he offered a psychological explanation and solution. To live in and be protected by civilization against the cruelties of Nature requires sublimation of a primal instinct, which "is [an] especially conspicuous feature of cultural development."[41] Human beings are obviously animals, but we are a kind of animal that can sublimate our instincts for the sake of creating a civilization that protects us from the vagaries of Nature. Yet, as much as we might sublimate our instincts, our animal instincts continue to exist. Freud, then, recognized that sublimation, while providing protection, does not eliminate the fractious or aggressive and destructive nature of human beings. Indeed, he presciently noted that human beings "have gained control over nature to such an extent that with their help they would have no difficulty in exterminating one another to the last man."[42] But not only are human beings in danger. Western civilization is well on its way to exterminating half of the known species by the end of this century.[43]

Arguing from a different angle, Karl Popper contended that the origin of civilization's strain "is most closely related to the problem of the tension between the classes."[44] Like Rousseau and later Karl Marx, Popper viewed the tension that attends civilization as rooted in manufactured inequalities—inequalities produced and maintained by the apparatuses of civilization.[45] Decades after Popper, Chris Harman argues that the very instantiation of civilization is fraught with tension and conflict that results from society organized by class.[46] I will say more about the tension between classes below; for now the strain, for both Popper and Harman, is due to how society is organized by class, creating hierarchies and material and political inequalities. Persons of the lower classes are constructed as uncultured and uncivilized (and often unculturable—e.g., India's untouchables[47]). The strain between those inside and those outside the walls of the town is due to the

41. Freud, *Civilization and Its Discontents*, 44.
42. Freud, *Civilization and Its Discontents*, 92.
43. Wilson, *Future of Life*; Wallace-Wells, *Uninhabitable Earth*.
44. Popper, *Open Society*, 168.
45. Popper begins his chapter on classes by quoting Engels: "The history of all hitherto existing society is a history of class struggle." I think it would be more accurate to replace "society" here with "civilization," since there are also "primitive" societies. In so doing, this replacement will suffice to respond to Popper's criticism of Engels's oversimplification of history. Popper points out that focusing on the struggle between the rich and the poor tends to overlook other conflicts that take place between political and economic elites. Yet, if we consider that civilization is wedded to the idea of sovereignty, then class conflict exists within states and between states (Popper, *Open Society*, 321).
46. Harman, *People's History of the World*.
47. Wilkerson, *Caste*.

perennial need to construct those outside as primitive, insignificant, and impermanent so that "civilized" human beings can retain a measure of existential or ontological value.

Hobbes, Freud, Popper, and Harman recognize and try to account for what they view as the inevitable strain that comes from human beings moving from small groups to towns and cities. Their differing accounts share something in common, namely, human domination. For Freud, human beings, while unable to control Nature completely, have come a long way in doing so through science, technology, and extractive capitalism. The irony and tragedy of our attempts to dominate and control Nature is they will likely bring about our demise, the evidence being the climate emergency. For Popper and Harman, it is not that humans seek to dominate Nature, but rather that one class of people seeks to dominate another, "lower" class in order to secure power, privileges, and positions. Put another way, the apparatuses of civilization, which human beings constructed to live in larger diverse groups, came with a psychosocial binary schema, namely, civilized-uncivilized, which is also evident, in part, in class conflict. Features of this construction include beliefs in superiority and inferiority, and while this schema and attending beliefs may have aimed at differentiating those within the city from those outside, the self-same schema has characterized and does characterize human civilization in general. Examples abound, but let me offer three illustrations of the inherent strain of domination linked to civilization. Isabel Wilkerson writes about castes in India and how stratified Indian society is. The Dalits are and have been among the most exploited and subjugated group.[48] To turn to the US, Nancy Isenberg provides a history of how poor White people are constructed as "white trash."[49] Charles Mills has written about racist ideas and their impacts on African Americans.[50] Ibram X. Kendi, as well, illustrates the impact of White supremacy.[51] In these accounts we note relations of domination, whether we are referencing classism,[52] racism, sexism, or some other form of subjugation that is part of what we call civilization.

We might wonder, then, if domination is an inevitable feature and central tension of civilization, whether we are trying to dominate "Nature," "primitive" peoples, or groups of "uncultured" people within civilization. In other words, perhaps the inherent strain within civilization and between

48. Wilkerson, *Caste*.
49. Isenberg, *White Trash*.
50. Mills, *Racial Contract*.
51. Kendi and Reynolds, *Stamped from the Beginning*.
52. Žižek, "From Democracy to Divine Violence," 120.

those constructed as civilized and uncivilized depends not only on property, class, and vicissitudes of the social contract, but, more fundamentally, **on** relations of domination that must continually be reproduced and maintained. This is where the story of civilization shifts to a story of sovereignty and its religious and philosophical roots and attributes.

Recall that the origin of civilization is approximately five thousand to ten thousand years ago, though we know human beings existed in groups long before that. What preceded the Neolithic revolution was the prevalence of tribes or small groups of human beings, cooperating together to survive and thrive. These groups possessed the capacities for language and ritual, and there is plenty of evidence of their capacities for technology and art, which includes the creation of stories. Put differently, they had oral traditions, stories, and rituals that answered existential questions about who they were, where they came from, and how they were to dwell together. We see examples of these stories in the oral traditions of native peoples in the US and Canada, traditions preserved by ancestors and passed on by descendants.[53] These ancient stories and rituals represent indigenous peoples' collective philosophies, theologies, or wisdom sayings about themselves and their world. To be sure, these stories and rituals are not "philosophy" like pre-Socratic and Socratic philosophies of the West and Mideast, and these are not "theology" like the theologies of Israelites. Still, indigenous traditions represent human capacities for philosophizing and theologizing—asking and answering questions about how we are to live and flourish together. My point is, first, that there is a continuity between so-called primitive and civilized peoples, as both groups constructed stories and rituals to make sense of the world; second, the stories that emerged vis-à-vis civilization were and are radically different from these earlier pre-Neolithic stories or the stories of indigenous peoples, who are often constructed as uncivilized. In my telling, the Neolithic revolution and the emergence of civilization led to the making of new stories and rituals that reflected challenges and opportunities resulting from all the changes that accompanied the development of civilization. To be sure, existential questions that "primitive" peoples addressed were also the questions "civilized" peoples answered in their myths and ritual practices: Who are we? Where are we from? What is our place in

---

53. See Kerven, *Native American Myths*; Erdoes and Ortiz, eds., *American Indian Myths*. In mentioning these native stories, I am in no way implying that these are pre-Neolithic. Rather, these stories and traditions have been considered by Western colonizers to be "primitive" and the people uncivilized. I would argue that native peoples reveal a civilized belonging that contradicts, if not threatens, Western civilization and sovereignty, though to make this case would take me far afield. See also Deloria, *God Is Red*.

the world? How are we to live in this world? What is the good? However, the resulting answers from Western philosophies and theologies were radically different vis-à-vis ways of being in and relating to the world. More specifically, a central premise of this book is that Hebrew scriptures (and later Christian and Islamic scriptures) and Western philosophies and theologies are stories that emerged in relation to the realities and strains of civilization, which also means that these stories have served and still do serve as apparatuses that produce, legitimate, and maintain a particular iteration of civilization—one that produces the belief that sovereignty is absolutely necessary for political belonging, which includes religious belonging. Richard Horsley makes a similar point, arguing that the collected texts of "the Hebrew Bible were evidently produced in scribal circles that served the Judean monarchy and temple state centuries before [these documents] were recognized as books of the Bible."[54] More broadly, I suggest that pre-Socratic and Socratic political philosophies, along with religious narratives and theologies emerging in the same period, can be seen as arising in and after the Neolithic Age, heralding and instantiating civilization. Indeed, these philosophical and theological stories, rituals, and practices reproduced the binary construction "civilized and uncivilized," and this binary continues today along with its inherent strains of domination and exclusion.

Before attending further to the radical differences between "primitive" organizations of peoples and "civilized" peoples, who depend on sovereignty for belonging and identity, I want to take a brief detour to indicate both continuity and discontinuity within the history of civilization. Whatever we call civilizations, we note great diversity diachronically and synchronically. A civilization changes over time, and historians, sociologists, and others comment on those changes. For instance, Max Weber argued that after the Enlightenment and its apotheosis of reason, Western civilization experienced the loss of an enchantment that had previously existed in Christian and "pagan" Europe.[55] More recently, Charles Taylor follows suit in seeing Western civilization as one of disenchantment in a secular age.[56] There certainly are important shifts to note in Western civilization (as well as in Asian, South American, and African civilizations), yet even in the secular West, there is a great deal of enchantment that continues to permeate societies. The pageantry around sports, entertainment, and political events demonstrates the presence of enchantment and an almost religious fervor. We can also browse the children's literature section at a bookstore and see

54. Horsley, *You Shall Not Bow Down*, 47.
55. Weber, *Protestant Ethic*.
56. Taylor, *Secular Age*.

the enchantment displayed by adult authors who write for children. There are several points to make here. First, despite "civilized" persons' attempts to (negatively) differentiate between civilized and "primitive" peoples, it is clear that civilized and tribal people are more alike than different. Indeed, the binary opposition is a false one, even though we can identify differences or make distinctions. Second, while it is important to distinguish between civilizations or between periods of civilization, and to note changes within civilizations over time, such differences all occur under the umbrella of what we call civilization. In other words, the core features of Western civilization remain the same, which I discuss in greater detail below. Third and relatedly, the differences between "primitive" and civilized cultures become significant not from any essentialist attributes of being human (or from any essentialist attributes of Nature). Rather they become significant because of constructed beliefs that are ensconced in narratives, rituals, and social-cultural apparatuses that shape subjectivities and organize intergroup and extragroup relations—a group's habitus. These beliefs and practices, then, reveal radical artificial differences that, when imbued with significance by Western civilized people, have been terribly destructive to Othered human beings, Othered species, and the Earth.

To depict the radical differences that emerged with the rise of civilization, I turn to the issue of sovereignty, the foundational organizing principle in the rise of what we call Western civilization. Let's begin with so-called primitive peoples who have to answer and live out the questions: How are we to organize ourselves so that we can cooperate toward our collective survival and flourishing? Who will be the leaders who facilitate collective cooperation? As social and communal creatures, humans found that these existential questions continued to be foundational when they began to live in towns and cities. From reading hundreds of native peoples' stories, I have discovered that these questions are answered in myriad ways, yet most indigenous stories focus on the importance of leadership, and leaders can be women or men or other species, depending on the task or issue at hand. What I contend is that, in contrast to organizations of indigenous people, Western civilization answered the questions of dwelling and leadership by focusing on sovereignty. In Plato and Aristotle, for example, there are varied types of sovereignty, which both philosophers had reasoned opinions about; but what was unquestioned and unquestionable was the necessity of sovereignty for civilization—a sovereign was believed to be necessary for the existence of a stable and secure civil society. Western philosophers after Plato[57]

---

57. Alfred North Whitehead noted that "The safest general characterization of the European philosophical tradition is that it consists of a series of footnotes to Plato," which indicates his belief that Western political philosophies are beholden to Plato,

and Aristotle may have argued over varied kinds of sovereignty that are best for a society, but as it is for their predecessors, so for them sovereignty, as existentially necessary, is largely unquestioned.[58] All of this indicates, in part, a confusion between and conflation of leadership and sovereignty.

Since I have mentioned Plato and Aristotle, let me offer a few thoughts about the Greek roots of the idea of sovereignty. Democracy, oligarchy, aristocracy, monarchy, plutocracy, and other forms of sovereignty have their origins in the Greek *archē*. What is interesting is that the Greek has two meanings that are, at times, in conflict, which I will say more about in the last chapter. For now, the Greek definition of *archē* covers (1) beginning/origin, foundation, first principle/element, and (2) first place/power, sovereignty, rule, empire/realm, magistracy/office, authorities/magistrates, command, and heavenly powers.[59] I suggest that these two meanings can be understood to be present in Western iterations of sovereignty. By this I mean that sovereignty means to rule, and it is believed to be the existential foundation for any polis, any group of human belonging. *Archē*, as both rule and foundation/command, encompasses a central anthropological category in Western political philosophies (and theologies).

While the origins of *archē* lie in Greek thought, it is important to note that we see a similar trend regarding the inherent necessity of sovereignty for political belonging in Abrahamic scriptures and subsequent political theologies. From the earliest scriptural passages to the final passages in the Torah, God's sovereignty is proclaimed, unquestioned, and unquestionable. While God is sovereign over creation, human beings are given sovereignty

---

and I would add Aristotle. The legacy of Plato and Aristotle (and I would include the Abrahamic traditions) is that "the very threshold of the political order was never called into question" (Whitehead, *Process and Reality*, 39). Agamben, *Homo Sacer*, 12.

58. I will return to the idea of anarchy in the last chapter, but for now it is important to mention that during the time Hobbes was writing, the idea of anarchy must have made its way into the consciousness of some people. Hobbes associated anarchy with chaos and uncontrolled violence. He feared anarchy, and this fear continues in many circles today. Rousseau, while criticizing civilization, did not question the necessity of sovereignty, which is evident in his view of the general will. In the nineteenth century, political philosopher and activist Pierre-Joseph Proudhon was one of the first persons to embrace anarchy, arguing that society or civilization could be organized without having a sovereign. Let me add that evidence of the sovereignty of sovereignty is evident in A. C. Grayling's tome on Western philosophy, where there is not one mention of anarchy or of Proudhon. Alan Ryan's volume on political philosophy does mention both anarchy and Proudhon (and others), but there is a negative slant when he mentions the failed utopias in the nineteenth century, which to my ears shows an unconscious bias toward democratic forms of sovereignty. Grayling, *History of Philosophy*; Ryan, *On Politics*, 880–95.

59. For this definition, I have relied on Dr. Clayton Jefford's personal communication regarding the meaning and origins of this term.

over other species and the Earth (Gen 1:28). Nevertheless, it is God's ontological sovereignty that binds the people together and insures their survival and flourishing—their significance and permanence. Gideon affirms God's sovereignty when he is confronted by elders who want him to be not simply their leader but their sovereign. Gideon responds by saying, "I will not rule over you, and my son will not rule over you; the LORD will rule over you" (Judg 8:23). Gideon was adhering to the traditional story that God is the only sovereign—the sole ruler of the universe and its foundation.

Of course, the story does not end there. Later, the elders of Israel ask Samuel to "appoint for us . . . a king to govern us, like other nations" (1 Sam 8:5). This is not a rejection of God's sovereignty, but an amendment. The elders want a human being to be sovereign; though a human being, the king would be under the ontological sovereignty of God. Eventually, God relents to their demands, though God has Samuel warn them of the consequences of having a human sovereign. Samuel tells them that

> These will be the ways of the king who will reign over you: he will take your sons and appoint them to his chariots and be his horsemen, and to run before his chariots; and he will appoint for himself commanders of thousands and commanders of fifties, and some to plow his ground and to reap his harvest, and to make his implements of war and equipment of his chariots. He will take your daughters to be perfumers and cooks and bakers. He will take the best of your fields and vineyards and olive orchards and give them to his courtiers. He will take one-tenth of your grain and of your vineyards and give it to his officers and his courtiers. He will take your male and female slaves, and the best of your cattle and donkeys and put them to his work. He will take one-tenth of your flocks, and you shall be his slaves. (1 Sam 8:11–17)

It is no surprise that the warning proves to be true, but this does not diminish the desire to have a human sovereign or the belief that sovereignty is necessary for human dwelling (civilization) and civic cooperation. Indeed, these stories (and later political theologies) and their attending rituals have served and do serve as apparatuses that produce our assumptive world, founded on the necessity of sovereignty for living in community and society. In short, the idea of and belief in sovereignty as universally and essentially necessary for human ways of being in the world accompany the emergence of civilization, and the idea of sovereignty and belief in sovereignty are evident in most Western philosophical or theological political anthropologies.

The key claim here is that the rise of "civilization" in the Mideast and West accompanied the rise in the notion of sovereignty.[60] Civilization and sovereignty were wedded in the birth and aftermath of the Neolithic revolution. The metaphor of a "wedding" provides a way of skirting the chicken-and-egg question: did civilization come before the idea of sovereignty, or did sovereignty precede the emergence of civilization? In my story, they appeared concurrently, though, in saying this, I am not arguing or suggesting that sovereignty and civilization are existentially entwined, except in our "civilized" imaginations. Indeed, as this book aims to argue, it is the illusory belief in the necessity of sovereignty for belonging and cooperation vis-à-vis civilization that needs to be exposed in order for humans to be open to or to create other stories and practices in the Anthropocene Age[61] that reject exploitative and extractive relations vis-à-vis Othered human beings, Othered species, and the Earth. That is, can we find ways of belonging and cooperation that do not depend on the necessity of sovereignty and its accompanying apparatuses?

Sovereignty: Its Attributes and Dynamics in Everyday Life

To understand the radical aspects of Western civilization's answer to the questions of dwelling and leadership, it is necessary to delve more deeply into the meaning and attributes of sovereignty. What is this thing we call sovereignty, and what are its attributes? Merriam-Webster's online dictionary defines sovereignty as "supreme power over the body politic"; "freedom from control"; and "controlling influence."[62] The term is derived from the Latin, *superanus*, which means supreme or paramount. Implicit are questions: Who rules? Who exercises this supreme power over the body politic? Additional questions arise: What laws and juridical and nonjuridical

60. I have placed "civilization" in quotes here to suggest two things. First, Western civilization is not the only possible view of civilization. I suggest that native peoples, prior to the arrival of European colonizers, had their own kinds of civilization. Second, what passes for civilization in the West has been and is incredibly destructive to Othered human beings and, as we now are aware, other species and Earth. The civilization of native peoples was more sustainable vis-à-vis planet Earth.

61. Since its coinage by Paul Crutzen and Edward Stoermer, the term "Anthropocene Age" has generated considerable discussion among scientists, philosophers, and scholars from other fields. The term refers to moving from the Holocene period to the current age, which entails the sixth mass extinction, caused by human activity. Crutzen and Stoermer, "'Anthropocene.'" See also Hamilton et al., comps., *Anthropocene and the Global Environmental Crisis*.

62. *Merriam-Webster*, s.v. "sovereignty (*n.*)," https://www.merriam-webster.com/dictionary/sovereignty/.

institutions support and legitimate the ruler(s)? Who has the authority to make the laws or construct the institutions, practices, and beliefs that undergird a particular instantiation of sovereignty?

Of course, answers to these questions vary according to geography, culture, and era, wherein we note versions of monarchy, aristocracy, oligarchy, plutocracy, democracy, tyranny, and so forth. They also vary within the same region, culture, and era. Socrates's students, Plato and Aristotle, for example, provided very different answers to questions of sovereignty. Interestingly, Aristotle had his students research the various constitutions throughout Greece to determine the best form of rule, leaving aside any question about ruling itself. Despite this plurality regarding sovereignty, we can identify some of its key attributes. In the sixteenth century, Jean Bodin, a French jurist and political philosopher, sought to explain what sovereignty is, perhaps because of the political instability resulting from the Protestant Reformation.[63] For Bodin, sovereignty is power that is (1) supreme, (2) absolute, (3) indivisible, and (4) perpetual. One can easily imagine these traits relating best to God, but for Bodin they are also features of human sovereignty. The king has no superior (except God), is absolute in his rule, holds power and exercises rule that cannot be divided, and holds power and exercises rule that is perpetual—handed down to his sons (and in rare cases, to his daughters). This pre-Enlightenment formulation of sovereignty remained part of political discourse long after Bodin's death. For instance, in the twentieth century, German jurist Carl Schmitt picks up on Bodin's work, pointing out that it is widely referenced in works on sovereignty.[64] More recently, political philosopher Wendy Brown claims that "classical theorists of modern sovereignty, including Thomas Hobbes, Jean Bodin, and Carl Schmitt, suggest that sovereignty's indispensable features include supremacy (no higher power), perpetuity (no term limits), decisionism (no boundedness by or submission to law), absolutism and completeness (sovereign cannot be probable or partial), nontransferability (sovereignty cannot be conferred without cancelling itself), and specialized jurisdiction (territoriality)."[65] Some of these features beg for further explanation.

To return to Carl Schmitt, a noted (and notorious) political jurist, he argued that the sovereign is "he who decides on the exception,"[66] which re-

63. Bodin, *On Sovereignty*.
64. Schmitt, *Political Theology*, 8.
65. Brown, *Undoing the Demos*, 22.
66. Brown, *Undoing the Demos*, 83. Agamben provides a brief modern history of the state of exception and its connection to the traditional Roman idea that necessity has no law. In this case, necessity produces the state of exception (Agamben, *State of Exception*, 24).

veals the supremacy feature of sovereignty. This means that the sovereign, who is sovereign precisely because of the juridical reality of the state,[67] possesses the power to suspend the law but does not abolish the law. Schmitt stated that "Because the state of exception is always different from anarchy and chaos, in a juridical sense, an order still exists in it, even if it is not a juridical order."[68] Put another way, "The state of exception is not a dictatorship (whether constitutional or unconstitutional, commissarial or sovereign) but a space devoid of law, a zone of anomie in which all legal determinations—and above all the very distinction between public and private—are deactivated."[69] One immediately can see the paradox here. For Giorgio Agamben, the "paradox of sovereignty consists in the fact that the sovereign is, at the same time, outside and inside the juridical order. The sovereign, having the legal power to suspend the validity of the law, legally places himself outside the law."[70] "The sovereign," Sergei Prozorov writes, "remains a borderline or threshold figure at the limit of order."[71] As a threshold figure, the sovereign "is both the sign of the rule and the jurisdiction of law, and supervenes the law."[72] What is interesting and important here is that the sovereign possesses the supreme (legal) authority to set aside laws, because sovereigns are given the legal power to decide on the exception. Add to this the idea that the state of exception is at play in the very creation of the law itself. That is, the establishment of the law already reveals the state of exception. I stress here that the state of exception does not mean the law is invalid, but rather that in the exception, the law simply is not applicable. The law remains in effect, but is set aside.

Naturally, the sovereign need not act on the state of exception. It can simply be potential, which is not to suggest a lack of power or force. Prozorov writes, "even when exceptional or emergency measures are not actualized in policies, they remain potentialities of state action and may indeed be more effective as potentialities, capable of regulating conduct by sheer threat of their actualization."[73] This is analogous to the IRS not auditing someone despite having the ability to do so. The very possibility of being audited motivates many people to make sure they pay their taxes. The state

---

67. For an excellent explanation of the differences between the "state" and "government," see Skinner, "Genealogy of the Modern State."
68. Agamben, *State of Exception*, 33.
69. Agamben, *State of Exception*, 50.
70. Agamben, *Homo Sacer*, 15.
71. Prozorov, *Agamben and Politics*, 99.
72. Brown, *Undoing the Demos*, 59.
73. Prozorov, *Agamben and Politics*, 101.

of exception that remains potential is, in short, still powerful in organizing the polis.

Let me pause here and note that the state of exception, as a defining feature of sovereignty, is applicable not simply to human sovereigns[74] but to God (in Abrahamic religions), as the sovereign over all creation and, therefore, over all human sovereigns. Indeed, the theological tenets around God's sovereignty are inextricably intertwined with Western civilization and its religious and secular dimensions. As Carl Schmitt recognized, "all significant concepts of the modern theory of the state are secularized theological concepts."[75] Similarly, Wendy Brown argues that "sovereignty secularized for political purposes *does not lose its religious structure or bearing*, even as it ceases to have the direct authority of God at its heart."[76] Saul Newman also noted, "Secularism itself retains a certain theological impulse, a trace of the sacred which is internalized within social structures and becomes the foundation for new forms of economic and political power."[77] *But what is this structure* that Brown and Newman refer to?[78]

Giorgio Agamben can help us here. He argues that a key feature of the sovereign's state of exception, from the beginning, is "bare life," which reveals the type of political power wielded by the sovereign in executing the state of exception. The notion of "bare life" exposes the intersection of sovereignty and political violence used to organize society.[79] Stated differently, bare life concerns persons "caught up in the sovereign ban . . . stripped of all protections and abandoned to the force of law."[80] Stated more starkly, "The sovereign sphere is the sphere in which it is permitted to kill without

---

74. Most of the history of sovereignty is patriarchal—centering on rule by men. Feminist theologians and philosophers have rightly condemned patriarchy and its negative impacts on girls and women (and in the end, also on boys and men, resulting in toxic masculinity). While I agree with their critiques, I am pointing to a deeper and more extensive problems with any form of sovereignty. See Reuther, *Sexism and God Talk*; Mann, *Sovereign Masculinity*.

75. Brown, *Walled States*, 59.

76. Brown, *Walled States*, 70 (italics added).

77. Newman, *Political Theology*, 155.

78. Newman uses Lacanian theory to posit that religion "continues to provide the ground or structure of symbolic authority, regardless of whether we consciously believe or not" (Newman, *Political Theology*, 75). Newman's argument is interesting, but one I cannot take up here.

79. Karl Jaspers makes a similar point, noting "Where sovereignty remains . . . there also remains a source of unfreedom; for it [state sovereignty] must assert itself as a force against force." "Force" here can be understood as violence, which is inherent in sovereignty. Young-Bruehl, *Why Arendt Matters*, 208.

80. Prozorov, *Agamben and Politics*, 102.

committing homicide . . . What is captured in the sovereign ban is a human victim who may be killed but not sacrificed."[81] That is, "it is the sovereign who, insofar as he decides on the state of exception, has the power to decide which life may be killed without the commission of homicide."[82] Put differently, the *homo sacer* (bare life), Agamben's term, is doubly excluded in the sovereign's use of the state of exception vis-à-vis political violence. The person "is excluded from human law, because that law does not protect him from being killed, and he is excluded from divine law, because he cannot be offered to the gods as a sacrifice—he is not worthy of being given to the gods."[83] Instead of *homo sacer*, Orlando Patterson uses the term "social death" when referring to the political reality of slaves in the United States, who could be killed with impunity, and who were denied political agency and recognition.[84]

Social death or bare life reveals not simply the sovereign's use of political violence or threat of political violence, but also that the sovereign's use or threat of political violence takes place in conjunction with sovereign classes. In brief, there is no such thing as a sovereign without sovereign classes and the attending apparatuses to support and facilitate the exercise of political violence and the state of exception. In the Judeo-Christian scripture, God's sovereignty is depicted as the ultimate state of exception, wherein God sets aside natural and God-given laws whenever God wishes. Sending the flood (Gen 7), parting the Red Sea (Exod 14), and halting the movement of the sun (Josh 10:1–15) are three cases in which natural "laws" are set aside, resulting in the killing of human beings and other species. In the ten plagues of Exodus, God kills animal and plant species, not to mention Egyptians, and then in the conquest of Canaan, setting aside the commandment against killing, God orders the Israelites to slaughter the inhabitants of the "promised land" (a label that would be disputed by its previous inhabitants).[85] But as sovereign, God makes an exception that does

81. Agamben, *Homo Sacer*, 83.
82. Agamben, *Homo Sacer*, 142.
83. Ugilt, *Giorgio Agamben*, 43.
84. Patterson, *Slavery and Social Death*.
85. At a conference, the issue of political violence was raised with regard to the exodus story. One scholar noted that the Israelites did not commit violence, God did. His point was that Israelites were innocent and that God killed Pharaoh to free the people. He seemed to unwittingly accept the notion that God's violence in freeing people was morally acceptable. I find this reasoning to be a convenient rationalization for the use of political violence and the state of exception, as well as a way to overlook that God's violence extended to the Egyptian people and other species. Making allowance for God's violence also overlooks God's commanding the Israelites to slay the inhabitants of the promised land.

not invalidate natural or divine law, but sets it aside. In so doing, God (and human sovereigns and sovereign classes) remains just because God is above and exceeds the law. We read, "Shall not the Judge of all the earth do what is just?" (Gen 18:25). And, if we return to Samuel's warning about the consequences of having a human sovereign, we see the sovereign's exercise of the state of exception and political violence in his exploitation of citizens, extraction of resources, and expropriation of wealth, all of which could not have taken place without sovereign classes and police/military apparatuses. If we turn to later scriptures, God's commands can be carried out by angels, which can be understood as sovereign classes that implement God's state of exception—the idea of virgin birth is a positive illustration of the state of exception and of the participation of sovereign classes in announcing God's command. In brief, as Guy Debord writes, "Religion justified the cosmic and ontological order that corresponded to the interests of the masters."[86]

Someone may point out that Samuel's warning merely highlights the radical difference between the sovereignty of God and human sovereignty. God's sovereignty, while at times displaying violence, is not exploitative, extractive, or expropriative, but liberative—at least with regard to the chosen people.[87] God has no need for anything human beings possess, except perhaps our worship.[88] Instead, God is interested in and cares for the well-being of, in this case, the Israelites—at least those who obey God. These circumstances might make a plausible case for God's sovereignty alone, but I do not think so, on two grounds. First, I contend that God's sovereignty is simply and solely a human creation that has been used to legitimate established leaders (sovereign classes) and, later, human sovereigns' control over peoples, the employment of political violence, and use of the state of exception to maintain order. Surely one can affirm that God created the universe without concluding necessarily that God has sovereignty over creation. (By analogy, consider an artist who creates a beautiful work. The artist does

---

86. Debord, *Society of the Spectacle*, 8. See also Boorstin, *Image*.

87. God legitimates the violence of ethnic cleansing of the promised land. The Israelites are given permission by God to extract and exploit, which in my view is evidence that the Abrahamic God can be extractive and exploitive in the service of God's chosen people.

88. The command that human beings worship the sovereign God strikes me more as a human construction that sneaks in not only the adoration of God's sovereignty, but also the necessity of human sovereignty. "Worshiping" God in our liturgies reinforces the very idea of sovereignty and its necessity for human belonging. The secular form of this "worship" is seen in the pageantry and ceremony associated with the British monarchy. A sovereign God may demand and "need" to be worshiped, but a nonsovereign God, as depicted in the last chapter of this book, does not.

not have sovereignty over her creation. Indeed, I have never heard an artist describe their relation to their works of art in terms of ruling over the art.)

Second, a plausible case for sovereignty cannot come from Israel's scriptures because the scriptures themselves ontologize sovereignty, reflecting a human belief that belonging and being are themselves dependent on sovereignty. Indeed, God's sovereignty vis-à-vis the kingdom of God secures the belief in communal-political being after death, which further cements the notion that sovereignty is necessary for human existence and the existence of creation. There are, however, plenty of instances of so-called civilized and primitive groups where sovereignty is not necessary for belonging or well-being or for creation itself. Having read numerous creation myths of North American indigenous peoples, I find in these stories an absence of the idea of the sovereignty of God or gods.[89] It is, then, possible to imagine a nonsovereign God's creative care for all creation, which does not legitimize the necessity of sovereignty and the concomitant exercise of the state of exception and political violence for political belonging.

After this sidebar, let me return to identifying and discussing other related attributes of sovereignty that are integral to Western civilization. The persistent belief in God's sovereignty accompanies the belief in God's superiority (omnipotence, omniscience) over all creation, which implies that creation is inferior to or lower than God on the cosmic hierarchy. When it comes to human sovereigns, the same valuative dynamic is at play. The sovereign, by virtue of the state of exception, is believed to be superior, while citizens and residents of the realm are deemed to be inferior, possessing less political significance than the sovereign and sovereign classes. When Chris Harman[90] depicts the history of class, for example, he also details the hierarchical valuation between sovereign classes, which have power, privilege, and prestige, and lower classes have significance to the extent that they accept being ruled. Put differently, the structural inequalities that are established between so-called upper classes and lower classes are legitimized by the beliefs in the sovereign classes' superiority, which is inextricably yoked to the state of exception and the use of political violence. To return to Samuel, only a sovereign and attending sovereign classes hold the belief in their superiority, which entitles them to extract from and exploit nonsovereign classes.

Beliefs in superiority and inferiority vis-à-vis sovereignty shape recognition, perception, relations, and behavior. Those who are constructed as superior, whether the sovereign or sovereign classes, recognize and perceive

---

89. See Kerven, *Native American Myths*; Erdoes and Ortiz, eds., *American Indian Myths*.

90. Harman, *People's History of the World*.

themselves to be of greater significance, while those of the lower or non-sovereign classes are regarded as less significant or completely insignificant. This recognition is dependent on apparatuses (collective stories, rituals, and the like) and disciplinary regimes and can be observed in the material inequalities inherent when sovereignty is the organizing principle of civilization. A stark illustration is the enslavement of persons. In Aristotle's civilization, slavery is justified by indicating that some human beings are existentially inferior and, therefore, fitted to be slaves.[91] Of course, it is almost certain that only members of the sovereign classes would be capable of possessing enslaved people. But we need not stop here. Western political philosophies and theologies have for millennia constructed females as inferior to males. Racism is yet another pernicious labeling of a people group as inferior. Members of the oppressing group/class recognize themselves as superior. The apparatuses of "civilized" societies, imbued with racism, sexism, and other forms of misrecognition, function to humiliate[92] and materially deprive target populations, with the aim of making beliefs about their inferiority seem "natural"—or, worse, with the aim of ontologizing the status of these populations, as Aristotle did, and as many Christians did during slavery and Jim Crow in the US. When "inferior" or "insignificant" persons resist or rebel, sovereign classes use political violence or the threat of political violence to enforce their beliefs. For instance, widespread lynching of African Americans in the US by White supremacists during the nineteenth and twentieth centuries has come to be understood as the exercise of the state of exception by White persons, with the aim of terrorizing and humiliating the Black population; this aim accompanied the goal of retaining belief in White superiority—even if the White people doing the lynching were on the lowest rung of the economic ladder and were constructed and perceived to be inferior by sovereign political and economic elites.[93]

It is important to stress that the construction of people as inferior occurs by virtue of a sovereign state of exception and the use or threat of political violence. Enslaved people or other marginalized, oppressed, and exploited people within a civilization are constructed as inferior by a sovereign's apparatuses. And for those who attempt to rebel, the sovereign exercises the state of exception and violence to insure state order. The violent defeat of rebels or the political humiliation of those who speak out

91. Barker, trans., *Politics of Aristotle*, 9–18.

92. Israeli philosopher Avishai Margalit argues that indecent societies humiliate groups of citizens. I suggest that the rise of civilization and sovereignty is built on apparatuses of humiliation (political violence) in order to ensure the stability and security of society's sovereign classes. See Margalit, *Decent Society*.

93. See Isenberg, *White Trash*.

serves as a warning to members of the nonsovereign classes to accept their inferior status.

There are two other attending features of sovereignty.[94] The second, recognizing some people as inferior, implies the presence of relations of subordination and, at times, of subjugation. Everyone is subordinate to the sovereign, including the sovereign classes, though the members of sovereign classes are not without their own power that may be used to keep the sovereign in check. Indeed, sovereigns must recognize that they are dependent on the sovereign classes for their ruling, even as sovereigns also see the sovereign classes as subordinate. Those who are subordinate are also one step away from subjugation. In the exodus story, the people of Israel live in Egypt and are subordinate to the Pharaoh. When one Pharaoh dies and a new one takes over, exercising his state of exception, the Israelites move from subordinate to subjugated status. Yahweh, as sovereign over all creation, exercises the state of exception, killing Egyptians and later giving Israelites permission to kill the inhabitants of the promised land. But it is not only the Pharaoh and other rulers who are subordinate to and eventually subjugated by God. The Israelites themselves are in a subordinate relationship with Yahweh, though this apparently did not sit well with all of them. They are repeatedly called a "stiff-necked people," ostensibly by God (Exod 32:9; 33:3, 5; 34:9; Deut 9:6, 13; 10:16).[95] (A synonym of "stiff-necked" might be "obstinate.") I suggest that being "stiff-necked" is an inevitable trait of people who are in a relationship where there is an enforced subordination between two (radically) unequal parties. One way to interpret the identifier "stiff-necked people" for the Israelites is that sovereignty and the theology of subordination/subjugation that legitimated it were onerous for some people. God's response, as sovereign over all creation, was to punish those who did not subordinate themselves to God (which included killing some). In Christian scriptures, one also observes the connection between sovereignty and relations of subordination and subjugation. Jesus was born and lived in a society that was subordinate to and subjugated by the Roman Empire. Within this society, Jewish sovereign classes (e.g., Herod, Pharisees, and Sadducees) could, with Rome's permission, exercise sovereign authority (e.g., see Herod's command to kill children around Bethlehem [Matt 2:16–18]), which meant producing

---

94. I stress that I am not saying these beliefs are simply or solely attached to phenomena of sovereignty. Hierarchical valuations seem to be an aspect of being human, though I think it is better to say that hierarchy is potential and not necessarily actual in some situations and groups. Nevertheless, although these beliefs are part of sovereignty, they must be seen as part of the constellation of attributes associated with sovereignty.

95. I use the term "ostensibly" to suggest that this is a theology that legitimates human rulers. It is part of the theological apparatus implemented to keep people in line.

and maintaining relations of subordination and subjugation within Jewish society, all under the thumb of Roman rulers. From my perspective, any cursory reading of the political philosophies and theologies of Western civilizations reveals the inevitable prevalence of subordinate and subjugated relations that attend varied iterations of sovereignty.

Forms of life that produce relations of subordination and subjugation are accompanied by a third feature of sovereignty, namely, instrumental epistemologies. To recognize other human beings as inferior and subordinate means that Othered human beings have, at best, use value. Their value is based on how they are "needed" to maintain the felt or psychosocial/political sense of upper-class superiority. But this is not the only use value of "inferior," subordinate, or subjugated people. Those in the subordinate, inferior classes are exploited to maintain the privileges and material well-being of the upper classes. Samuel's warning is a perfect illustration of how subordinate classes are used by the sovereign and sovereign classes to meet their own needs and fulfill their own pleasures. If we jump to the present, capitalism, which emerged from and depends on the sovereign political and economic elites, reveals the dominance of instrumental epistemologies in the expropriation, extraction, and exploitation of subordinate classes.[96] This subordination and subjugation includes the instrumental use of other species—who are constructed as inferior—to meet human needs and desires. To use human beings or other-than-human animals means to fail to recognize or treat them as singular beings or, more particularly, as persons or potential persons.[97] If they have value at all in this scenario, it is use value.

Another facet of instrumental epistemologies, which accompany beliefs in superiority and inferiority, is the construction of the Other as lacking personhood. Enslaved individuals are not, in the eyes of the superior caste, persons. If they have a self, it is inferior, which justifies and legitimates exploitation. This extends to other-than-human species that, at least for most Westerners, are not persons and do not have selves. While I will say more about this in Chapter 3, for now let me simply state that instrumental epistemologies that deny selfhood to other species and Othered human beings accompany a zone of nonjustice. That is, the notion of justice simply does not apply, because Othered human beings and other-than-human species are constructed as not being persons, as not possessing unique selves.

---

96. See Dufour, *Art of Shrinking Heads*; Frank, *One Market under God*; Fraser and Honneth, *Redistribution or Recognition?*; Klein, *This Changes Everything*; Valencia, *Gore Capitalism*; Wolff, *Occupy the Economy*.

97. See Castro, *Cannibal Metaphysics*. Castro argues that indigenous peoples construct other-than-human animals as having selves or persons—potentially or actually.

CIVILIZATION, SCRIPTURE, AND THE RISE AND ARTIFICE OF SOVEREIGNTY 39

Instrumental epistemologies and relations of subordination/subjugation—two features of sovereignty that are intertwined with the beliefs in superiority and inferiority—can also be depicted in terms of care and faith.[98] Members of the so-called lower classes can be exploited, but this often accompanies instrumental-contractual care and faith. The sovereign classes must demonstrate some modicum of care if the lower classes are to provide use value. In other words, persons in subordinate classes are provided sufficient material goods to perform their roles. Similarly, people within the lower classes are trusted and deemed loyal to the extent that they maintain their subordinate status. This is a foundation of the social contract: obey authority to receive a modicum of care. When the sovereign God kills and punishes stiff-necked people, it is because they are not fulfilling the contract—if you obey the sovereign, you will be cared for (if not in this life, in the next life). If people refuse to abide by the contract, they are constructed as unfaithful, stiff-necked, disloyal, and untrustworthy. Hobbes's leviathan and social contract are secular versions of a sovereign God who has a contractual relationship with members of the subordinate classes. By contrast, the sovereign God of the Israelites appears more concerned about collective freedom and well-being than about the Enlightenment's focus on the individual.

History is replete with stories of sovereigns who failed to provide sufficient care for the lower classes, which led to rebellions and revolutions. Indeed, Samuel's warning ushers in an era of prophets who call sovereigns and sovereign classes to account for their lack of care for and fidelity to those who are subordinate. Yet, these prophets never question sovereignty itself—divine or human. And revolutions, which often emerge as a result of carelessness, marginalization, and oppression vis-à-vis the lower classes, seem only to replace one form of sovereignty with another. Karl Marx predicted the withering away of the state and the emergence of a classless society, but the Russian and Chinese communist revolutions never rejected the necessity of sovereigns and sovereign classes.

A fifth feature of sovereignty is its exclusionary focus. But before discussing this focus, it is important to differentiate between sovereignty before and after the Enlightenment. Sovereignty, I have been arguing, has been integral to Western peoples since the Neolithic revolution, but in the seventeenth century, with the Treaty of Westphalia, sovereignty became associated with the nation and its government,[99] which is tasked with preserving the sovereignty of the nation. So, in the US, we do not have a sovereign,

---

98. See Niebuhr, *Faith on Earth*.
99. See Skinner, "Genealogy of the Modern State."

but we have a government that is charged with securing US sovereignty over its territories and its peoples.[100] Assigned to maintain and expand a superpower, US governments have worked diligently to extend the nation's sovereignty by expanding its political and economic control over client states.[101] Of course, the absence of a sovereign does not mean there is a corresponding absence of sovereign classes. A nation-state, whether democratic or totalitarian, has political and economic elites who exercise a great deal of sway in securing material wealth, political power, and social-political prestige. These sovereign classes support the government's task of securing national sovereignty, which means constructing apparatuses that promote national identity, while also maintaining territorial integrity. To be sure, before the rise of nation-states sovereigns sought to preserve their own sovereignty, which included maintaining the political belonging of the people and the country's geographical boundaries. In contrast, the sovereignty of nation-states does not depend on an individual sovereign, but rather on the government to secure the sovereignty of the nation and care for its citizens. If it fails to do so, the government loses its legitimacy.

Sovereignty, past and present, is fundamentally exclusionary, which can be understood in several ways. First, a sovereign cannot be divided. There cannot, in other words, be two sovereigns ruling over the people. In terms of nation-states, there cannot be multiple governments within territorial boundaries exercising sovereignty. In the US, individual states exercise limited sovereignty vis-à-vis their boundaries and citizens, but they are subordinate to the national government. These states, in other words, are excluded from exercising sovereignty over the nation. Exclusion is also noted in who is deemed to be a citizen and who is not, which is the second type. Noncitizens may reside within a nation's boundaries, but they have limited rights and can be expelled. Persons living outside the geographical boundaries of the state must be granted the right to visit or to reside within the nation. Perennial hand-wringing in the US about so-called illegal immigrants illustrates not only the link between sovereignty and its exclusionary powers, but also the legitimacy of the government to exercise sovereignty's state of exception in labeling people "illegal" and expelling them. For many conservatives, "securing" the borders is the responsibility of the US

---

100. Hannah Arendt recognized the exclusionary feature of sovereignty, as well as its tendency toward violence vis-à-vis other sovereign states. "Sovereignty means," she notes, "that conflicts of an international character can ultimately be settled only by war" (Arendt, *Last Interview*, 101).

101. See Bacevich, *American Empire*; Bacevich, *New American Militarism*; Chomsky, *Imperial Ambitions*; Johnson, *Sorrows of Empire*; Johnson, *Dismantling the Empire*; Kinzer, *Overthrow*; Klein, *Shock Doctrine*.

government and its apparatuses. In their view, the government's failure to stem the tide of foreigners crossing the border threatens US sovereignty and in turn threatens their own understanding of US national identity (which is connected to the nation's White majority). The relation between sovereignty and "building walls" (literally and in other ways) to exclude other peoples (noncitizens) is not simply a US phenomenon. Political philosopher Wendy Brown points to other nation-states exercising their sovereignty by building walls to keep undesirable people out (e.g., Israel and Egypt keeping Palestinians out).[102] Of course, sometimes nation-states exercise sovereignty by building walls to keep citizens from fleeing, as well as to keep real and imagined threats from entering into the country (e.g., the Berlin Wall).

Closely associated with exclusion based on identity is exclusion based on property. All sovereigns seek to maintain (and in many cases extend) territory. This territory is considered to be the property of the nation and its peoples. It is our land. Outsiders may visit, even dwell, but because they do not share in the identity of the nation, it is not their land. More often than not, the idea of property vis-à-vis sovereignty is ontologically justified. God gives the Israelites the promised land, which today conservative Israeli Jews consider to be their land, which provides them with the "legal" basis for excluding Palestinians and marginalizing Palestinian citizens of Israel. The religious pilgrims to America carved out the land, believing it to be God given and rightfully theirs, justifying ethnic cleansing of indigenous peoples. Even within a nation-state, property is held to be a God-given feature of human life. It is my property and the apparatuses of the state legitimate this, which is exclusionary in the sense that it is my property and not yours. I have certain rights, while you do not. As noted above, Rousseau believed the idea of property led to inequalities and class conflict—exclusions.[103]

A third kind of exclusion is founded in any form of sovereignty, whether that is monarchies or democracies. All forms of sovereignty are exclusionary with regard to the exercise of political power and agency. Monarchies, oligarchies, plutocracies, and tyrannies secure political agency and power to themselves and their attending sovereign classes. Citizens may have certain rights and may exercise some political agency and power, but only as granted by the sovereign or leviathan, and always to lesser degrees than the sovereign or leviathan. Other citizens and residents may be completely excluded from exercising agency, such as women were in the Greek polis. Is this kind of exclusion from agency present in democracies? Today the only large-scale operating democracies are representative democracies, and even

---

102. Brown, *Walled States*.
103. Ryan, *On Politics*, 556–72.

the democracies of Plato and Aristotle's era excluded women, children, "barbarians," and enslaved persons. In fact, those elected to represent people today are, more often than not, the political-economic elites, who have greater political power, privileges, and agency than average citizens do. Naturally, citizens can exercise political agency and power by protesting or rebelling, but these means may be constructed as illegitimate (e.g., as riots) or may be sidelined—undermining their effectiveness. Poor people, many African Americans, and native peoples are just some of those who, as a result of apparatuses of sovereign classes, have little political power.

The fundamental reality of sovereignty's exclusion, combined with beliefs in the superiority of the sovereign (and sovereign classes), instrumental epistemologies, and accompanying relations of subordination and subjugation, give rise to perpetual mimetic violence, which is a feature of the inherent strain of civilization. Above I have indicated that the state of exception is the core attribute of sovereignty and that it is accompanied by the use or threat of political violence. Sovereignty's appearance, alongside civilization, could only have been accompanied by the use or threat of force/violence. Hobbes's leviathan uses the threat of violence to keep citizens themselves from exercising violence to achieve individual self-interests. Freud's patriarchal tale of humankind's origin is one in which the sons kill the ruler-father to establish their own sovereignty. From a different angle, Agamben points out that sovereignty contains both law-making and law-preserving violence, and what the "law can never tolerate ... is the existence [of violence] outside the law."[104] Violence outside the law "neither makes nor preserves law, but deposes it."[105] Only the sovereign and sovereign classes can legitimately use or threaten violence. Violence outside the law is a threat to the sovereign.

What I wish to suggest is that political violence, which is at the core of sovereignty, results in what René Girard calls mimetic violence.[106] The sovereign's law-making and law-preserving violence, in other words, sets the stage for the reality of violence outside the law. To establish societal-political belonging through violence means that the objects of violence—nonsovereign classes—must submit; otherwise, they become targets to be disciplined, humiliated, or killed—*homo sacer*. Of course, many citizens accept the social contract and relations of subordination, because the sovereign

---

104. Agamben, *State of Exception*, 53.

105. Agamben, *State of Exception*, 53.

106. Girard focused on mimetic violence and the sacred. While he does not address sovereignty, the sacred often attends formulation of sovereignty, even in the modern period, as both Wendy Brown and Saul Newman note. Put differently, if all modern concepts of the state are secularized theological concepts, then the sacred is latent. See Girard, *Violence and the Sacred*.

and sovereign classes ideally provide security and stability for people to go about their daily lives—much like Hobbes's leviathan. But the looming threat of violence is ever present—to secure the sovereign and sovereign classes. I want to suggest that the reality of political violence at the heart of sovereignty establishes a mimetic relation between sovereignty and violence and a contradiction between the two, founded in violence. The subordinate and subjugated classes may submit, but not always happily. God the sovereign expects people to submit, but stiff-necked people resist, evoking God's wrath and violence. Those rebels (heretics, apostates, infidels) who are killed are made examples. Richard Horsley points out this contradiction in his analysis of peasant life during the time of Jesus. The exploitation of peasants by Imperial Rome and the Jewish state led to numerous political crises in the form of rebellions.[107] Jesus was seen by Roman authorities as undermining Rome's (and the Jewish state's) sovereignty, and he was publicly executed—as many other colonized people were—with the political aim of terrorizing people into submission. Richard Ford also takes note of the mimetic feature of sovereign authority, writing that it "is perennially vulnerable to overthrow by greater violence . . . Because we gain our position by violence, not collaboration, we too will be subject to retaliation by greater violence."[108] Ford notes that the "question is no longer whether God will intervene; the question becomes, 'How can any intervention transform the endless revival of violence in which even the divine can be implicated?'"[109] This question I intend to address in the last chapter.

Naturally, the sovereign's political violence is effective, at least in the short term. But extralegal violence subsists, eventually making its appearance in rebellions and revolutions. This is why there is a contradiction between sovereignty and its dependence on political violence, which can be understood in two ways. First, the use of political violence is, in itself, antipolitical in the sense that the objects of violence are denied political agency.[110] Put differently, the exercise of political violence places the objects of violence outside political spaces of speaking and acting together.[111] This is clearly evident when the state executes citizens who are constructed as criminals (*homo sacer*) or those who are considered to be enemies of the state/sovereign. Second, the threat or use of political violence breeds violence in the forms of rebellions and revolutions, which are, in turn, attempts

---

107. Horsley, *You Shall Not Bow Down*, 55–57.
108. Ford, *Jesus' Parables*, 3.
109. Ford, *Jesus' Parables*, 11.
110. LaMothe, "Pastoral Theology."
111. Arendt, *On Violence*.

to deny political agency to sovereign and sovereign classes. Saul Newman notes this mimetic relation, arguing that

> Revolutions and counterrevolutions often share the same structure—both gravitate around sovereignty and both affirm its place of transcendence and authority. While counterrevolution safeguards the constitutional state order by suspending it in the state of exception—thus creating, artificially, a situation that resembles a revolution—a revolution destroys an existing constitutional state order only to erect a new one in its place. The core of sovereignty is retained in both.[112]

The core of sovereignty is the state of exception and its attending political violence, which creates mimetic dynamics between the ruled and the rulers. It also reveals a fundamental contradiction between sovereignty and violence, namely, political crises.

US Representative Adam Schiff remarked, after the January 6 insurrection, that every generation has to fight for democracy—a form of sovereignty where the *demos* rules. On its face, this seems to be true, but it reveals the contradiction at the heart of *all forms* of sovereignty. Consider Judeo-Christian scriptures as replete with stories of political crises centered on sovereignty, culminating in the final victory of the cosmic sovereign God over Satan and his minions. The birth of Jesus takes place in the context of a possible political crisis. In Matthew's Gospel, the magi inform Herod of the birth of a king, which impels Herod to massacre children "to prevent the deliverance from imperial domination that Jesus is born to lead."[113] In the Oedipal myth, King Laius, not unlike Herod, has his aides kill his son, because Tiresias predicts the king's son will grow up to kill his father (a political crisis, at least from Laius's point of view), which his son eventually does. Socrates was put to death because the male leaders of Athens feared he was undermining their power, their sovereignty. Plato's elaborate imagination concocted a republic where violence would be mitigated. John Milton's *Paradise Lost* is an epic poem about sovereignty and violence. Even in a so-called modern democracy political violence founds and maintains the political order. The state and its apparatuses can legitimately use or threaten violence, while all other violence is labeled illegitimate—riots, insurrections, rebellions. Sovereign violence begets mimetic violence, leading to one political crisis after another.

To return to Adam Schiff, he overlooks the fact that the American Revolution was an illegitimate rebellion against the British Empire. Many colonists felt oppressed and marginalized by the British sovereign and his

---

112. Newman, *Political Theology*, 106.
113. Horsley, *You Shall Not Bow Down*, 44.

attending apparatuses of the state. They rebelled, establishing a "democracy" that excluded poor men, women, native peoples, and enslaved persons. Yes, many of these groups, through political agitation and sometimes violence, gained political rights. But, what Adam Schiff's quote points to is the violence at the very heart of sovereignty, whether we are talking about monarchy or democracy. Put another way, a hidden belief lies at the foundation of all forms of sovereignty, which is the belief that violence and the threat of violence are essential for political belonging and the exercise of political agency. This belief tends to give birth to political crises,[114] even as it coexists with another belief: that sovereignty is necessary for political belonging.

Let me summarize the main points about sovereignty before briefly shifting to how the marriage of civilization and sovereignty has implications for other species and the Earth, which the climate emergency reveals. First, I claimed that the emergence of civilization accompanied the notion of sovereignty, which was and is believed to be existentially and ontologically necessary for human belonging. Second, the attributes of sovereignty entail a state of exception, instrumental epistemologies, the use and threat of political violence, beliefs in superiority and inferiority, and relations of subordination and subjugation. That is, the attributes of sovereignty reflect forms of life that exhibit these attributes. Third, at its core, sovereignty is exclusionary. Fourth, sovereignty propagates perpetual mimetic violence, which reveals the inherent contradiction and strain at the heart of sovereignty, namely, perpetual political conflicts and crises. In other words, sovereignty and its dependence on violence lead to a perpetual contradiction vis-à-vis its putative stability, which predisposes it to political crises.

All of these attributes and dynamics have referenced human beings, but sovereignty and civilization negatively impact other species and the Earth. While I will say more about this in coming chapters, for the moment I want to acknowledge briefly that the preponderance of Judeo-Christian scripture and Western political philosophies[115] and theologies that deal with civiliza-

---

114. In her excellent book, Nancy Fraser argues persuasively that "every form of capitalism harbors a contradiction that inclines it to political crisis" (*Cannibal Capitalism*, 117). I agree, but capitalism emerged as a result of political classes linked to a monarchal parliamentary system and spread as a result of sovereign imperial nations colonizing other nations and peoples. I am arguing that sovereignty is a more fundamental problem, which precedes any economic system.

115. Aristotle claimed that human beings have dominion over other species and in so doing can improve them. "Tame animals have a better nature than wild, and it is better for such animals that they should be ruled by man because they get the benefit of preservation" (Barker, trans., *Politics of Aristotle*, 13). The climate emergency and attending vast numbers of extinctions, not counting factory slaughterhouses, belie this claim.

tion and sovereignty excludes other species, except to the extent that they are instrumentally useful for meeting human needs and desires. Since other species and the Earth are constructed as insignificant or inferior, they can be used or ignored. In being given dominion over "Nature" by a sovereign God, human beings who act out of this dominion are at odds with "Nature" in that we differentiate between "Nature" and humanity, between inferior, subordinate animals and superior human beings. We forget that we, too, are animals, facing the same existential vulnerability and dependency, as well as existential insignificance and impermanence that other animals do. Our dominion has limits, as Freud recognized; yet, for Freud, civilization, with its attempt to have dominion over "Mother Nature" is nevertheless necessary to protect humans from the vicissitudes of "Nature," as if "Nature" is cruel and indifferent. Yet, "Nature" is neither cruel not indifferent; it is human beings that proclaim dominion (and violence) over other species, projecting onto them existential insignificance and impermanence. What climate change reveals is that our attempts (mainly from Western countries) to have dominion over Nature (instead of adapting to "it") have led to catastrophic changes in the environment, threatening the very foundation of a biodiverse Earth that is essential for civilization, for human habitation. The irony and tragedy of this is not that "Nature" is cruel and indifferent; it is civilized-sovereign human beings who are ruthless and indifferent to the sufferings of other species and the degradation of the Earth.

While many human beings believe and act as if we have dominion over Nature and that this dominion is necessary for human survival, flourishing, and belonging, civilization's mimetic features and contradictions reveal that civilization in fact depends on sovereignty—that civilization is, in the end, self-defeating vis-à-vis sustainable human dwelling with other-than-human beings and the Earth. As Jonathan Schell writes, "If we conquer nature, we will find ourselves among the defeated."[116]

Conclusion

Our God-given sovereignty over other species and the Earth is produced and maintained by religious apparatuses (scriptures, rituals, and theologies), as well as apparatuses associated with capitalism, colonization, and science, which I will say more about in the next chapter. That is, the marriage of civilization and sovereignty and the apparatuses that generate and sustain this marriage create a climate wherein the nonsovereignty of God and humanity become seemingly unthinkable. And yet, the revelation of the climate

116. Schell, "Human Shadow," 19.

emergency invites, if not demands, that we critically examine our past and present forms of life and ways of ordering human belonging—which in this chapter includes the ideas of civilization and sovereignty—so that we can reimagine our answers to the political questions of human belonging. Critiquing and reimagining includes developing apparatuses for producing human belonging that exemplify noninstrumental, inclusive caring relations that respect the singularities of all human beings, of all other species, and of the Earth. This reimagining is not simply and solely based on the hope that human beings survive (as if we are again privileging human existence over all other life), but on the categorical existential demand to care, as best we can, for the singularities of all species. The Earth is not simply our home, on which our material existence depends; it is the home of millions of other species.

2

Climate Calamities

Iterations and Consequences of Western Sovereignty

The original sin of sovereignty threatens to contaminate the history which flows from it, and so must be suppressed.[1]

I do not mean that our times are particularly corrupt . . . all times are corrupt.[2]

The beating heart of sovereignty is political violence.[3]

One can stroll through a forest, stooping here and there to examine a plant, and be oblivious to what appears to be a singular stem when it is actually a shoot of a massive underground plant—a rhizome—that extends for many yards. Rhizomes, unlike trees and most other plants, grow laterally with varied shoots, here and there, pushing above ground. Philosophers Deleuze and Guattari argue that a "rhizome" is an apt metaphor for conceptualizing knowledge: they point out that Western epistemologies are hierarchal, suggesting that the metaphor of a tree

---

1. Eagleton, *Tragedy*, 101.
2. T. S. Elliot, quoted in Eagleton, *Critical Revolutionaries*, 21.
3. These are my own words.

is apt in conceptualizing human knowing.[4] In considering the epistemologies linked to the apparatuses of sovereignty, it would appear more fitting to a hierarchical metaphor, like a tree, instead of the metaphor of rhizome, because sovereignty establishes relations of subordination/subjugation. Yet, the notion of sovereignty and its attending apparatuses is more rhizomic in nature than treelike. This is not because the shoots of sovereignty are manifold, such as monarchy, oligarchy, plutocracy, democracy, and so forth. If we saw these shoots, we would naturally think that they are part of the underground rhizomic plant of sovereignty, but we might also overlook other shoots that do not at first glance appear to be connected to this rhizome. We might then think that these shoots are distinctly different and unrelated, when, in fact, they have grown from the same source.

Chapter 2 furthers the diagnosis, contending that nationalism, imperialism, capitalism, and some forms and practices of science are all shoots of the same source, namely, the rhizome of sovereignty's epistemologies and its accompanying apparatuses. They undergird civilization and forms of life that are wedded to power over Othered human beings, more-than-human species, and the Earth. To be sure, each of these iterations of sovereignty is distinct, but all are rooted in and depend on sovereignty and its epistemologies. It is important to recognize the intersectionality of these systems because they are implicated in fostering forms of life that are, in the end, destructive to the planet,[5] undermining the dwelling and well-being of human beings and other species. If we simply focus on one or two, we will overlook their connectivity and unwittingly risk colluding in their continuance. By acknowledging their connectivity and rootedness in sovereignty and its apparatuses, we might begin to imagine forms of life that eschew illusions of human superiority and the inferiority of other species. We could develop forms of life that reject relations of subordination and subjugation. We might foster forms of life rooted in epistemologies that recognize and respect the singularities of all species. These inoperative forms of life will be considered in the last chapter.

Several clarifications are needed before plowing the ground. First, while I begin with the issue of nationalism and end with a brief discussion of some practices of science, I am not suggesting any kind of priority or hierarchical valuation of these shoots of sovereignty. In other words, I do not view nationalism as more important than imperialism or capitalism vis-à-vis the destruction of the planet's biosphere and its inhabitants. Instead, I see all of these as interconnected and, therefore, equally destructive. Indeed,

4. See Deleuze and Guattari, *A Thousand Plateaus*.
5. Gardner, *Perfect Moral Storm*.

the intersection of these ways of life are exponentially destructive than one alone; that is, if we could actually tease them apart. Second and relatedly, I begin with nationalism because it arose in the West at about the same time that European states developed their imperial ambitions. Capitalism also emerged around this time, slowly becoming imbricated with nationalism and imperialism. Western science has ancient roots, but the Enlightenment birthed an explosion of scientific discoveries, many of which fueled imperialism and capitalism. Third, I recognize that each of these shoots comes with some positive features, particularly for some human beings and with few benefits for other species. Nationalism, for instance, helped colonized people resist and then shed the yoke of their oppressors by forming a collective and liberating sense of identity and purpose. Imperialism, especially American imperialism, has many supporters, who cite world stability, security, economic growth, and other consequences as the positive results, though I suspect most of those who have been the objects of American imperialism might take a different view.[6] Capitalism, as Karl Marx noted, produces tremendous wealth, benefitting political and economic elites.[7] The sciences, which often rely on experimentation of other-than-human species, have been responsible for achievements leading to better health and longer lives for human beings and some other species (e.g., pets). These positive features pale in comparison to the wide and deep destruction that the iterations of sovereignty produce, which the climate emergency reveals. Fourth, it is impossible to offer an exhaustive depiction of each of these four shoots on the rhizome of sovereignty, since they and their consequences, individually and collectively, are complex. My approach is heuristic, highlighting the main features of each, their links to the notion and attributes of sovereignty, and the destructive environmental aftermath. Finally, readers will note that I have omitted religion, in particular Christianity, from the list. The truth is that many Christian leaders and their followers have used scripture and theologies to support, if not ontologize, nationalism, imperialism, capitalism, and science. To demonstrate the link between Christianity and these shoots of sovereignty would take me far afield. Instead, I simply rely on the argument of the last chapter regarding sovereignty and its connection to Abrahamic traditions. More specifically, the shoots from the rhizome of sovereignty—nationalism, imperialism, capitalism, and science—give rise to forms of life that exhibit relations of power over Othered human beings, other-than-human species, and the Earth. These prevailing forms of life enable adherents of Western Abrahamic traditions to more

---

6. Fergusson, *Colossus*, 4–7.
7. Eagleton, *Why Marx Was Right*, 11.

readily link religious beliefs to nationalism, imperialism, and capitalism. So, in a sense, my view is analogous to Carl Schmitt's view that "all significant concepts of the modern theory of the state are secularized theological concepts."[8]

The Shoots of Sovereignty and Their Contribution to the Climate Emergency

Nationalism

Before delving into the notion of nationalism, it is important to explain what the terms nation and state mean. Steven Grosby concisely defines the nation "as a territorial community of nativity."[9] Implied here is a unique type of kinship that differs from other types, such as family, tribe, and so forth because "the centrality of territory" encompasses many families and tribes.[10] He clarifies further that a nation "differs from other territorial societies such as a tribe, city-state, or various 'ethnic groups' not merely by the greater extent of its territory, but also because of its relatively uniform culture that provides stability, that is, continuation over time."[11] This suggests that there is a collective memory of the people and the nation. This group memory and identity are fostered by oral traditions, written stories, and collective or public rituals that facilitate collective identification with the nation.[12] What is clear here is that "nations are the artefacts of men's convictions and loyalties and solidarities."[13] As Grosby claims, "*The nation is a social relation of collective self-consciousness*,"[14] and this self-consciousness is connected to socially constructed, shared identity and loyalties.

This does not mean that nations are monolithic or homogeneous with regard to identity and memory.[15] Within the circumscribed territory of a nation, there can be many tribes or ethnic groups. But those within a nation, despite plurality, must "recognize certain mutual rights and duties to each other in virtue of their shared membership . . . It is their recognition of each other as fellows of this kind which turns them into a nation, and not other

---

8. See Brown, *Walled States*, 59.
9. Grosby, *Nationalism*, 7.
10. Grosby, *Nationalism*, 7.
11. Grosby, *Nationalism*, 7.
12. Gellner, *Nations and Nationalism*, 6.
13. Gellner, *Nations and Nationalism*, 7.
14. Grosby, *Nationalism*, 11 (italics original).
15. See Smith, *Nationalism*.

shared attributes, whatever they might be, which separate that category from non-members."[16] This recognition, it must be stressed, is founded on the artifice of nation and its attending social constructions. Moreover, this recognition of shared membership is supported by state and nonstate apparatuses, such as state institutions that determine citizenship, as well as nonstate public events (e.g., memorial parades, sports, and standing for the national anthem).

Since I mentioned "state," it is important to differentiate between state and nation, while recognizing their connectivity. Nations, Grosby argues, "have been consolidated through a state's exercise and extension of sovereignty over time."[17] The state entails varied institutions that, while having many functions, are aimed at securing the nation's stability and, ideally, the well-being of its citizens. Governments may come and go, but the state and its institutions remain, unless they are overthrown or defeated by enemies from other nations. A nation may, then, perdure even if the state falls by a revolution (e.g., France underwent the French Revolution in 1789), but this revolution will necessarily have to construct a state and its apparatuses to govern people (e.g., the French Consulate was formed in 1799). A recent example is the collapse of the Soviet Union. Previous republics split off and formed new nations, but it was clear that Russia and the Russian people continued to exist, even as new institutions or agencies were being developed or transformed.

Another distinction between the nation and the state is that the state has legitimacy with regard to the exercise of political violence,[18] whether it is perpetrated within its nation's borders or directed toward other persons or other nations outside its nation's borders. Hobbes's leviathan, for instance, represents the state and not the nation. The leviathan exercises violence or threatens violence with the purported aim of societal stability. This stability, founded on the social contract that one must subordinate oneself to the leviathan/state, ideally provides the nation's citizens with the freedom to pursue their self-interests, as long as these citizens accept the social contract and do not interfere with or harm the interests of others. Of course, there are numerous examples in history when a nation's state apparatuses exercised (or exercise) violence toward citizens who were (or are) constructed as a danger to the nation, when, in fact, these citizens have endangered the power, privileges, and positions of political-economic elites. For example, the current state-sanctioned violence against Iranian citizen

---

16. Gellner, *Nations and Nationalism*, 7.
17. Grosby, *Nationalism*, 22.
18. Gellner, *Nations and Nationalism*, 3.

protestors is aimed at maintaining the Islamic state and its sovereign classes. The United States also has a long record of exercising state violence and sanctioning, tacitly and overtly, extralegal violence against native peoples, African Americans, unionists, and others.[19] In addition, the state may decide to exercise violence toward an enemy, by using state apparatuses to form and train armies, raise money, produce weapons, and the like. But soldiers do not fight on behalf of the state, but rather on behalf of the nation against an outside enemy. The relation between the state and the nation becomes more complicated and murkier when the state exercises violence toward citizens and residents.[20] The police and military may commit acts of violence on behalf of and for the state and not necessarily the nation. The use of state violence against trade unions in the late nineteenth and early twentieth centuries is an example of how those who exercised violence were acting not for the benefit of the nation, but for the benefit of political and economic elites.[21]

What I hope is noticed here is that both the state and the nation are inextricably linked to the idea of sovereignty. A monarch is seen as sovereign over the peoples, but the nation itself has sovereignty with regard to its territory. The sovereign acts (ideally) on behalf of the people to secure the territory from other nations and groups. In more modern democratic states and nations, the people are deemed to be sovereign, and elected representatives exercise the state's sovereignty by protecting territorial integrity. The claim here is that both nation and state are intertwined with the idea of sovereignty, which means that both nation and state possess the same attributes of sovereignty as outlined in the previous chapter, namely, exclusion,[22] exceptionalism (belief in superiority), and relations of subordination and subjugation. For instance, both nations and states exclude people from other nations, unless the state constructs laws that allow for some foreigners to live within the boundaries of the nation or to visit or to trade. There may also be legal processes whereby an "alien" may become a citizen of

---

19. See Zinn, *People's History of the United States*; Wilkerson, *Caste*.

20. Boris Groys argues that Alexander Kojève believed "classes constitute themselves not through their relation to the process of production but through their relation to direct violence and political power." His is a view that I take in this chapter. Sovereignty's apparatuses of political violence preceded the emergence of capitalism. Groys, *Philosophy of Care*, 36.

21. See Zinn, *People's History of the United States*.

22. See Auestad, *Nationalism and the Body Politic*. Auestad, using psychoanalytic concepts and theory, indicates the exclusionary features of nationalism, evident in ethnocentrism and xenophobia.

the nation.²³ There is also a tendency among nations to produce apparatuses that promote citizens' identification with the nation and its citizens. This is done, in part, through cultivating types of exceptionalism or group pride.²⁴ It is not simply that we are a particular people who dwell within this specific territory, but rather we perceive ourselves to be extraordinary for this or that reason. Exceptionalism is the glue that binds a nation's peoples together, while also subtly or overtly constructing noncitizens as inferior. The Israelites viewed themselves as the chosen people. Roman citizens took pride in being an empire. French people may take pride in their "superior" cuisine and art. Americans tout US superpower status and boast of its relatively long period of democracy.²⁵ Naturally, there may be nations and individuals that do not view themselves as special, exceptional, or superior, but I would argue that, by and large, exceptionalism accompanies both nations and their states. Closely associated with exceptionalism are relations of subordination and subjugation. Those who are excluded and constructed as less-than are by definition subordinate and at times subjugated. People who live in the US and are without documents are easily exploited, because they are not seen as citizens and therefore lack legal protections.²⁶ While I will say more about imperialism, nation-states that endeavor to expand their territorial boundaries, to rule over other peoples, or both, construct such other peoples as both subordinate to and subjugated by the "exceptional" or superior nation-state.

As political constructions, nations and states also exclude other-than-human species. By this I mean that other species, whether within and outside the territorial borders, are not considered to be integral to the nation

---

23. It is important to note that people who live within the nation's territory may also experience marginalization and oppression. Aristotle's polis viewed women as citizens, but they were excluded from the polis's spaces of speaking and acting together, as were barbarians, who were simply seen as noncitizens.

24. Grosby, *Nationalism*, 93.

25. Alexis de Tocqueville made note of this deeply embedded, grandiose exceptionalism in the middle of the nineteenth century: "If I say to an American that the country he lives in is a fine one, aye he replies and there is none its equal in the world. If I applaud the freedom its inhabitants enjoy, he answers 'freedom is a fine thing but few nations are worthy of it.' If I remark on the purity of morals that distinguishes the United States he declares 'I can imagine that a stranger who has witnessed the corruption which prevails in other nations would be astonished at the difference.' At length I leave him to a contemplation of himself. But he returns to the charge and does not desist until he has got me to repeat all I have been saying. It is impossible to conceive of a more troublesome and garrulous patriotism" (quoted in Niebuhr, *Irony of American History*, 28).

26. As I mentioned in the previous chapter, groups of citizens can also be subjugated by fellow citizens.

or the state. To be sure, some species may be seen and used as totems or national symbols (e.g., the bald eagle in the US), but they are not integral to the nation itself. Some species may be protected because they are in danger of extinction. Nevertheless, millions of other-than-human species are exploited within (and outside) the nation's borders for the real and imagined benefits or pleasures of citizens who, in large part, consider other species to be inferior to human beings, who are deemed to be existentially and ontologically exceptional. The reality, which the disasters of the climate emergency demonstrate, is that the very existence of nations and states depends on a biodiverse Earth.

Nations, I argue, are political artifices founded on the idea of sovereignty, its attending apparatuses, and forms of living. If this is the case, then did nations arise with the emergence of civilization? Prior to the Neolithic revolution, people lived in relatively homogenous groups or tribes. After this revolution, people began to live in larger, more diverse groups, such as towns or city-states, which competed with and warred against other city-states. In my telling of this story, the rise of sovereignty and civilization accompanied the gradual emergence of the idea that this group of tribes, towns, and city-states fell under the umbrella of a nation and its territory. Grosby highlights the nations of ancient Egypt, Israel, early ninth-century England, and the fourth-century Yamato Kingdom in Japan as illustrations of nations that existed before the seventeenth century in Europe and the 1648 Treaty of Westphalia. Nevertheless, important distinctions can be made between nations that existed before and after the Treaty of Westphalia. Nations like ancient Egypt and Israel were theocratic, which indicates the intersection of religion and nation.[27] While territory was an important piece of a theocratic nation, the boundaries were not always clear and were easily contested by neighbors. The focus was primarily on the people of the nation. The Treaty of Westphalia affirmed nations' territorial integrity and noninterference of other nations in the domestic affairs of a sovereign nation. This affirmation did not mean that nations after the treaty did not seek to war against other nations or attempt to interfere in the domestic life of other nations. As the Enlightenment emerged around the same time, close identification of religion with a nation and state gradually loosened. So, states and nations became linked by secular political philosophies, though, as I mentioned above, "all significant concepts of the modern theory of the state are secularized theological concepts."[28] Of course, today we continue to see in some places the close connection between religion and some

27. Grosby, *Nationalism*, 80–90.
28. See Brown, *Walled States*, 59.

nation-states (e.g., in Islamic nation-states, among Christian nationalists, and among Israeli religious conservatives).

Benedict Anderson's work further elaborates the idea of the nation before and after the Enlightenment. Anderson argues that there were three key cultural features of nationhood prior to the seventeenth century. "The first of these," he writes, "was the idea that a particular script-language offered privileged access to ontological truth," which grounded and legitimated the nation and its territory.[29] The second "was the belief that society was naturally organized around and under high centres—monarchs who were persons apart from other human beings and who ruled by some form of cosmological (divine) dispensation."[30] Anderson goes on to remark that relations were "hierarchical and centripetal because the ruler, like the sacred script, was a node of access to being and inherent in it."[31] The last "was a conception of temporality in which cosmology and history were indistinguishable."[32] In my view, this last feature provided people of the nation a sense of continuing to exist even given the fact of their impermanence—that they will die. God's pledge to Abraham (Gen 12:1–3) is an example of promised continuity in the face of finitude. These three conceptions of nationhood fell away in Western Europe during and after the Enlightenment, fueling "the search . . . for a new way of linking fraternity, power and time,"[33] which took the form of nationalism.

Like Schmitt, I believe these ideas remained, though in secular form and in the background. Nationalism, in other words, provides an imagined sense of belonging or community that links cherished (not ontological) truths about the nation and shared loyalty among citizens. The hierarchical dimension clearly continues in nationalism in that the state legitimately exercises political violence. And while cosmology and history are not united, there certainly is the belief in the continuity of one's nation, which citizens out of love and devotion will sacrifice themselves to insure.[34] As Anderson notes, "nationalism thinks in terms of historical destinies."[35]

All of this, even with the distinctions, can be attributed both to nations and forms of nationalism that preceded Western Enlightenment. Hannah Arendt addresses a key feature of Western nationalism. She argues that the

29. Anderson, *Imagined Communities*, 36.
30. Anderson, *Imagined Communities*, 36.
31. Anderson, *Imagined Communities*, 36.
32. Anderson, *Imagined Communities*, 36.
33. Anderson, *Imagined Communities*, 36.
34. Anderson, *Imagined Communities*, 141.
35. Anderson, *Imagined Communities*, 149.

rise of ideas linked to liberal individualism accompanied an atomized society and the loneliness that comes with it.[36] "Nationalism," she writes, "became the precious cement binding together a centralized state and an atomized society."[37] She continues, "Nationalism always preserved this initial intimate loyalty to the government and never quite lost its function of preserving the intimate balance between nation and state on the one hand between nationals of an atomized society on the other."[38] In one sense, Anderson's imagined community is a way of understanding Arendt's perspective on an atomized society where loneliness abounds. Nationalism gives citizens a sense of belonging to an imagined community that mitigates loneliness, while also screening citizens from recognizing how atomized the society is.

This imagined community, with its shared loyalty, collective memory and identity, and common purpose, can evoke strong emotions and identifications, which are especially intense in nationalistic fervors. Nationalism, for Gellner, "is a very distinctive species of patriotism,"[39] which is love of and for one's country. Love for one's country may be a common enough claim, but it is also imaginary in the sense that the object "nation" is an abstraction.[40] Nationalists may love their country, while despising many of its citizens. That love of country or community is imaginary does dilute its power. Nationalism can motivate people to extraordinary feats of altruism, as well as horrendous acts of brutality, all in the name of love and loyalty to a nation.

While one can live in a nation and not succumb to nationalistic fervor, the tendency of nation-states is to fan the flames of nationalism. When this occurs, the world becomes divided—"one's own nation in opposition to all other nations."[41] "Nationalism," Grosby writes, "repudiates civility and the differences that it tolerates by attempting to eliminate all differing views and interests for the sake of one vision of what the nation has been and should be."[42] China and Russia are seen as a threat by the US and some of its allies. Russia violated the sovereignty of the nation of Ukraine, initiating a war that has resulted in NATO nations providing weapons and other resources to combat Russia. In the US, Florida governor Ron DeSantis and like-minded

36. Arendt, *Origins of Totalitarianism*, 317.
37. Arendt, *Origins of Totalitarianism*, 231.
38. Arendt, *Origins of Totalitarianism*, 231. While not the focus of this chapter, it is nevertheless important to point out the Arendt persuasively argues that an atomized society leads to a form of nationalism in the guise of totalitarian states.
39. Gellner, *Nations and Nationalism*, 132.
40. LaMothe, "Patriotism."
41. Grosby, *Nationalism*, 17.
42. Grosby, *Nationalism*, 17.

Republican nationalists are promoting a vision of the US that marginalizes and oppresses LGBTQI persons and seeks to exclude educating children about the long history of racism in this nation. Nationalism is fundamentally exclusionary, though there may be times when nations decide to conditionally accept people from other nations or to work in cooperation with other nations, as long as their interests align.

The problem is not simply that nations and nationalism are fundamentally exclusionary; it is also that nations, because of their inherent sovereignty, retain the right to exercise violence within and outside their borders in the pursuit of territorial integrity and other rationalized illusory interests. For instance, the US has a sustained history of using violence to extend its borders and advance its economic interests and reach into Central and South America, as well as into the Pacific. Political leaders, legislators, and others have concocted fictions such as the Empire of Liberty (1780), the Monroe Doctrine (1823), Manifest Destiny (1845), and the like to rationalize their use of political violence. A nation's right to exercise violence is unquestionable, though in actual practice it may come under scrutiny or be questioned. For instance, Russia's political leaders have said that they have sovereign right to conduct a "special operation" in Ukraine, because Ukraine's close ties to the West threaten the sovereignty of Russia. Western nations scoffed at this fabrication yet never questioned a nation's right to use political violence, because this is unquestionable dogma.

It is difficult to conceive of something like a nation where there is no right to exercise political violence. Indeed, it seems to be a truism that when you have borders, a shared identity, and a common history, you need to have state apparatuses that have a duty and function to protect the nation. From Anatol Lieven's perspective, those who critique nationalism tend to be naïve or utopian, imaging some cosmopolitical world without nations.[43] For Lieven, nations must create institutions to protect citizens, which may include institutions that exercise violence toward other nations or those within the nation-state. Yet, consider the US as a nation composed of fifty states (and territories). Each state exercises limited sovereignty, and while a US state is not a nation, citizens often identify themselves as belonging to their state and sharing its identity and loyalties. States have armies, which are called national guards, but states do not have a right to declare war or send their guard units into neighboring states. They may deploy their armies within the state's territory to safeguard people and institutions.[44] However,

---

43. Lieven, *Climate Change and the Nation State*, xxv.

44. Sometimes, in incidents of environmental racism, police brutality, classism, and so forth, certain people or places are not safeguarded. Not all residents within a state are protected.

if states disagree about territorial boundaries, trade, or what have you, they settle these disputes through legal and extralegal processes. Contra Lieven, what I am suggesting is that it is possible to imagine a federation of states that do not have the right to exercise political violence. Of course, the issue of sovereignty and its attributes would remain.

Let me turn to the issue of nationalism and climate change. I have argued that nationalism is a shoot of the rhizome of sovereignty, which poses a significant obstacle to climate action. Nations are focused "naturally" on their self-interests, which may or may not result in cooperation between nations who have similar self-interests. When it comes to the reality of global warming and attending disasters, one would think that all nations would have a vested interest in working together to mitigate the trajectory of climate change. Working together and meeting are not necessarily the same thing. There have been global meetings among world leaders since the 1990s. Treaties have been signed and promises made, but the reality is that little to no progress has been made toward reductions in greenhouse gas emissions, sustainability, or resiliency. Wealthy nations of the global north have not contributed their promised aid to nations already suffering from the effects of climate change.[45] This suggests that although political leaders from wealthy nations may recognize the dangers of global warming, their loyalty and commitment lie with their own nations and people. This is completely understandable, given the logic of sovereignty and nationalism; however, these priorities are significant obstacles to genuine cooperation among nations. Add to this that major powers (the US, China, Russia, and also India) aggressively compete against one another, and also two of these are pursuing global economic hegemony (China and the US). Their ongoing contributions to greenhouse gas emissions dwarf those of other nations, and there is neither motive nor action toward cooperation to aid poorer nations or to find ways to drastically reduce emissions. Instead, trillions are spent on weapons and military forces, which worsens climate change and diverts financial and other resources that might be used to mitigate effects of the climate emergency.[46]

Anatol Lieven would partially agree with this assessment, though, seeing the positives of nation-states and nationalism, he advocates for a Western civic nationalism that steers clear of a defense of liberal democracy and toward an ethic of shared responsibility, whereby state and nonstate leaders motivate people to make shared sacrifices with the aim of reducing emis-

---

45. Kamal, "Revealed."
46. The military's contribution to climate change—CEOBS.

sions.[47] He argues that social-national solidarity can be realized vis-à-vis the Green New Deal. In short, Lieven believes that Western civic nationalism, which is neither imperialistic nor chauvinistic, is what a realist should choose for the path ahead. Yet, I think Lieven is naïve to think that civic nationalism is somehow the answer. After providing numerous examples of the problems associated with nation-states and nationalism, he advocates for a kind of almost humanist nationalism that creates strong identities and motivates people to make sacrifices. In a telling quip, Lieven says, "To defeat the Trumps and Bolsonaros on climate change, it is necessary to seize the weapon of nationalism from their hands and turn it against them."[48] Whether he uses "weapon" metaphorically or not, he has hit on a truism. Weapons are constructed and used to overcome and defeat an enemy. Weapons are used not to encourage cooperation, but to subordinate and subjugate. Even if we think of weapons solely as a means of defense, the enemy still must be defeated. There is no evidence in history of nations surrendering their weapons and their "sovereign right" to exercise violence (including exploitation of other species and the Earth) to advance their real or imagined interests. As Wendy Brown notes, "if nation-state sovereignty was always something of a fiction in its aspiration to absolute supremacy, completeness, settled jurisdiction, monopolies of violence, and perpetuity over time, the fiction was a potent one."[49] This is true, and as long as we continue to depend on apparatuses associated with the production of nationalism and its forms of life, we will find ourselves on the wrong end of climate action and, in the end, ironically and tragically holding on to weapons as we fall to extinction.

Imperialism

Another related shoot of the rhizome of sovereignty is imperialism. Not all nations are imperialistic, but some nations seek to extend their territory and power. Imperial nations are of course, nothing new in history. Alexander sought, for a time successfully, a Hellenistic Empire that extended to India. Additional examples include the Roman Empire, varied empires in the history of China and India, and a plethora of competing Western empires (Spain, Portugal, Britain, France, Germany, Austria-Hungary, and Belgium, to name a few). The imperialistic states of Western Europe (especially England) laid the foundation for US imperialism. Since US imperial ambitions have been dominant since the nineteenth century and since it is one of main

47. Lieven, *Climate Change and the Nation State*, 139.
48. Lieven, *Climate Change and the Nation State*, xvi.
49. Brown, "We Are All Democrats Now," 48–49.

contributors to greenhouse gas emissions, I want to focus the discussion on the US Empire. This will serve to illustrate the problems associated with other imperial nations, which today also include China and Russia.

One more comment is in order before beginning: Lest one think that the discussions about nations and imperialism have little to do with Christianity, let me be clear. Christianity is imbricated in the enthusiastic rise of and support for the imperialism of European nations and the US.[50] As was mentioned earlier, Catherine Beecher, the nineteenth-century advocate for women, believed that the mission of the United States was to demonstrate "to the world the beneficent influences of Christianity, when carried into every social, civil, and political institution."[51] On the political stage, this was echoed by Senator Albert J. Beveridge of Indiana, who believed that the US had a moral "duty to bring Christianity and civilization to 'savage and senile peoples.'"[52] This kind of language shifted in the twentieth and twenty-first centuries from promoting Christianity to advocating a kind of secular evangelical democracy, which retained loose connections to Christianity. Chalmers Johnson turned to Woodrow Wilson's "hyperidealistic, sentimental, and ahistorical idea that what should be sought was a world democracy based on the American example and led by the United States" as an illustration of this kind of discourse.[53] Decades later, Ronald Reagan continued this legacy, saying, "I have always believed that this anointed land was set apart in an uncommon way, that a divine plan placed this great continent here between two oceans to be found by people from every corner of the Earth who have a special love of faith and freedom."[54] Reagan merely echoed Wilson's salvific belief in the US's global mission to democratize the world and bring about the "ultimate peace of the world."[55] Similarly, Bill Clinton viewed the end of the Cold War as "the fullness of time" and the US as an "indispensable nation."[56] The triumphalism of George W. Bush's administration and his moral justification for military interventions in the Middle East and elsewhere are the most current illustrations of democratic evangelism and free market fundamentalism.[57] The mixed secular-Judeo-Christian discourse,

---

50. See Hughes, *Christian America*; Merry, *Sands of Empire*; Rieger, *Christ and Empire*.
51. Kaplan, *Anarchy of Empire*, 29.
52. Johnson, *Sorrows of Empire*, 43.
53. Johnson, *Sorrows of Empire*, 51.
54. Quoted in Lundestad, *American "Empire,"* 17.
55. Johnson, *Sorrows of Empire*, 47–48.
56. Quoted in Bacevich, *American Empire*, 1.
57. See Ryn, *America the Virtuous*; West, *Democracy Matters*.

which has its roots in the founding of the US, is exemplified in Herman Melville's comment: "We Americans are the peculiar chosen people—The Israel of our time. We bear the ark of the liberties of the world."[58] In my view, Christian support for US imperialism, bolstered by scripture and theology, has been and continues to be an easy hermeneutical stance, since Christian scriptures themselves tout sovereignty, and given the evangelical conviction that Christians are in possession of the universal Truth.

When we consider the imperialistic ambitions that led the US to become an empire, we note that imperialistic desires and attitudes do not necessarily result in a nation becoming an empire. Mussolini's government had imperialistic aims that motivated it to take over Ethiopia, though Italy fell far short of being an empire. Imperialism is defined as a nation-state's policies and apparatuses aimed at extending political, military, and economic control over other nations and peoples. A nation cannot become an empire without imperialistic narratives, policies, and the political, economic, and military resources needed to extend its territory, influence, or both. There is, then, a close relation between imperialism and empire. If we turn to the US, imperial ambitions were present at the birth of the new nation,[59] though it lacked the resources to be an empire. George Washington presciently called the United States a "nascent empire." His compatriot Thomas Jefferson dubbed the US an empire of liberty, arguing, with typical American exuberance and grandiosity, that "no constitution was ever before as well calculated as ours for extending extensive empire and self-government."[60] The imperialistic seeds began to take root very quickly. Less than a decade after Jefferson's hubristic, ironic, and tautological claim that the United States is an empire of liberty, Secretary of War (a post now euphemistically called Secretary of Defense) John C. Calhoun "inaugurated the policy of removing 'Indians' to the ninety-fifth line of longitude, a policy that became law in 1825."[61] This brutal form of ethnic cleansing extended into Spanish-held Florida, where, in 1818, Andrew Jackson led soldiers to subdue ostensibly rebellious Seminole tribes and protect (that is, advance) US interests.[62] The Monroe Doctrine (1823) and then, in the 1840s, Manifest Destiny were embodiments of Washington's and Jefferson's imperialistic narratives, which served to justify not only concrete actions of westward expansion, but also a trumped-up war with Mexico that resulted in the US acquisition of huge

58. Quoted in Bacevich, *American Empire*, 43.
59. Chomsky, *Imperial Ambitions*.
60. Quoted in Fergusson, *Colossus*, 34.
61. Fergusson, *Colossus*, 36.
62. Zinn, *People's History of the United States*, 127.

swaths of territory. Narratives supporting and maintaining the beliefs in the uniqueness and entitlement of the United States served to justify numerous interventions in South America, Central America, the Caribbean, and the Pacific in the nineteenth and twentieth centuries,[63] which, after two world wars, eventuated in the rise of the American Empire.[64]

What is important to note in the history of the rise of the US Empire is the change in how empire is understood and lived out. Empires of the seventeenth, eighteenth, and nineteenth centuries established, through force, "the formal political control of one state over another's external and internal policy."[65] European empires had direct rule over peoples of other countries. Given Western political and economic changes in the twentieth century, a broader definition of empire replaced the earlier conventional view. An empire in the twentieth and twenty-first centuries, Lundestad argues, seeks to enforce "a hierarchical system of political relationships with one power clearly being much stronger than any other."[66] So, the US Empire, generally speaking, does not have "formal" political control over other nation-states, but it uses its military and economic power to create client states or allies. Consider the following illustrations: Prior to World War II, while still on active duty, major general Smedley Butler made an after-dinner speech in front of seven hundred guests. He told the guests "how Marines had cynically rigged elections in Nicaragua in 1912, and how they controlled the client president and manipulated politics in Haiti."[67] Later, in an article published in *Common Sense*, Butler wrote:

> I helped make Mexico and especially Tampico safe for American oil interests in 1914. I helped make Haiti and Cuba a decent place for the National City Bank boys to collect revenues in. I helped the raping of a dozen Central American republics for the benefit of Wall Street. The record of racketeering is long. I helped purify Nicaragua for the international banking house of Brown Brothers in 1909–12. I brought light to the Dominican Republic for American sugar interests in 1916. I helped make Honduras "right" for American fruit companies in 1903. In China in 1927 I helped see to it that Standard Oil went its way unmolested . . . Looking back on it, I feel I might have given Al Capone a few

---

63. See Kinzer, *Overthrow*; Zinn, *Twentieth Century*.

64. See Van Alstyne, *Rising American Empire*; Bender, "New Rome"; Fish, *Path of Empire*; Herring, *From Colony to Superpower*.

65. Lundestad, American "Empire," 37.

66. Lundestad, American "Empire," 37.

67. Schmidt, *Maverick Marine*, 204.

hints. The best he could do was to operate his racket in three city districts. We Marines operated in three continents.[68]

The use of the military did not necessarily involve "formal" political control over other states, but the threat and use of force made possible, as Butler noted, the expansion of US markets—an expansion that could have happened only as a result of force or the threat of force.

This naked use of US military force shifted after World War II. Before the end of that war, the United States organized a financial conference (Breton Woods) that was instrumental in creating international financial institutions (e.g., the World Bank and the International Monetary Fund), which ensured the supremacy of the United States and its European client states. This expansion of capitalism was not confined to the creation of global financial institutions. Naomi Klein painstakingly documents the collusion of US government leaders and economic experts to destabilize foreign governments and economies (in Chile, Argentina, Brazil, and other countries) during the latter half of the twentieth century in an effort to install in these countries capitalistic systems that favored US and European interests.[69] All this was accomplished without the use of military force, and it must be noted that the US is the only nation with approximately 725 known military bases in over thirty-eight foreign countries and over 254,000 military personnel in 153 countries.[70] The US is not an occupying force in these countries, at least currently. This is clear evidence of the continued international reach and influence of the United States. In brief, the use of "proconsuls"[71] and economic power to alter the policies and actions of foreign countries are signifiers of the presence of an American Empire.[72] As Rhodes writes, "The new world order is possible because America's global military power allows it to dictate the rules of international discourse and the means by which political actors can adjudicate their differences."[73] Thus, the definition of empire vis-à-vis the US is a country that uses economic, military, and political power to dominate the rules of international discourse and to influence—directly and indirectly—the domestic policies of foreign nations in order to maintain and further its economic and political hegemony.

---

68. Quoted in Schmidt, *Maverick Marine*, 231.
69. Klein, *Shock Doctrine*; see also Reich, *Supercapitalism*, 44–45.
70. Johnson, *Sorrows of Empire*, 154.
71. Bacevich, *New American Militarism*.
72. Young, "Imperial Language," 40.
73. Rhodes, "Onward Liberal Soldiers?," 230.

While it is important to note the difference between empires of old and the US Empire, a sobering fact remains.[74] We may not have direct political control over other nations, but the reality is that the US often relies on the use of military force. A blue-ribbon commission noted that "since the end of the Cold War, the United States has embarked upon nearly four dozen military interventions . . . as opposed to only sixteen during the entire period of the Cold War."[75] Since this commission, the US invaded Iraq and Afghanistan, exercised military operations in Syria, Somalia, Pakistan, and Yemen, to name a few.

Before shifting to the relation between imperialism and climate change, I want to briefly comment on the particular form of life that accompanies an imperium. As mentioned earlier, empires depend on apparatuses, which shape social-political psyches/subjectivities.[76] As Amy Kaplan noted, "international struggles for domination abroad profoundly shape representations of American national identity at home."[77] We might also say that national identities formed by imperial apparatuses shape behaviors toward other nations and legitimate varied forms of domination. I suggest that there are core features of imperial forms of life or subjectivity that have implications with regard to climate change. Above I indicated that nationalists tend to possess a sense of exceptionalism, which is inherently exclusive. Imperial subjectivities take exceptionalism to a new level—exceptionalism on steroids.[78] This is accompanied by cultural-imperial chauvinism, which undergirds a sense of entitlement and arrogance.[79] Because we consider ourselves to be superior (a new chosen people), we are entitled to act with impunity and, of course, we merit the riches that come from being an empire.[80] Max Boot's comment is a good example of this. He said, "We are an attractive empire . . . Afghanistan and other troubled lands today cry out for the sort of

---

74. In *Patterns of Empire*, Julian Go explores the patterns of the British Empire in the nineteenth and twentieth centuries, demonstrating that military interventions increase as empires begin to decline, which reveals the desperate attempt to hold on to power.

75. Bacevich, *New American Militarism*, 143.

76. Societal psyche is a term that signifies the collective sharing of particular representations, beliefs, values, expectations, and attitudes, in this instance, regarding the American Empire. See Samuels, *Political Psyche*.

77. Kaplan, *Anarchy of Empire*.

78. Walker, "Empire Unlike Any Other."

79. See Fulbright, *Arrogance of Power*.

80. Ikenberry, "America's Imperial Ambition."

enlightened foreign administration once provided by self-confident Englishmen in jodhpurs and pith helmets."[81]

On the more positive side, chauvinism and exceptionalism can also serve to motivate what at first appears to be altruism. The US, for instance, sent tons of aid and expertise to countries impacted by the 2004 Indian Ocean tsunami. While there are more examples of the US aiding other nations, I argue that this "appears" to be altruistic, because it only reinforces US exceptionalism. It simply "proves" that we are exceptional people. Moreover, in cases where we "altruistically" intervene to stop an atrocity (e.g., in Kosovo) or to help defeat an aggressor country (in Kuwait to help defeat invaders from Iraq), national security and economic interests are core features of these decisions. One would expect this to be the case, but it is altogether another thing to suggest these actions are altruistic.

Another feature of this form of life is simplification. Simplification is a cognitive operation that bifurcates the world into "us" and "them" and is linked to both asserting one's own moral superiority and reducing complexity into either/or thinking.[82] For example, shared hostility from many Americans toward "Old Europe" for disagreeing with Uncle Sam's relentless march toward another war with Iraq in 2003 illustrates a way of reducing complex reality into simplistic, often moralistic slogans that become shields from doubts or questions about reality and the consequences of one's actions. George W. Bush's crude categorization of Iran, Korea, and Iraq as the "axis of evil" is another example of this tendency, which Douglas John Hall identifies as a strand of simplism in evangelical Christianity, where the "faithful" bifurcate the world into good and evil.[83] In short, simplification, which is inextricably linked to a belief in the inherent goodness of American policies and intentions and to a grandiose sense of entitlement, becomes a key factor in screening the messiness of our motives and actions in the world and serves to keep dissenters at bay by turning them into "bad" objects (disloyal Americans).

---

81. Quoted in Johnson, *Sorrows of Empire*, 70.

82. Charles Krauthammer's argument for and justification of the United States' unipolarity ("Unipolar Era") is an excellent example of the tendency to see ourselves as morally superior, which serves to reduce complex reality and to avoid taking responsibility for problems and disasters that resulted from US policies. In proclaiming the benignity of the US Empire, he cites US help in establishing a democratic Germany, South Korea, and Taiwan. Not only does he overlook the decades of dictatorships in South Korea and Taiwan, but also numerous other negative examples of US policies and interventions (e.g., Central America, Diego Garcia, and Native Americans, to name only a few).

83. Hall, *Thinking the Faith*.

These features work together to make imperialistic subjectivities or ways of living highly resistant, if not impervious, to change. It has taken decades for British citizens to let go their imperialistic ambitions, though there likely are some who continue to long for the old days of the British Empire. Some writers argue that the US Empire is in decline,[84] but one would not know this when listening to other citizens or the media. The strength of the US Empire over the last few decades has shown no signs of diminishing, as the US seeks to stop or undermine the rise of China.[85]

Imperial apparatuses and their attending forms of life are not only resistant to change, but highly dangerous when we consider the present and future realities of climate change. Of course, any of a number of scholars have pointed out the dangers of empire. Chalmers Johnson presciently wrote that America's imperial ambitions would come back to haunt us in the form of terrorist attacks.[86] Gabriel Ash later argued that the US Empire faced a coming crisis, which he framed largely in terms of economics.[87] Michael Hardt and Antonio Negri are rightly very critical of present-day empires and their dependence on global capitalism.[88] These writers never mention the relationship between empire and global warming, which is an existential crisis that all life is currently encountering and will continue to face. Imperial ambitions, apparatuses, and forms of life are significant obstacles to getting any traction on action to mitigate climate change. The US and China are the two behemoths that are the largest emitters of greenhouse gasses.[89] Their drive to maintain or gain hegemony only serves to impede cooperation between themselves and other nations around climate action. Many of their citizens are complicit, precisely because of their close identification with and attachment to their respective nation and imperial sovereignty. In addition, like other forms of sovereignty and its accompanying forms of political-public life, other-than-human species are not considered in terms of their singularities and needs. Nationalism and imperialism give no thought to the needs of Othered human beings and other-than-human species. Of course, in the US Empire, there are groups trying to protect endangered species, but this is never a concern for the imperium.

84. Fergusson, *Colossus*.
85. Milbank, "Sovereignty"; North, "America's Drive."
86. Johnson, *Blowback*.
87. Ash, "Empire's Coming Crisis."
88. Hardt and Negri, *Empire*.

89. The old empires of Europe are also implicated, because greenhouse gas emissions accompanied the rise of capitalism and industrialization. See Mason, *Turbulent Empires*; Moore, "Name the System!"

This lack of concern about or attention to climate change and its impacts on human beings and other-than-human species are also evident in the building up of armies, navies, and intelligence institutions for the sake of maintaining or extending the empire. Armies and navies have to practice continually to maintain proficiency in the arts of war. Not only is the cost of maintaining armies, air forces, and navies hugely expensive, but it also drains resources that could be used to combat climate change. Moreover, the practices of military forces in peacetime lead to significant greenhouse gasses and escalate the destruction or degradation of the Earth.[90] Of course, when nations do go to war, as we currently see in Ukraine, the environmental damage is even worse.

Capitalism and Present-Day Market Societies

A third pernicious shoot of the rhizome of sovereignty is capitalism. Briefly, capitalism is a complex semiotic system or social imaginary[91] composing ideas, narratives, treatises, rituals, and other practices that order relationships and institutions vis-à-vis financial exchange, with the primary aim of profit. In moving toward a clearer definition, we immediately discover that there is no single definition or type of capitalism. There are instead various kinds of capitalism, and even within these various types there is often no clear consensus on definitions. There is, for instance, classical capitalism,[92] laissez-faire capitalism, supercapitalism,[93] neoliberal capitalism,[94] state-corporate capitalism,[95] state-run capitalism (e.g., in China), democratic

---

90. See Crawford, *Pentagon, Climate Change, and War*.

91. The term "social imaginary" is taken from Charles Taylor's work, *Modern Social Imaginary*. The concept suggests that capitalism is a human construction, which rejects the idea that capitalism is natural, inevitable, or ontological.

92. For example, the works of Adam Smith and David Ricardo reflect the period of capitalism that was emerging from mercantile capitalism to industrial capitalism. See Mann, *Disassembly Required*; Wolff and Resnick, *Contending Economic Theories*.

93. Reich, *Supercapitalism*.

94. See Birch, *Research Agenda*; Harvey, *Brief History*; Wolff and Resnick, *Economics*. Neoliberal capitalism, at times, falls under the heading of late capitalism. The adjective "late" seems to suggest that we are either in the midst of the most recent form of capitalism or that this is the final stage of capitalism wherein it collapses under its own contradictions. I prefer the term "neoliberal capitalism" because it points to the underlying ideology of the most recent edition of capitalism. Moreover, while Marx revealed the contradictions of capitalism, the proponents of capitalism have proven to be remarkably resilient in ensuring capitalism survives. A recent example of this is Robert Reich's book *Saving Capitalism*.

95. Duménil and Lévy, *Crisis of Neoliberalism*.

capitalism,[96] and so forth. Recognizing that capitalism is complex and contested will not deter me from attempting to provide a brief sketch of capitalism and its attributes, with the goal of indicating its imbrication with other shoots of sovereignty and the destructive forms of life it manufactures. I begin by addressing the historical origins of capitalism, which lays the groundwork for identifying its attributes and forms of life—ways of living that are ecologically destructive.[97]

Ellen Meiksins Wood argues that capitalism has its roots in sixteenth-century England with changes in enclosure laws and agrarian "reforms."[98] Enclosure "meant not simply a physical fencing of land but the extinction of common and customary rights on which many people depended for their livelihood."[99] The first set of changes "occurred in the sixteenth century, when landowners sought to drive commoners off lands that could be profitably put to use as pasture for increasing lucrative sheep farming."[100] She adds that "there was increasing pressure to extinguish customary rights that interfered with capitalist accumulation,"[101] and this pressure came from political and economic elites. Katharina Pistor details how the emergence of capitalism, in England and elsewhere, was accompanied by and further entrenched through the use and promulgation of laws, court actions, and government policies and programs.[102] Add to this the works of Adam Smith and David Ricardo. These public intellectuals and others were highly influential in laying the groundwork for the philosophical and legal principles of what became known as classical capitalism. What is notable here is that agrarian "reforms," enclosure laws, and related policies could not have been enacted without propertied classes and their close alliance with sovereign elites. The sovereign nation-state, then, was necessary for the emergence and expansion of capitalism.

Wood points out that the agrarian reforms in England slowly expanded to other European countries. During this same period, we also note the

---

96. Wolff, *Democracy at Work*.

97. John Bellamy Foster, *Return of Nature*, 179–81, shines a light on the historical roots of ecological socialism. William Morris and Frederick Engels cared not only about the environment in which workers' struggled, but also about how capitalism was polluting the air, rivers, forests, and oceans. They could not have known about climate change, but they certainly observed firsthand just how destructive capitalism was and is to the environment.

98. Wood, *Origin of Capitalism*, 95–121.

99. Wood, *Origin of Capitalism*, 108.

100. Wood, *Origin of Capitalism*, 108.

101. Wood, *Origin of Capitalism*, 108.

102. Pistor, *Code of Capital*. See also Mattei, *Capital Order*.

rise of nationalism and imperialism, as England, Spain, France, and other European states sought wealth and profit, not only by exploiting their own citizens, but also by colonizing other lands and peoples. Put another way, the proliferation of capitalism had its roots not simply in the rational ethics of liberal Protestantism as Max Weber argued,[103] but also in Western imperialism and industrialization during the nineteenth and twentieth centuries.[104] This was a period wherein mercantile capitalism and imperialism eventually changed to industrial capitalism.

Briefly, early and later forms of industrial capitalism were intricate economic-political symbol systems focused on the dynamics and ends of financial exchanges between persons within the nation and between societies. Even though the state was considered to be distinct from the market, industrial capitalism was deeply dependent on state apparatuses for its legitimation and enforcement. More particularly, industrial capitalism is a state-dependent semiotic system "organized . . . around the institution of property and the production of commodities,"[105] which is determined by a "rational" calculus of cost and price—the commodification of goods and services—and the market law of supply and demand.[106] As Wood writes, "it is a system in which the bulk of society's work is done by propertyless labourers who are obliged to sell their labor-power in exchange for a wage in order to gain access to the means of life . . . In the process of supplying

---

103. See Weber, *Protestant Ethic*.

104. See Stone and Kuznick, *Untold History*; Zinn, *People's History of the United States*.

105. Bell, *Cultural Contradictions of Capitalism*, 14. The "institution of property" cannot exist without laws and mechanisms of enforcement that are provided by the state. Laissez-faire and later neoliberal capitalists incessantly argue for deregulation or for the state to remove itself from "interfering" in the market. As Anita Chari notes, this obfuscates the state's role in regulating markets by suggesting the "market" and the state are two completely different entities when, in fact, the market could not exist without the state. Indeed, pointing to Krippner's research, Chari writes that "neoliberal politicians and elites pursue policies that obscure the state's role in regulating markets, allowing them to govern the economy at a remove while avoiding political responsibility for economic policies and outcomes" (Chari, *Political Economy of the Senses*, 30).

106. I have placed the term "rational" in quotes to suggest the underlying illusion that the so-called market or those involved in the market make rational, objective decisions. Any casual observer of the rises and falls of the stock market notes the presence of greed, fear, hubris, anxiety, and anger, which all play a large role in making "rational" decisions, which Alan Greenspan realized only after the financial collapse of 2008 (King, "Greenspan"). I would add here that the notion of "rational" vis-à-vis capitalism is a kind of rationalism that is associated with the advancement of each individual's self-interest. It is instrumental and individualistic. This is decidedly different from rationalism associated with making decisions with regard to the interests and needs of others.

the needs and wants of society, workers are at the same time inseparably creating profits for those who buy their labour-power."[107]

According to Peter Hudis, "Marx insisted that the aim of capitalist society is not to enrich human needs and capabilities, but rather to augment value. Capitalism ... has one over-riding goal: to accumulate value for its own sake."[108] Put another way, the core aims and values of any iteration of capitalism are productivity and profit—or the accumulation of capital for the purposes of reinvestment, market expansion, and greater profits, all of which relies principally on instrumental epistemologies. Profit, then, is the central value, motive, and *telos* that largely determines "rational" decisions vis-à-vis expanding production, seeking larger market share, wages, hiring, benefits, expenditures, and so forth. Labor and wages, for instance, are inextricably linked to and ostensibly determined by material production, services, supply and demand, and, naturally, the overarching aim of securing profit.[109] Surplus labor and value are integral to the profit, which is legally kept by those who are owners or shareholders of the profiting business. In addition, the means of production in classical or industrial capitalism are privately owned, whether by an individual, a family, or a number of stockholders (more precisely, by socially constructed legal entities called corporations, which have stockholders). In terms of the relation between consumers and producers, Adam Smith touted the "invisible hand" of the market, whereby each individual "rationally" maximizes self-interest in a milieu in which supply will equal demand, increasing the wealth of producers and shareholders while providing goods and services to consumers.[110] One can hear Thomas Hobbes and John Locke in the capitalist idea that each individual is self-referential, maximizing their self-interest, which, it is believed, will lead to an overall "good" for the society. This "good" is understood primarily in terms of economic wealth, which is measured by what we call the GDP (gross domestic product). The good of wealth is also dependent on the good of societal-market stability (and expansion) and individual freedom,[111] which is brought about by the leviathan/state and its attending nonstate apparatuses—the not-so-invisible hand or fist that insures compliant yet purportedly free workers/citizens. In short, agrarian and industrial capitalism, then, could not have emerged without the work of the

107. Wood, *Origin of Capitalism*, 3.
108. Hudis, *Marx's Concept*, 176.
109. Wolff and Resnick, *Contending Economic Theories*, 39.
110. Hendricks points out that John Maynard Keynes dismantled this claim, indicating that "supply cannot be counted on to create its own demand" (Hendricks, *Universe*, 152).
111. Hayek, *Road to Serfdom*.

sovereign and sovereign classes who created laws, policies, and programs that primarily benefited them.

While the market may function as an invisible hand, suggesting its autonomy from the state, the state, in classical and laissez-faire capitalism, still retains power and control. Indeed, the "invisible hand" is inextricably linked to and dependent on the arm of the state and its exercise or threat of political violence. For instance, in laissez-faire capitalism, the state is seen as restricting its power by not interfering with so-called "market forces," though the state will interfere when workers strike or show other forms of resistance.[112] Of course, this does not mean the state does not continue to use its power, even in situations of deregulation, which actually is another form of regulation. The very creation and sustenance of classical capitalism, then, depends on the state to create legal fictions such as corporations, as well as to use the police and military to insure the security and stability of the national and international commercial exchanges, property rights, and other mechanisms of capitalism.

Wood locates the origin of capitalism in England, which quickly became imbricated with nationalism and imperialism in the seventeenth century, spreading capitalism across the globe. Let me leap to the twentieth century when significant, pernicious alterations in capitalism ensued. Socialism and communism arose in the nineteenth and twentieth centuries largely in response to the rampant poverty, the terrible exploitation of workers, and political violence[113] that attended the proliferation of laissez-faire capitalism. Before, during, and after World War II, some economic and political elites gathered to address their growing concerns about the rise of socialism and (Keynesian) economic policies that aimed at reducing capitalism's numerous boom-and-bust cycles. At the same time, the US Empire continued to rise and dominate, especially after the ashes of World War II. Before the end of the war, the US organized a financial conference (Breton Woods) that was instrumental in creating and imposing international financial institutions (e.g., the World Bank and the International Monetary Fund) that were created to stabilize the international markets, which, in turn, would insure the supremacy of capitalism and largely benefit the US. and its European client states through the expansion of empire and profit.[114]

At that time, the US Empire (and client states) was operating mainly out of a Keynesian-style capitalism, wherein the state promulgated laws and

112. Zinn, *People's History of the United States*, 225–51.

113. What is often ignored is the capitalist-imperialist exploitation of colonized peoples.

114. For a history of capitalism in the twentieth century, see Jones, *Masters of the Universe*.

policies that offered some limited protections for workers and unions, as well as regulations vis-à-vis businesses. Governmental "intrusions" in the market (e.g., taxes, protections/regulations, legitimation of unions) did not sit well with some economic and political elites. One particular group would have far-reaching impacts through changes to capitalism. Pierre Dardot and Christian Laval point out that the "creation of the Mont Pelerin Society in 1947 is often incorrectly cited as marking the birth of neoliberal capitalism. In fact, the founding moment of neoliberal capitalism came earlier: it was the Walter Lippmann Colloquium," which was held in 1938.[115] Of course, the colloquium and its attending economic theories were decades in the making, reacting to the trends toward "policies of redistribution, social security, planning, regulation and protection that had developed since the end of the nineteenth century,"[116] in response to the crushing and extensive economic injustices citizens experienced as a result of laissez-faire capitalism. The colloquium attenders and later the Mont Pelerin Society were reacting against these social-economic trends and, in particular, Keynesian economic policies—policies aimed at greater regulation of the markets and wealth redistribution through tax reforms to limit the inevitable boom-and-bust cycles associated with classical capitalism.[117]

The Mont Pelerin Society included such luminaries as Milton Friedman, whose Chicago school played a central role in destabilizing various nation-states in the attempt to establish neoliberal capitalism during the 1970s and 1980s.[118] The catalyst for the flowering of neoliberal capitalism and the meteoric rise of its proponents to positions of power and influence in the United States and Britain was the economic crisis of the 1970s in the United States and Britain.[119] Through the creation of think tanks,[120] popular publications,[121] schools of business, and the IMF (International Monetary Fund),[122] and by attaining government positions, neoliberal capitalists and their ideas took hold. This resulted in the undermining of regulations, protections, and social programs.[123] The election of Ronald Reagan is usually

115. Dardot and Laval, *New Way of the World*, 49.
116. Dardot and Laval, *New Way of the World*, 49.
117. See Wolff and Resnick, *Contending Economic Theories*, 320–35.
118. Harvey, *Brief History*, 20. See also Klein, *Shock Doctrine*.
119. Harvey argues that the power and influence of neoliberal ideas came to fruition in the 1970s and eighties with the proliferation of conservative think tanks, as well as the elections of Margaret Thatcher and Ronald Reagan.
120. See Jones, *Masters of the Universe*, 134–79.
121. Hayek, *Road to Serfdom*; Friedman, *Capitalism and Freedom*.
122. See Mann, *Disassembly Required*, 141.
123. See Slobodian, *Globalists*.

cited as the beginning of neoliberal economic policies, but Jimmy Carter, who inherited the economic crisis from Gerald Ford, instituted a series of deregulatory policies and appointed Paul Volcker as chairman of the Federal Reserve.[124] Nevertheless, the Reagan administration rapidly extended neoliberal policies. As Anita Chari points out, "In the 1970s and 1980s, neoliberalism in the Euro-American context was associated with a set of policies known as the Washington consensus, which carried out policies of fiscal austerity, privatization, and pro-corporate policies through institutions such as the World Bank, IMF, and Federal Reserve."[125]

While there is no clear consensus on the attributes of neoliberal capitalism,[126] I nevertheless identify ten central features of this social imaginary.

1. Human well-being, understood almost exclusively in economic terms, is best achieved by providing entrepreneurial freedoms so that individual actors (includes corporations) can act out of their "rational" self-interests.[127]

2. Social goods will be maximized by expanding the reach and frequency of market transactions.[128]

3. Anything and anyone can be commodified.[129]

4. The state is not to intervene to control markets or restrict the reach of commodification.

5. The state functions to ensure private property rights and deregulation so that there can be free markets and free trade.

6. Where markets do not exist, entrepreneurs and the state work together to privatize and deregulate (e.g., through privatization of public education, prisons, healthcare, and other sectors).[130]

7. Corporations are to inform the state as to the laws that will enhance profit and market expansion.

---

124. Jones, *Masters of the Universe*, 248–53.
125. Chari, *Political Economy of the Senses*, 27.
126. See Birch, *Research Agenda*.
127. Implicit here is that individuals are largely responsible for their economic failures and successes, which is a core tenet of neoliberalism.
128. Rieger, *No Rising Tide*, 15.
129. See Sandel, *What Money Can't Buy*.
130. The market, in other words, becomes the organizing principle of the state, not citizenship and the common good.

8. Greed benefits society.[131]
9. "Market freedoms are natural and political restraints on markets are artificial."[132]
10. Individual citizens are to be entrepreneurs in a competitive state—*homo oeconomicus*.[133] *Homo oeconomicus* is a "hypermobile, entrepreneurial neoliberal subject who must assume the burden of risk that the state no longer shoulders."[134]

Neoliberal capitalism, Terry Eagleton writes, "wants men and women to be infinitely pliable and adaptable."[135]

The rise of neoliberal capitalism resulted in significant changes to society. First of all, while the state has always been implicated in the rise, expansion, and changes to capitalism, the state in neoliberal capitalism is inextricably yoked to capitalist elites and their institutions. This is especially evident in the erosion of the commons through marketization. Accompanying this change is the shift from a society that has markets to societies that are markets, wherein capitalism and its apparatuses dominate social life. Indeed, capitalism, especially after the fall of the Soviet Union and the rise of China's state-controlled capitalism, became unquestioned and unquestionable. Margaret Thatcher's campaign slogan, "There Is No Alternative," is an example of this. Neoliberal capitalism became the new dogma, or what Harvey Cox calls the market god.[136] Thomas Frank makes a similar observation in his examination of "extreme" capitalism, which operates like a religion.[137] As Tony Benn comments: "If I look at the world today it seems to me that the most powerful religion of all—much more powerful than Christianity, Judaism, Islam, and so on—is the people who worship money . . . The banks are bigger than cathedrals, the headquarters of the multinational companies are bigger than mosques or the synagogues. Every hour on the news we have business news—every hour—it is a sort of hymn to capitalism."[138] Cox, Frank, and Benn are not simply using theological metaphors to depict the

---

131. See Duménil and Lévy, *Crisis of Neoliberalism*; Couldry, *Why Voice Matters*; Harvey, *Enigma of Capital*.

132. Gray, *False Dawn*, 17.

133. See Chari, *Political Economy of the Senses*, 28; Dardot and Laval, *New Way of the World*, 104, 255.

134. Chari, *Political Economy of the Senses*, 9.

135. Eagleton, *After Theory*, 118.

136. Cox, *Market as God*.

137. Frank, *One Market under God*.

138. Tony Benn in Carrette and King, *Selling Spirituality*, 23.

secular phenomena of capitalism. Religion, especially in some Christian denominations in the US, has become an apparatus promoting capitalism. While capitalism has, in one form or another, always been connected to Western religious traditions,[139] the rise of neoliberal capitalism was accompanied by the growth of the prosperity gospel movement,[140] which has served as a cheerleader or apologist for capitalism. Indeed, theological support for capitalism tends to ontologize capitalism (to make capitalism equivalent to God's sovereignty), overlooking that capitalism is strictly an artifice based on powerful illusions.

This quick overview has demonstrated, in part, how the rise of and changes in capitalism are intertwined with the other shoots of the rhizome of sovereignty, namely, nationalism and imperialism. I should add that while there are distinctions between these shoots of sovereignty (on the one hand) and the Abrahamic traditions (on the other), they are all connected by way of the apparatuses of sovereignty. Indeed, the often close relationship between the Abrahamic traditions and apology for capitalism (and nationalism) result from the forms of life dependent on sovereignty—dependent on the sovereignty of God. Even having said all this, I have not yet depicted the negative impacts of capitalism on human beings, other species, and the Earth.

Long ago Jean-Jacques Rousseau noted the destructive impacts of capitalism, which "bound new fetters on the poor, and gave new powers to the rich . . . fixed forever the laws of property and inequality; converted clever usurpation into an inalienable right and for the sake of the few ambitious men, subjected all mankind to perpetual labour, servitude and misery."[141] A contemporary of Rousseau, Voltaire held similar views. Terry Eagleton writes, "Voltaire believed that the rich grew bloated on the blood of the poor, and that property lay at the heart of social conflict."[142] He contended "that property brings war, exploitation and class conflict in its wake."[143] Similarly, in the late nineteenth century, William Morris, in referring to a British market society, said, "The truth is that our system of

---

139. See Weber, *Protestant Ethic*; Agamben, *Creation and Anarchy*; Tanner, *Christianity*. It is necessary to point out that religious leaders, communities, and organizations have often taken a critical stance toward capitalism. For a depiction of the last 130 years of Roman Catholic criticisms of capitalism, see LaMothe, "Least of These."

140. See MacDonald, *Thieves in the Temple*; Novak, *Spirit of Democratic Capitalism*; Novak, *Toward a Theology of the Corporation*; Tanner, *Christianity*; Carrette and King, *Selling Spirituality*.

141. Eagleton, *Why Marx Was Right*, 199.

142. Eagleton, *Why Marx Was Right*, 32.

143. Eagleton, *Why Marx Was Right*, 117.

Society is essentially a system of *waste*."[144] This system of waste, for Morris, was imbricated with nationalism and imperialism: "The Commercial War is simply the agony of capitalism driven by a force it cannot resist to seek for new & ever new markets at any price, at any risk."[145] While the degree of social regulations and protections varies between market countries, capitalism in every form depends on instrumental epistemologies and establishes relations of subordination and subjugation, which drive profit and wealth toward economic and political elites, leaving the majority of the population to fend for themselves—more on this below.[146] Thomas Piketty's extensive global research demonstrates massive disparities in wealth and income throughout the world's capitalist countries, which are only worsening.[147] Despite capitalism's ability to create vast wealth (for a few), it has chewed up and spit out billions of people.[148]

Apologists for capitalism, whether secular or religious, seem to think that the sufferings of human beings (other species are not even recognized) are simply the price of doing business. Hayek and Friedman, for instance, were aware of the sufferings of poor people, but, as evangelizers for neoliberal capitalism, they focused on the creation of wealth, while sacrificing millions of lives on the altar of capitalism. Still, not only secular disciples of capitalism justify its destructive consequences. Theologian Michael Novak uses scripture and tradition to construct a theological anthropology that ontologically legitimates capitalism and its corresponding practices of exploitation.[149] As an apologist for capitalism, he recognizes that millions of human beings suffer as a result of capitalism. But this is dismissed by his theological rendering of suffering. He writes, "If God so willed his beloved Son to suffer, why would He spare us?"[150] Of course, the "us" really does not include him, since Novak is well ensconced among the political and

---

144. Quoted in Foster, *Return of Nature*, 132 (italics original).

145. Quoted in Foster, *Return of Nature*, 136.

146. Maurice Hamington and Michael Flower note the rise in precarity for human animals and other species as a result of the proliferation of neoliberalism and neoliberal capitalism. In addition, Sarah Clark Miller argues that neoliberal capitalism has given rise to a crisis of care in market societies, undermining social relations and our relations to other species and to planet Earth. (Hamington and Flower, eds., *Care Ethics*; Miller, "Neoliberalism, Precarity").

147. Piketty, *Capital in the Twenty-First Century*; Piketty, *Capital and Ideology*.

148. See Baptist, *Half Has Never Been Told*; Dufour, *Art of Shrinking Heads*; Fraser, *Cannibal Capitalism*; Valencia, *Gore Capitalism*.

149. Novak, *Spirit of Democratic Capitalism*; Novak, *Toward a Theology of the Corporation*.

150. Novak, *Spirit of Democratic Capitalism*.

economic elites. Novak and others manifest the cruel logic embedded in capitalism and the prosperity gospel movement.

Embedded in the exploitation of human beings is a form of life that mirrors the attributes of sovereignty, namely, instrumental epistemologies, relations of subordination/subjugation, and implicit hierarchical valuations (superiority/inferiority). Over a century ago, Georg Lukács used the term "reification" to depict the kind of rationality at the heart of capitalism. Reification, he wrote, "requires that a society should learn to satisfy all its needs in terms of commodity exchange."[151] For Lukács, reification "becomes the central social pathology of capitalist society."[152] This social pathology is manifested in the reality that the "social relation is consummated in the relation of a thing, of money, to itself."[153] Reification is a central feature of instrumental epistemologies, which are esteemed by economists like Gary Becker.[154] In his book, Becker "rejects the old-fashioned notion that economics is 'the study of the allocation of material goods.'"[155] Instead, he advocates a kind of economic, calculative approach to all aspects of life. "I have come to the position that the economic approach is a comprehensive one that is applicable to human behavior."[156] Reification or objectification means that the apparatuses of capitalism form the residents of market societies into *homo economicus* (i.e., into entrepreneurs, consumers, workers, idle poor—Marx's reserve army), objectifying or reifying themselves, other human beings, and other species.

The employment and continuance of capitalism's instrumental epistemologies require the ongoing production of apparatuses that establish and maintain relations of subordination/subjugation and their accompanying hierarchical valuations. Every market society and its accompanying apparatuses establish classes, wherein most residents are subordinate to and, more often than not, subjugated by political-economic elites. When Thomas Piketty empirically lays out the data regarding the extreme disparities in wealth and income across market societies, he implicitly highlights the fact that funneling material and financial distribution toward the elites depends on subordinating and subjugating the lower classes. Put another way, subordination and subjugation require the threat or exercise of political-economic violence, which is legitimated by the sovereign and sovereign

---

151. Lukács, *History and Class Consciousness*, 91.
152. Chari, *Political Economy of the Senses*, 5.
153. Lukács, *History and Class Consciousness*, 94.
154. Becker, *Economic Approach*.
155. Quoted in Sandel, *What Money Can't Buy*, 49.
156. Sandel, *What Money Can't Buy*, 49.

classes, insuring their class position. Within market class hierarchies are valuations of superiority and inferiority. The upper classes are deemed superior, and this becomes part of their sense of self-esteem, self-respect, and self-confidence. Members of the so-called lower classes are regarded as inferior, and the proof of their inferiority is evident in their lack of financial success. Sociologist Jennifer Silva, for example, researched working-class young people who were in debt and had low-paying jobs. These young people tended to blame themselves for not being entrepreneurial enough and, not surprisingly, had a lower sense of self-esteem than upper-class or middle-class young people, while also seeing financially well-off people as superior.[157] In one sense, a market society wants, if you will, the members of the lower classes to accept their inferiority, making their subordination and subjugation all the easier.

There are, as many commentators have noted, material and psychological consequences of a market society's reification of human beings,[158] relations of subordination/subjugation, and hierarchical valuations based on wealth and power. Gilles Deleuze and Felix Guattari address the connection between capitalism and schizophrenia, indicating that capitalism shapes subjectivity in such a way as to contribute to a split subject, who is alienated from others and self.[159] Silva provides evidence of this social alienation, noting that "the only way to survive in such a competitive and bewildering labor market is to become highly elastic and unencumbered by other obligations," including family obligations.[160] Sociologists Arlie Hochschild and Eva Illouz depict the alienation that takes place through capitalism's subjective coercion of workers' emotional lives.[161] From another angle, Dany-Robert Dufour describes capitalism's production of an acritical subject with psychotic tendencies, reemphasizing the alienated features of social life and relations of subordination and subjugation.[162] Echoing Dufour, Henry Giroux identifies not only the rise of the acritical subject but the cruel reality of disposable youths in neoliberal capitalistic societies and evokes a sense of helplessness and worthlessness present among lower-class

---

157. Silva, *Coming Up Short*.

158. Guy Debord writes that "the first stage of the economy's domination of social brought about an evident degradation of being into having" (Debord, *Society of the Spectacle*, 4–5). This is an objectification or reification of the human and I would add of other species.

159. Deleuze and Guattari, *Anti-Oedipus*. See also Fromm, *Dogma of Christ*.

160. Silva, *Coming Up Short*, 31.

161. Hochschild, *Managed Heart*; Illouz, *Cold Intimacies*.

162. Dufour, *Art of Shrinking Heads*.

and minority youths.[163] In a different vein, Ann Cvetkovich explored the way capitalism produces depression, a condition related to both a relatively high level of economic insecurity (including food insecurity) and feelings of helplessness.[164] Finally, Jerry Mander listed numerous studies pointing to rising violence, anxiety, depression, and suicide in the United States, which he attributes to the dominance of neoliberal capitalism.[165]

But it is not only human beings we need to be concerned about. Capitalism, as a shoot of sovereignty's instrumental epistemologies, of its relations of subordination and subjugation, and of its accompanying ontological rift,[166] also lays waste to billions of ("inferior") species and the Earth, in its pernicious pursuit of profits.[167] Decades ago, T. S. Elliot presciently noted this. He said, "The organization of society on the principle of profit, as well as public destruction, is leading both to the deformation of humanity by unregulated industrialism, and so to the exhaustion of natural resources . . . a good deal of our material progress is a progress for which succeeding generations may have to pay dearly."[168] I am confident that if he were alive today, he would say that in our market societies, succeeding generations of human beings and other species will bear the consequences of our profligacy.

Nevertheless, critics of capitalism rarely consider the sufferings and deaths of billions of other-than-human animals, which is a symptom of anthropocentrism (of believing human beings to be higher on the evolutionary scale than nonhumans) and capitalism's calculative thinking and relations. Factory farms, factory fishing ships, strip mining, Mountain Top Removal (MTR) mining, and mass use of fertilizers are incredibly destructive to other species, local inhabitants, and the Earth. Indeed, Jason Moore, some years ago, made the case that the current geological age should be named Capitalocene, because, from his perspective, capitalism is the main culprit in climate change and a major obstacle to climate action.[169] I basi-

---

163. Giroux, *Disposable Youth*.

164. Cvetkovich, *Depression*. See also Rogers-Vaughn, "Blessed Are Those Who Mourn."

165. Mander, *Capitalism Papers*.

166. Briefly, the ontological rift refers to the radical separation between "human beings on the one hand" and more-than-human on the other (Latour, *We Have Never Been Modern*, 10–11). Chapter 3 will take up this idea and develop it.

167. Since the nineteenth century, scholars and public intellectuals have observed the destructive power of capitalism vis-à-vis the environment. See Foster, *Return of Nature*.

168. In Eagleton, *Critical Revolutionaries*, 27.

169. Moore, "Name the System!"

cally agree with Moore, though I would stress that capitalism, nationalism, and imperialism are all shoots of the rhizome of sovereignty.

One may point out that other-than-human species were exploited long before capitalism made its appearance. This is, of course, true, but as I noted in Chapter 1, this is due largely to the apparatuses that produced the ontological rift, which became intertwined with the emergence of sovereignty during the Neolithic period. Capitalism simply takes the exploitation and destruction of other species and the Earth to levels unimaginable to previous generations. All of this is done without a hint of remorse by most human beings, because the belief in our dominion justifies or legitimates our treatment of Othered human beings, Othered species, and the Earth.

My presentation of capitalism is obviously negative, so it is necessary to mention that some economists, such as Gernot Wagner and Matthew Weitzman, argue that the market can be harnessed to reduce greenhouse gas emissions and slow, if not curtail, the rise of global warming.[170] Matthew Paterson and Peter Newell pose a similar argument. For them, "the issue is less whether we have climate capitalism or not, but what sort of climate capitalism we end up with. Capitalism of one sort or another will provide the context in which near-term solutions will have to be found."[171] While markets can lead to significant changes, these authors, it seems to me, are so focused on the rubrics of capitalism that they ignore the long history of exploitation by human beings in capitalist societies. And if they were to acknowledge it, I am confident that the sufferings of other species would not make it onto their radar screens. In addition, they overlook the fact that capitalism is fundamentally exploitative and extractive in its relations, whether we are talking about human beings, other species, or the Earth. Some people may genuinely believe that the state can initiate regulations and protections to mitigate and even harness the effects of capitalism in order to provide benefits for the majority of people (other species are ignored). But a cursory look at the history of capitalism and state protections simply reveals that political and economic elites will seek to hold on to and further their privileges and wealth. Even those nation-states that have more social protections and equitable distributions of wealth continue to operate within the capitalistic model, which inevitably privileges those who possess economic and political power. I am not at all sanguine that capitalism can be reformed, and given the dire realities of climate change, we need to radically reimagine economies that take into account other species and the

---

170. Wagner and Weitzman, *Climate Shock*.
171. Newell and Peterson, *Climate Capitalism*, 161.

Earth—economies that eschew relations of subordination and subjugation, the primacy of instrumental epistemologies, and hierarchical valuations.[172]

Sciences

Many people believe science is separate from political, cultural, and religious realities. To be sure, science and scientists can engage in and be influenced by these systems, but science itself retains its purchase on dealing with universal facts/truths.[173] Experimental results, if accurate, can be replicated anywhere in the world. Scientific "laws" (e.g., Ohm's law, Poiseuille's law, Stoke's law) are based on repeated observations or experiments and are applicable throughout the world. There is, then, some truth to this view, but I suggest that much of what passes for science is imbricated with the belief in human sovereignty or dominion over other species. Of course, not all scientists accept this view, being sure to utilize science to understand and care for the well-being of other species and the Earth. Yet, when we consider the close relation between the rise of science in the West and the attending growth of nationalism, imperialism, and capitalism, then we can see that some of the sciences operate as an offshoot of sovereignty. Let me briefly attempt to make this clear.

We might consider that Western science arose with the Enlightenment, but Armand Marie Leroi argues that Western science began with Aristotle.[174] Aristotle conducted dissections of other species, sought to understand them, and offered taxonomies of animal and plant species. This quest to know, however understandable, was rooted in instrumental epistemologies that justified the objectification of other species and, correspondingly, denied their singularities. Put another way, to kill and dissect any animal is to deny the singularity of that living being, which is made acceptable precisely because it is constructed as less-than, inferior, and lower on the taxonomic tree. Millennia later, Francis Bacon, a devout Anglican philosopher, is credited with having proposed the "inductive-experimental method as a replacement for Aristotle's methods."[175] Bacon was not alone in making significant changes to science, and, like others, he believed that "the practical aim of improving humanity's lot [depended on] the increased understanding and *control* of nature."[176] What is retained, despite the changes, are instrumental

---

172. See Posner and Weyl, *Radical Markets*; Piketty, *Time for Socialism*.
173. Polkinghorne, *Methodology*, 86–87.
174. Leroi, *Lagoon*.
175. Polkinghorne, *Methodology*, 16.
176. Grayling, *History of Philosophy*, 197 (italics added).

epistemologies and attending hierarchies that legitimated experimenting on other species and destructive extractions of materials from the Earth. In the twentieth century, Sigmund Freud followed this tradition, believing that science, while having some limits of control vis-à-vis nature, had proven to be instrumental in protecting and improving human life.[177] Freud's scientific training and his desire to be seen as a scientist himself meant he accepted Western science's hierarchical taxonomies, which, in part, is reflected in the near-complete absence of the importance of other species in his theories of psychosocial development.[178]

These views of science exhibit several important features. First, while Aristotle considered human beings to be (political) animals, human animals are placed at the apex of the taxonomic tree of life. As indicated above, they are believed to be superior. Bacon, Freud, and innumerable other scientists retained, consciously or unconsciously, this hierarchical view, but also differentiated human beings from nature itself.[179] Indeed, Freud pitted human beings against Nature, which he anthropomorphized as cruel and indifferent—unsurprisingly he constructed "Nature" in terms of the maternal. Lulu Clark Miller furthers this point in her recent book. Miller contends that, in general, human beings tend to elide similarities between human beings and other species, which justifies or legitimates the instrumental use of other species. She writes, "Scientists, Frans de Waal points out, can be some of the worse offenders—employing technical language to distance ourselves from the rest of animals. They call 'kissing' in chimps 'mouth-to-mouth contact'; they call 'friends' between primates 'favorite affiliation partners'; they interpret evidence showing that crows and chimps can make tools as being somehow qualitatively different from toolmaking said to define humanity. If an animal can beat us at a cognitive task . . . they write it off as instinct, not intelligence. This and so many more tricks of language are what de Waal has termed 'linguistic castration.' The way we use our tongues to disempower animals, the way we invent words to maintain our spot at the top."[180] It is not simply to disempower other species; it is an attempt to secure a sense of human superiority, which then serves to legitimate or justify exploitation. And it often accompanies projecting onto Othered species existential

---

177. Freud, *Future of an Illusion*; Freud, *Civilization and Its Discontents*.

178. Harold F. Searles recognized over six decades ago that psychoanalysis had overlooked the importance of other species in psychosocial development. His prescient book was ignored when it was published and is still largely overlooked today (Searles, *Nonhuman Environment*). See also Kassouf, "Psychoanalysis and Climate Change."

179. See Latour, *We Have Never Been Modern*.

180. Miller, *Why Fish Don't Exist*, 181.

impermanence and insignificance, while we secretly believe in our existential, if not ontological, significance and permanence.[181]

Of course, Miller is addressing Western science and Western apparatuses. Not all human beings or scientists linguistically castrate other species. As I mentioned in Chapter 1, some indigenous peoples believe neither in human dominion over Nature nor that human beings are separate from and superior to Nature. The fact that indigenous peoples have been and, in many cases today, are constructed as primitive and lacking scientific knowledge only furthers Miller's point about linguistic castration. Labeling indigenous people as primitive has been and continues to be a prelude to imperialism, ethnic cleansing, and other forms of cruelty. I add that some philosophers[182] and scientists eschew these Western views.[183]

Let me stress, though, that differentiation is not, in itself, a problem. One can differentiate between this or that animal without holding beliefs in human superiority and control (dominion) over "nature." These twin beliefs—a belief in human superiority and a kindred belief in human domination—coupled with instrumental epistemologies are features of sovereignty that for many legitimate and justify objectification and exploitation of other-than-human beings, Othered human beings, and the Earth. Experimenting on other species for human benefit or pleasure, developing technology for the mass killing of other species for human consumption, and using science and technologies to extract ores from the Earth, thus polluting air and lands, are examples of the forms of scientific life that are shoots of the rhizome of sovereignty.

---

181. Human beings are signifying and valuing creatures. In the West we make a categorical mistake, confusing our capacities to signify and value with our being existentially significant and valuable, which avoids coming to terms with collective existential insignificance and impermanence.

182. Philosophers Deleuze and Guattari agree with Agamben's claim, arguing that "We make no distinction between man and nature . . . man and nature are not like two opposite terms confronting each other . . . rather they are one and the same essential reality" (*Anti-Oedipus*, 4–5). These philosophers argue that the ontological rift and sovereignty are human constructions—constructions that together are, in the end, deadly for human beings and other species. Interestingly, precursors of this argument are evident in Ralph Waldo Emerson's writings about nature (see Emerson, *Nature and Selected Essays*). Chapter 3 of this book explores more fully the ontological rift.

183. See Singer, *Animal Liberation*; Nussbaum, *Justice for Animals*; Goodall, *In the Shadow of Man*.

Conclusion

We are used to thinking about sovereignty in circumscribed ways, usually assigning it to political philosophy or political theology. In this chapter, I suggested a much more complicated picture, wherein sovereignty is imbricated in the apparatuses associated with nationalism, imperialism, capitalism, and some sciences. Together these forces and the sovereignty that underlies them produce and maintain ways of living that while benefiting some human beings, are profoundly destructive to the well-being of other-than-human species and the flourishing of a biodiverse Earth. Recognizing the rhizome of sovereignty and its shoots in human life is a necessary step toward radically reimagining our ways of dwelling together with other species and the Earth.[184] To recall Clayton Crockett, we "need to experiment radically with new ways of thinking and living, because the current paradigm is in a state of exhaustion, depletion, and death."[185]

---

184. McKinnon, *Climate Change and Political Theory*, 27.
185. Crockett, *Radical Political Theology*, 165.

3

Sovereignty's Ontological Chasm and Its Psychosocial Dynamics

---

Our noblest virtues were enlisted in the service of these twin missions (nature's masters and owners), one in the political arena and the other in the domain of science and technology.[1]

The state necessarily introduces estrangement into social existence.[2]

Decades ago, I became interested in theology, which was followed by my growing intrigue with political philosophies. I found a certain creative, anarchic freedom in Western philosophical traditions that was lacking in the more hierarchical, creedal, and juridical forms of theology. This is not to imply that theologians are not creative, but their creativity tends to be confined to staying within the bounds of tradition and reinforcing the "truths" of that tradition. It seemed that in philosophy it is possible to think without a banister, as Hannah Arendt notes. While there is some truth to this, critical thinking always has banisters—concepts and premises that we inherit and internalize, and that often remain outside our awareness. These banisters are part of our assumptive world and ways of life.

1. Latour, *We Have Never Been Modern*, 9.
2. Kovel, *Radical Spirit*, 213.

Alfred North Whitehead confirms this view: "The safest general characterization of the European philosophical tradition is that it consists of a series of footnotes to Plato."[3] Many Western philosophers and theologians no doubt believed they were creating something new or at least different, only to perpetuate the premises that attend Plato's philosophy. This may be too strongly stated, but the thread of truth becomes apparent when one reads the political philosophies of indigenous peoples—philosophies that support neither the sovereignty of humanity nor its attending ontological rift.[4] One of the banisters or concepts I have been exploring and interrogating in the previous chapters is sovereignty—a central idea to political philosophies and theologies, and one that has largely proven to be destructive vis-à-vis Othered human beings, other species, and the Earth. As Albert Camus wrote, "When an abstraction starts to kill you, you have to get to work on it."[5] The Western banister or abstraction is sovereignty, and it gives rise to the ontological rift—a dangerous pathology that is revealed by the climate emergency.

In this chapter, getting to work on sovereignty's ontological rift and its attributes means understanding how sovereignty produces and attends the ontological rift between some human beings and Othered human beings, as well as between human beings and more-than-human beings. This rift is evident in and produced by Western political philosophies and is rooted in Abrahamic scriptures and political theologies. I begin by addressing what is meant by the ontological rift before depicting the psychosocial dynamics and functions of this rift. This background will help demonstrate the extent of human destructiveness toward other species and psychosocial resistance to change in the West. In addition, this chapter sets the stage for the next chapter's discussion of the theologizing that explains and offers an ontological remedy for alienation and destructiveness while paradoxically mystifying, unwittingly legitimating, and ultimately solidifying the ontological rift and its illusions.

Allow me a few thoughts before beginning. There are a couple of reasons for furthering the discussion of sovereignty vis-à-vis the ontological rift. First, in my storytelling, I want to emphasize the pervasiveness of this rift in Western forms of thinking and behaving. In so doing, I provide reasons for the intractable aspects of unethical Western approaches to other species and to "Nature,"[6] as well as portraying the tenacious systemic resistance to climate action. Second, having become aware of the prevalence

---

3. Whitehead, *Process and Reality*, 39.
4. See Castro, *Cannibal Metaphysics*; Kohn, *How Forests Think*.
5. Camus, *Plague*, 69.
6. See Latour, *Facing Gaia*.

of sovereignty and the ontological rift in Western life, we are invited to reimagine or jettison our stories, our political philosophies and theologies, our theories, our anthropologies, and our public and religious rituals—all of which the last chapter calls into question. Two other comments are in order. Without doubt, one can delve into Western philosophies and theologies and discover examples that contradict what I am arguing in this chapter: For example, Francis of Assisi showed his deep love for other species; Pierre Teilhard de Chardin's theology focuses on the unity of life and the cosmos;[7] Jeremy Bentham[8] and Arthur Schopenhauer[9] express concern for the rights of other species; Peter Singer argues for animal liberation;[10] and Martha Nussbaum advocates for justice for all other species[11]—these are examples that refute my discussion of the ontological rift. But I would argue that these wonderful outliers serve to prove the pervasiveness and staying power of the ontological rift and its apparatuses. That some sensitive, thoughtful, and compassionate people have made this rift inoperative or have been able to cross it only testifies to its presence in Western forms of life. These and other scholars, poets, and novelists look into the abyss of the suffering of other species (and Othered human beings) and offer ways to reimagine how we relate to one another, to other species, and to the Earth. Finally, and relatedly, the ontological rift suggests something unbridgeable, like the story of the rich man and Lazarus (Luke 16:19–31). Recall that in this story Lazarus, who is destitute and ignored, goes to heaven, while the rich man has warmer quarters. When the rich man beseeches Abraham for a bit of water from Lazarus, Abraham says, "Child remember that during your lifetime you received your good things, and Lazarus in like manner evil things; but now he is comforted, and you are in agony. Besides all this, between you and us a great chasm has been fixed, so that those who might want to pass from here to you cannot do so, and no one can cross from there to us" (vv. 25–26). This unbridgeable chasm is something that ostensibly God creates. The presence of such an unbridgeable chasm in this parable might raise questions about God's cruel justice or lack of mercy that prevents Lazarus or Abraham from compassionately comforting the rich man; further, the parable brings up the perplexing idea of eternal suffering for unjust actions over a short life span. The ontological rift, however, is merely a human creation; it can be crossed,

---

7. Teilhard de Chardin, *Divine Milieu*.
8. Sunstein, "Rights of Animals."
9. Puryear, "Schopenhauer on the Rights of Animals."
10. Singer, *Animal Liberation*.
11. Nussbaum, *Justice for Animals*.

though crossing it requires significant efforts, which I will address in the last chapter. Therein lies the flicker of hope.

The Ontological Rift: Sources and Attributes

Western political philosophies and Abrahamic theologies continually affirm the idea of sovereignty. In the last chapter, I indicated how the idea of sovereignty is imbricated with other macro ideas and systems, namely, nationalism, imperialism, capitalism, and some forms of science. What accompanies the idea of sovereignty is what Giorgio Agamben terms the "ontological rift." He argues that Western political theologies and philosophies function as apparatuses that produce and maintain a "deep ontological rift ... between animal and human," which is a part of the assumptive world of most Western persons.[12] Agamben writes:

> It is as if determining the border between human and animal were not just one question among many discussed by philosophers and theologians, scientists and politicians, but rather a fundamental metaphysico-political operation in which alone something like "man" can be decided upon and produced.[13]

Others have pointed to this rift. Jacques Derrida referred to it as an "abyssal rupture."[14] Bruno Latour makes a related claim, noting that there are "entirely distinct ontological zones: that of human beings on the one hand; that of nonhuman [beings] on the other."[15] Similarly, Eduardo Viveiros de Castro takes note of the "Great Divide" in Western engagements with other species and indigenous peoples.[16] These scholars claim that the ongoing drive in the West to differentiate between human beings and other species is a central project of Western theology, philosophy, and some of the sciences, which leads to "a radical and total discontinuity between human and nonhuman,"[17] and, consequently, a hierarchical privileging of human beings over all other species—anthropocentrism.[18]

12. Dickinson, "Absence of Gender," 173.
13. Agamben, *Open*, 92.
14. Derrida, *Animal That Therefore I Am*, 30.
15. Latour, *We Were Never Modern*, 10–11.
16. Castro, *Cannibal Metaphysics*, 45.
17. Kompridis, "Nonhuman Agency," 252.
18. This ontological rift also applies to those human beings who are constructed as absolutely Other and inferior, which we observe in varied forms of racism (and other types of oppression and marginalization such as sexism, classism, heterosexism, and so forth) and attending traumas. My focus in this chapter is primarily on the gap as it

Agamben and Latour rightly cast a wide net to demonstrate the depth and width of the ontological gap between human animals and other species. Let me offer some heuristic evidence that will illustrate some of the attributes of this rift. Plato and Aristotle have had, as Whitehead points out, a significant influence on Western political philosophies. Aristotle, in particular, argued that human beings are political animals, distinct from other animals by virtue of reason, language, and political agency.[19] Human beings, he argued, are "thus intended by nature to be part of a political whole."[20] If a human being exists outside the polis, that human being is either a beast or a god, according to Aristotle.[21] Furthermore, a beast is a creature—human or otherwise—that *lacks* the law or justice, which implies that everything outside the polis, including other animals, dwell outside the law and justice.[22] The notion of "injustice" does not apply to other species. Other species exist in the zone of nonjustice. Similarly, a beast or Othered animal is perceived to *lack* language, reason, and political agency, which means Othered animals are not part of or integral to the polis. We (wrongly, as the Anthropocene reveals) come to believe that the polis is not dependent on the survival and flourishing of other species. For Aristotle, then, human beings, as a result of possessing reason, language, and virtue, are "the best of animals."[23] Of course, Aristotle recognized that some human beings commit injustices in the polis and for the polis, but these human beings are not virtuous, and capacity for virtue is another feature that other-than animals lack. Only human beings, it is dogmatically believed, can actualize the potential capacities for language, reason, and virtue.

Aristotle and innumerable other Western philosophers who followed sought to differentiate between human animals and other species. This differentiation accompanies an existential hierarchical valuation, which we note in the comment that human beings are the best of animals. What other species "lack," in other words, becomes linked to the valuation of inferiority

---

pertains to other species and planet Earth. See Baptist, *Half Has Never Been Told*; Danner, *Stripping the Body Bare*; Mills, *Black Rights/White Wrongs*; Patterson, *Slavery and Social Death*; Wilkerson, *Caste*.

19. Barker, trans., *Politics of Aristotle*, 6.
20. Barker, trans., *Politics of Aristotle*, 6–7.
21. Barker, trans., *Politics of Aristotle*, 6.
22. One could argue that a god is outside the law and justice to the extent that a god is not commanded by the law or justice. This is evident in Abrahamic scriptures where God can set aside the law and justice. Consider, for instance, God's killing of Egyptians and their livestock.
23. Barker, trans., *Politics of Aristotle*, 7.

and, by implication, with the idea that human beings are superior.[24] As remarked in Chapter 2, above, differentiation is not a problem in and of itself. Rather, hierarchical valuations and beliefs that can attend differentiation are problematic because they create the ontological rift. Let me explain. We can safely claim that there are differences in communication vis-à-vis human beings and other animals. Human beings apparently have complex symbol systems while other species rely on *seemingly* less complex semiotic forms of communication. While this is a distinction, it does not necessarily follow that this makes us "best," better, or higher/superior to other species. Indeed, many species have communicative capacities that human beings do not have, which does not mean they are existentially superior because of what we lack. What accompanied Aristotle's (and other Greek and Western philosophers') philosophical (and scientific) perspective, in other words, depended on a hierarchical valuation that placed human beings on top of the taxonomic ladder. These valuations, I am arguing, are mere human constructions and not existential or ontological facts.

Aristotle's philosophical apotheosis of humanity has a religious counterpart. In the nineteenth century, Ludwig Feuerbach wrote "that religion itself, not indeed on the surface, but fundamentally, not in intention or according to its own supposition, but in its heart, in its essence, believes in nothing else than the truth and divinity of human nature."[25] And there is no greater inferiority than constructing other species as "lacking" souls, which means that they, in the end, have no ontological significance or chance of ontological permanence (though other species may have existential instrumental significance if they are seen as benefiting human beings). Or, as Feuerbach noted, "Religion has its basis in the essential difference between man and the brute—the brutes have no religion."[26] Following upon Aristotelian claims that animals lack reason, language, and political agency, Feuerbach argues that Judeo-Christian religions view animals as lacking both religion and souls. In Aristotle and in Feuerbach's depiction of religion, "lack" is imbricated with hierarchical valuations deemed either existential or ontological "truths." Western philosophy and religion both produce the rift between human beings and other animals.

While it is possible, with some caveats, to empirically show whether this or that species is sentient, the beauty of the idea that other species lack souls lies in its unfalsifiability: it is an idea impossible to debunk, because

24. This hierarchical valuation exists in relation to other human beings. Women, for Aristotle, do not lack reason and virtue, though theirs are deemed to be less than men's capacities, which therefore legitimate men's superiority.

25. Feuerbach, *Essence of Christianity*, xvi.

26. Feuerbach, *Essence of Christianity*, 1.

the existence of a "soul" cannot be proven empirically. It is an article of faith, which functions, in part, to separate ontologically human beings from other species, as well as to legitimize the nonrecognition of the singularities of other species. In addition, this belief exemplifies the hubris and narcissism associated with many Abrahamic political theologies—hubris and narcissism that these theologies mainly deny or overlook. How could one possibly know that other species do not have souls, except by saying that somehow God told us that, revealing a deceptive and, in the long run, tragic tautology.

This kind of differentiation often attends varied iterations of sovereignty, as I mentioned in Chapter 1. While sovereignty inevitably creates a rift between those who rule and those who do not, it is not necessarily the case that such a rift is constructed as ontological in the sense of being absolutely unbridgeable or impassable. Of course, from the theological perspective, the sole sovereignty of God over creation indicates an ontological rift between God and humanity. The cosmological ordering of the universe, according to Abrahamic traditions, places God on the top—as best, superior, and highest—but this rift is not insurmountable. The idea of the incarnation suggests this rift can be crossed with Jesus's taking on human flesh.[27] The divide is also bridgeable by humans who become members of the kingdom of God, which suggests some human beings can cross the rift by way of God's salvific grace.[28] When it comes to other species, however, the ontological rift is not bridgeable. Incarnation and the kingdom of God refer only to human beings, and not to all human beings at that. Human beings, in short, are believed to be ontologically different from other species, which is evident in beliefs that other species lack souls and, therefore, have no existence in the kingdom of God.

In Chapter 1, I also mentioned other features of sovereignty, namely, instrumental epistemologies and relations of subordination and subjugation, which are also attributes of the ontological chasm. Let me come at this from the perspective of the ideas of *imago dei* and soul. The notion of *imago dei* is usually attributed to human beings, though in practice we rarely live up to or out of this ideal. To be created in the image and likeness

---

27. Feuerbach argued that the "incarnate God is only the apparent manifestation of the deified man; the descent of God to man is necessarily preceded by the exaltation of man to God" (Feuerbach, *Essence of Christianity*, 50).

28. The notion of hell in the Abrahamic traditions illustrates to some degree the rift that exists between those who believe and practice according to these traditions and those who do not or have failed. It is an eternal rift that apparently cannot be crossed, at least not by those human beings residing in heaven. Perhaps other species are fortunate, in the sense that they are not subject to hell or heaven. The rift means they are not ontologically significant enough to merit either and, therefore, pass into oblivion—outside of time and place.

of God can mean many things, but it principally means that human beings are ontologically valuable and significant to the creator. Similarly, the idea that human beings have souls suggests that *ideally* each human being is recognized as unique, inviolable, and inestimably valued. Perhaps some people in the Abrahamic traditions believe that all creation is created in the image and likeness of God, which would suggest an appreciation of and for the singularity of other species. Yet, the idea that other species lack souls denies both in theory and in practice their singularities. This disavowal means that other species are deemed inferior and, therefore, subordinate to human beings, who have a higher place in the cosmic hierarchy. Moreover, this categorical disavowal, which is an inextricable part of the impassable ontological rift, justifies and legitimates relations of subjugation—exploitation (e.g., factory farms and slaughter factories) and extraction (e.g., mining, Mountain Top Removal). Just as destructive is the reality that the presence of the ontological rift means that other species and the Earth may be completely ignored because they have no political-economic value (e.g., ecological dead zones).[29]

Of course, Othered human beings can be constructed such that they, too, are part of the impassable ontological rift, but there is a difference. Let me first turn to Greek political theorizing. Some Greek philosophers, including Alkidamas, argued that "The deity gave liberty to all men, and nature created no one a slave."[30] His argument was set against a recognizable danger in the polis: "Whenever the poor are vulnerable to contracts that make them potentially liable to be used or sold as slaves, they cannot be equal citizens, because they cannot be secure in their status as citizens ... They are in these circumstances always at risk of falling into some form of bondage."[31] By contrast, Aristotle argued that some human beings are naturally suited to be slaves (animate instruments that are property of their masters).[32] "It is thus clear" Aristotle wrote, "that, just as some are by nature free, so others are by nature slaves, and for these latter the condition of slavery is both beneficial and just."[33] In Western political philosophy and theology, there have been numerous times when some human beings have been constructed as less than human and even as not possessing a soul;

29. Ecological dead zones, like the Mississippi Delta, drastically undermine aquatic life and are the result of human-caused pollution.

30. Quoted in Lane, *Birth of Politics*, 51.

31. Lane, *Birth of Politics*, 34. A modern version of this is seen in the brutal enslavement and exploitation of Africans in the United States and its close connection to capitalism. See Baptist, *Half Has Never Been Told*.

32. Barker, trans., *Politics of Aristotle*, 9–18.

33. Barker, trans., *Politics of Aristotle*, 14.

these alienating constructions of some humans by other humans reveal the impassable ontological rift between human beings and are a prelude to exploitation and death.[34] While Othered humans face one set of implications from the ontological rift, nonhuman species face decidedly different implications. Human beings who are Othered, more often than not, find ways to gather in groups to survive and attempt to thrive. They usually, in defiance of the larger political-economic system that denies their singularities, recognize and treat each other as persons. The long history of slavery and racism in the US testifies to the resilience and defiance of enslaved people who believed in their inherent ontological dignity.[35]

Daniel Black's novel *The Coming* illustrates this. He tells the harrowing story of the Middle Passage. In one scene, we learn of "a young man's calm,"[36] which captures the narrator's attention. The young man, Abuto, "studied our weary eyes, then nodded slowly as if knowing something we didn't. Distress and trauma had not broken him; he shared our rage, as any man would, but something else occupied his mind. Something deep in the soul that could not be spoken. Something the oppressors could not disturb or destroy."[37] His fellows knew when they looked into his eyes "that he would never, ever be another man's captive."[38] Although they were initially unsure of the source of this man's strength and *resilience*, the next morning they noticed Abuto's eyes meeting the eyes of a woman. "They said nothing, made no gesture of recognition, but their eyes bore desire and hope too strong to be concealed . . . Had the captors known, they surely would've tried to break this bond, to strip the lovers of the last vestiges of joy they knew, so we tried not to look at them or they at each other."[39] The other prisoners "tried to distract the captors' attention away from them that they might get a few precious moments of seeing and perhaps even brush each other's flesh."[40] For the captives, this "alone would be enough. At least for now. And it was. It was comforting to see these captive lovebirds refusing to deny the only thing they knew for sure."[41] These caged lovebirds were not the only manifestation of the dignity or singularity the brutish slavers could not control. At one point in the crossing, enslaved persons began to hum. "We hummed until

---

34. Castro, *Cannibal Metaphysics*, 52.
35. Robinson, *Black Marxism*.
36. Black, *Coming*, 37.
37. Black, *Coming*, 37.
38. Black, *Coming*, 38.
39. Black, *Coming*, 38.
40. Black, *Coming*, 38.
41. Black, *Coming*, 38.

we knew we'd survive. We hummed until we released mothers and fathers whom we'd never see again. We hummed until our love and gratitude to each other was clear."[42] Clearly, there is an ontological rift that is created by slavers and the larger economic and political-religious systems that justify and legitimate the exploitation and killing of other human beings. But this rift is not absolute. Othered people find ways to resist and overcome this rift. Put another way, while those who construct the ontological rift view it as unbridgeable—constructing apparatuses to make this a "truth" or "reality"—the reality is that Othered human beings find innumerable ways to defy it.

This is not the case for other species. To be sure, some species find ways to resist exploitation, but the only ones that can actually overcome this rift are human beings—the ones who created it. As the climate emergency demonstrates, other species are at the mercy of human actions, and the varied iterations or shoots of the rhizome of sovereignty discussed in Chapter 2 reveal the truly uncrossable ontological rift vis-à-vis other species. Generally speaking, Western human beings have created and maintain the ontological rift by way of various political, cultural, economic, and scientific apparatuses, and only human beings can deconstruct these apparatuses and their instrumental epistemologies in order to create spaces in which the existential singularities of other species are recognized and respected.

There is another important feature to highlight regarding the ontological rift, which can be understood in terms of an error in reasoning and its attending illusions. That human beings do construct one another and other species as respectively superior and inferior indicates that humans have capacities for signification and valuation. First, these capacities do not, in and of themselves, invariably lead human beings to create the ontological rift, especially given the numerous indigenous philosophies that do not establish the gulf between human beings and other species. These indigenous narratives reveal capacities for signification and valuation, but in these narratives these capacities do not lead to proclamations of human ontological superiority over so-called inferior animals. Indeed, some indigenous stories portray other species as possessing abilities, including knowledge and wisdom, that human beings lack, though these stories do not show other species as superior and human beings as inferior.[43] The point here is that capacities for valuation do not inevitably lead to an ontological rift between human beings and other species. Second, the presence of the ontological rift reveals

---

42. Black, *Coming*, 43–44.

43. See Kerven, *Native American Myths*; Erdoes and Ortiz, eds., *American Indian Myths*; Deloria, *God Is Red*.

an error in logic. Human beings think, consciously or unconsciously, that because we have the capacity to signify and value other creatures, we are necessarily superior existentially or ontologically to these other creatures. Our superiority and other species' inferiority is a mere belief. Our abilities to differentiate and evaluate are traits of human beings, just as the ability of bats to move and communicate with sonar is a trait of bats. Perhaps bats, because they have capacities human beings lack, consider themselves to be superior to humans, though this would remain faulty logic—because a species's possessing a capacity does not in itself prove the superiority of that species; nor does a species lacking a specific capacity prove the inferiority of that species. To assume superiority based on a capacity is a mental trick we play on ourselves as humans. Third, constructing other species in terms of what they "lack" does not necessarily lead to the ontological rift, unless what is perceived as a lack in some species is attached to the belief in the inferiority of those species.

This error in logic remains hidden, because the religious and political apparatuses that produce and maintain the rift operate to give each of us a felt sense of the existential or ontological truth of these beliefs. In other words, we internalize these beliefs and valuations without critically examining or questioning them. They become conscious or unconscious religious and/or secular dogmas. We go to the store and buy packaged meat without any thought to the suffering of the animal, and if we do give thought to the animal's suffering, we pass over it because we believe that we need to eat and that animals exist for that reason alone. Some scientists give no or little thought to experimenting on other species, which they justify, tacitly or overtly, by beliefs in human dominion and superiority. In our drive to make money and develop properties, we ignore the fact that other species (also, Othered human beings) may depend on habitat for their survival and flourishing.

The mental trick we Western humans play on ourselves includes grounding valuations and the ontological rift in ideas of Nature or God. Philosophers and theologians in the West have long anchored their arguments in Nature,[44] as if (1) Nature and culture are radically different,[45] and

---

44. Alfred North Whitehead was critical of Western philosophical constructions of Nature, as if human beings are to be differentiated from nature. Whitehead, *Concept of Nature*.

45. Bruno Latour discusses the problems associated with differentiating between nature and culture. "In the Western tradition," he writes, "most definitions of the human stress the extent to which it is distinguished from nature" (Latour, *Facing Gaia*, 14). "The concept of 'nature,'" he continues, "now appears as a truncated, simplified, exaggeratedly moralistic, excessively polemical, and prematurely political version of the otherness of the world to which we must open ourselves if we are not to become

(2) human superiority is a fact of Nature and not a mere human construct that has political-economic functions. In other words, a belief, attributed to Nature, comes to be treated as an existential fact, which then becomes an unquestionable premise and finally undergirds and makes normative a related claim. Worse, Abrahamic traditions, as I have indicated above, cement valuations in Nature *and* God. Such valuations and the ontological rift, then, are not considered mere existential facts; they come to be regarded as ontological facts—unquestionable norms. The logic systems built from these premises are formidable, if not impregnably dogmatic, becoming part of forms of life that dictate our exploitative relations with other species and the Earth. Western philosophical and theological apparatuses give rise to our assumptive world where we do not question the "truth" of human superiority and its attending ontological rift.

Someone might counter that human superiority certainly feels real or true. Just look around. Human beings have domesticated many other species. There are hardly any species we cannot control or destroy, despite the fact that they might be faster, larger, and more dangerous than ourselves. We can sequence the DNA of other species and clone some. What other species has made it into space, reached the moon and Mars? Are these not proofs of our superiority? I am arguing that all of these and other examples used to provide proof are not convincing, not simply because they reveal an error in logic, but especially because human beings are also vulnerable to extinction despite our creative attempts to avoid it. The Anthropocene Age, in short, reveals that human beings may go the way of the dinosaurs. That dinosaurs became extinct does not signal their inferiority but rather reveals only their finitude, their existential insignificance and impermanence. Further, the survival of cockroaches does not mean they are or will become superior to humans; their survival points to their adaptability.

If we concede that there is an error in logic, why consider this belief in superiority and ontological rift to be illusory? I approach this question in two ways. First, an existential fact does not have to be reproduced by any human apparatus. It is a universal or existential fact that human beings are animals that need air and water to survive. It is also an existential fact that human beings are altricial animals (creatures that need significant amounts of care to develop psychologically and physically). Even if we consider the tremendous variability in child-rearing practices throughout the world, these existential facts are true and universal. We do not need to construct apparatuses to prove them or to give us a felt experience of the truth of these

---

collectively mad—*alienated*" (*Facing Gaia*, 36, italics original). This alienation, which I will elaborate further, is another way of pointing to the ontological rift between human beings and other species. See also Cupitt, *Radical Theology*, 109.

statements. Illusions, on the other hand, must be continually produced, precisely because they are not existential facts. It is not a universal or timeless fact that human beings are superior to all other species. It is not, in other words, an existential truth that there is an ontological gap between humans and other species. These are illusions that must be continually manufactured and maintained by Western apparatuses, giving those who hold them a sense of their facticity.

There is another related angle to highlight regarding the illusions of superiority and the ontological rift. As I noted above, human beings have capacities for signification and valuation. The cosmos neither has these capacities nor confirms them. If anything, the universe or multiverse simply confirms the existential insignificance and impermanence of all life, including of the Earth. Western human beings have looked to Nature, God, or both, to confirm that human beings are significant and, for some, permanent (living in the divine eternal polis). Nature and God are part of the apparatuses that promote the "truth" of our belief in human superiority, which places a chasm between ourselves and other species. Put another way, we project, as Feuerbach noted, our desire for significance and permanence onto God, failing to note its illusory foundation. The wonderful thing about Western religions is that they continuously affirm ontological significance for some human beings while denying it to all other living beings. While I will return to this below, many scholars have noted that in the West Christianity is in decline, though capitalism and its spectacles,[46] while not affirming ontological significance, serve as distractions or even soporifics in the face of the stark reality of existential insignificance and impermanence.

Someone reading this might wonder if I am saying that God is an illusion. Millennia ago, Greek philosopher Xenophanes said that "if oxen and horses or lions had hands, and could paint with their hands, and produce works of art as men do, horses would paint the forms of the gods like horses, and oxen like oxen."[47] Since then, other philosophers (e.g., Feuerbach), theologians (e.g., Meister Eckhart, Don Cupitt), and those in the human sciences (e.g., Sigmund Freud, Ana-Maria Rizzuto) have noted that human beings create gods in their images and/or out of their fears, anxieties, and insecurities. Yet, like Xenophanes, accepting this fact does not necessarily mean one is an atheist—understood in the traditional sense. One can believe that there is a God beyond religion's social imaginary of God—a God beyond any notions of superiority or inferiority, ontology, and sovereignty.

---

46. See Debord, *Society of the Spectacle*; Boorstin, *Image*.
47. Quoted in Grayling, *History of Philosophy*, 24.

Whenever in history other human beings and other species are constructed as insignificant, existentially or otherwise, we can be assured that exploitation and death are not far behind. Here is where we see the "utility" of the ontological rift and its attributes. What is deemed insignificant is alien to me and is available for my use, to meet either my needs or desires. Even better, since there is a radical gulf between us, I am free of any responsibility or remorse for the consequences of my actions as they relate to what is insignificant. For instance, the radical gulf between the scientist and the rat she dissects keeps the scientist from recognizing the singularity of the rat and, consequently, protects her from feelings of remorse for the suffering she has caused. The radical chasm between human beings and, say, cattle, means I can ignore the massive suffering that accompanies their slaughter. I feel no remorse as I pick up a pound of steak. Indeed, I do not even have the thought that the meat I purchase comes from a singular creature. It is simply meat, and its significance is only for my well-being and pleasure. Because we are superior, we can exploit the Earth, causing great devastation to the local environment and ignoring the loss of habitat for other-than-human species. The ontological rift legitimizes and justifies all manner of instrumental uses of Othered human beings, other species, and the Earth. And if the climate emergency has revealed anything, it is that this way of thinking and relating is incredibly destructive, endangering not only our lives, but the lives of millions of other species. Western errors in logic and illusions may, in the end, bring us all more quickly to the existential realities of insignificance and impermanence. As Jonathan Schell remarks, "If we conquer nature, we will find ourselves among the defeated."[48]

Let me stress here that illusions can have very serious and very real consequences, positive and negative. The belief in Santa Claus is *mostly* a benign illusion, which can motivate people to be charitable. The illusions created by Marvel comics are, for many, enjoyable and entertaining, generating billions of dollars. All kinds of illusions are attached to capitalism and nationalism, some positive, mostly not. The illusion of the ontological rift has proven to be incredibly damaging to other species and the Earth, for millennia. Only with the arrival of the Anthropocene have many of us become aware of how dangerous this error in logic and attending illusions are for life on Earth.

There is one more facet to tease out regarding beliefs in human sovereignty, instrumental epistemologies, and their relation to the ontological rift. Earlier, I mentioned Whitehead's view that "the European philosophical

---

48. Schell, "Human Shadow," 19. Alan Watts, *Way of Zen*, 174–75, also points out the Western preoccupations with conquering nature, as if nature is an object to serve the needs of humanity.

tradition is . . . a series of footnotes to Plato."[49] While this may be an exaggeration, there is some evidence for this. Western political philosophers and theologians have been obsessively preoccupied with the interrelated ideas of Being and the Truth, despite Heidegger's claim that Being was forgotten in the West. That there is Being and Truth is the foundational premise underlying instrumental epistemologies, and many Western philosophers and theologians are fixated on these ideas, constructing elaborate and complex theories about them.[50] This kind of thinking makes use of bifurcation or binaries (exemplified in pairs such as Being and nonbeing and Truth and falsehood). In addition, the uppercasing of the first term in each pair suggests a hierarchical valuation of the first term over the second (where the first term functions as a Platonic form); such valuation deepens the chasm between Being and nonbeing, between Truth and lies, for instance. The result of such valuation in the study of Being (ontology) and truth, and its bifurcation of reality, is the eclipse of perspectivism, variability, and multiplicity.[51] In the West, there is only Being and The Truth. There cannot be multiple truths or multiple perspectives, because they would contradict the foundational premises of Being and Truth. There can only be one Truth. All other partial truths must not contradict The Truth.

Lest one think this is mere philosophizing, many of us in the West have grown up being told in thousands of ways not only that there is the Truth, but also that we have it and Others do not. Western colonization of Othered peoples has been partially fueled and justified by instrumental epistemologies with foundational philosophical and theological premises about what is The Truth and what it is Not. Consider that indigenous peoples, who tend to embrace the pleasurable, creative messiness of multiple perspectives, including the varied truths of other species, are constructed as *lacking* The Truth. It is believed that their stories have nothing to do with the "sophistication" of Western philosophies. Indigenous stories are considered mere myths, fanciful. Their lacking the Truth becomes a motive for religiously or secularly evangelizing them, for bringing them into the Truth of civilization. There is, in other words, a rift that emerges out of Western premises about Being and Truth, and ironically (and tragically) this rift between human beings who

---

49. Whitehead, *Process and Reality*, 39.

50. Let me stress that I am not suggesting that Western philosophies and theologies that focus on Being and Truth are without value, which would be a myopic claim to say the least. I am simply pointing to the underlying problems with focusing on Truth/Being, problems that become more apparent given encounters with indigenous peoples with decidedly different philosophical views—views and apparatuses that do not produce the ontological rift.

51. See Castro, *Cannibal Metaphysics*.

have The Truth and those who do not can be bridged by forcing Othered human beings to adopt Western philosophies/myths and religions. Those human beings who do not can be dispensed with.

Further, since other species are constructed as lacking reason, they are logically lacking in Truth. Other-than-human species take part in creation, but they are judged incapable of possessing the Truth, which is yet another factor entrenching the ontological rift. Not having the truth, in other words, is the other side of not having a soul. Such palatial Western logic is absent in the philosophies of indigenous people, where other species are sources of revelation and wisdom. Other species have truths that can be discovered if human beings listen. But the ontological chasm deafens and blinds Westerners from these truths.[52] We take note of this rift and of the blindness and deafness that arise because of it in the instrumental exploitation of other species and the Earth.

In summary, it is one thing when human beings are capable of differentiating between themselves and other species; it is altogether another matter when (1) differentiation is linked to beliefs in human superiority (existential significance) and the inferiority (existential insignificance) of other species; (2) instrumental epistemologies determine how humans behave toward other-than-human species and the Earth; (3) beliefs in human dominion rule the day; and (4) subordination and subjugation characterize relations between humans and other-than-human species. This kind of differentiation, produced and maintained by varied apparatuses associated with sovereignty and its shoots, leads to an ontological rift between human beings and other species. We, who have internalized all these beliefs, become alienated from what stands on the other shore of the rift. The destruction from this rift is vast, and from most of those who live in the assumptive world where the ontological rift is operating, there is no remorse and no empathy for the past or present (or future[53]) sufferings of other species (and Othered human beings); such remorselessness simply confirms our state of alienation as a species.

A Psychosocial Analysis of the Ontological Rift

A psychosocial perspective can deepen and broaden our analysis of the dynamics and functions of the rift, as well as provide answers to just how

---

52. There are philosophers and scientists who are listening, but not enough of them. See Kohn, *How Forests Think*; Meijer, *When Animals Speak*; Meijer, *Animal Languages*.

53. Just as we have a moral obligation to nonexistent human beings (those who will be born), we similarly have a moral obligation for nonexistent other-than-human beings.

intransigent the ontological rift is in Western assumptive worlds and ways of living. Put another way, we obtain a better appreciation for how and why the ontological rift has been foundational in climate change and how it continues to function as an obstacle to climate action. The underlying premise in this discussion is that when we become aware of the sources of our resistance, we can choose to let go the ontological rift and take steps toward constructing other forms of living that respect the singularities of other species and the singularity of the Earth.

Above I mentioned that the reality of existential insignificance and impermanence is elided by apparatuses that alienate human beings from other species. What the rift manifests are the psychosocial operations of splitting and projection. Splitting "is an unconscious process that actively separates contradictory feelings, self-representations, or object representation from one another."[54] Projection is a psychological mechanism whereby split-off aspects of oneself are evacuated and projected onto other persons.[55] While both of these operations usually apply to individuals, they are also social or intersubjective operations. For instance, US history offers plenty of evidence of both operations in the varied ways White supremacists relate to people of color. White supremacists split off their anxieties and deep insecurities about their sense of worth and project these anxieties and insecurities onto people of color.[56] In terms of the ontological rift vis-à-vis the assumptive world of most Westerners, anxieties and fears founded in our existential insignificance and impermanence are split off, evacuated, and projected onto other species. We engage other species in terms of their perceived insignificance and existential impermanence when compared to ourselves, and the comparison leaves us seemingly secure in the illusions of our significance and permanence. In other words, Abrahamic traditions, including their political theologies, secure (not all) human significance and permanence in ontology while "proving" the insignificance of other species.

Let me explicate this further. The origin myths of the Abrahamic religions are thoroughly anthropocentric, fostering beliefs that the Earth, if not the cosmos, was created for human beings, which clearly establishes the ontological significance of human beings. Similarly, the idea of the kingdom of God in Christianity implies that some human beings are significant enough to obtain everlasting life—ontological permanence—while other species are left completely outside the eternal kingdom. These myths not only reveal *in themselves* splitting and projection, but they also function as apparatuses to

---

54. Gabbard, *Psychodynamic Psychiatry*, 44.
55. Gabbard, *Psychodynamic Psychiatry*, 48.
56. See Kovel, *White Racism*; Altman, "Black and White Thinking."

maintain these psychosocial defenses. Let's return to Ludwig Feuerbach's critique of Christianity to illustrate this: "But we nowhere read," Feuerbach writes, "that God, for the sake of brutes, became a brute—the very idea of this is, in the eyes of religion [Christianity], impious and ungodly; or that God ever performed a miracle for the sake of animals or plants."[57] The Christian idea of incarnation, like the corresponding notion of the kingdom of God, is understood to be strictly for the sake of human beings, since "brutes" or other species are deemed soulless and thus insignificant and impermanent. In short, Abrahamic religious stories reveal the splitting and projection that secures the illusion of human ontological significance and permanence, which wards off anxiety and fear about the existential reality of human insignificance and impermanence. This splitting and projection results in alienation between human beings and other species but also in intrapsychic alienation in that keeps us out of touch with the reality of our own existential insignificance and impermanence.

While Western religious apparatuses continuously affirm ontological significance for some human beings by projecting insignificance and impermanence upon all other living beings, these are not the only apparatuses. In this reputedly secular age dominated by the decline of Christianity's hegemony in the West, nationalism and capitalism step into the breach, though in different ways. Nationalisms often have a religious function in that a person obtains a sense of existential significance and permanence by way of the nation and its continued existence in history. Splitting and projection are present in the very absence of other species from the national identity. Capitalism is different. Capitalism and it spectacles,[58] while not consciously affirming ontological significance,[59] serve as a distraction from or even a soporific in the face of the stark reality of our existential insignificance and impermanence. Still, the attributes of the ontological rift remain, given how other species and the Earth are exploited. Put differently, capitalism does not offer existential significance and permanence, but it maintains the operations of splitting and projection that are evident in the instrumental use of Othered human beings, Othered species, and of the Earth. In brief, modern Western political philosophies have not lost their religious structure, which means that they carry forward, overtly or covertly, the operations of splitting and projection vis-à-vis human existential insignificance.

57. Feuerbach, *Essence of Christianity*, 104–5.
58. Debord, *Society of the Spectacle*.
59. Capitalism, unlike Abrahamic traditions, does not affirm ontological significance or permanence. However, it perpetuates the attributes of the ontological rift, which is why I suggest it is unconsciously present in the way we instrumentally treat other species and planet Earth.

To carry this further, the defensive operations of projection and splitting can be depicted in terms of Donnel Stern's notion of weak dissociation, for which he is indebted to Herbert Fingarette's philosophical analysis of routine self-deception. Fingarette wrote, "It is when we judge that there is a purposeful discrepancy between the way the individual really is engaged in the world and the story he tells himself that we have the complex but common form of self-deception in which we are interested."[60] This self-deception, from Fingarette's perspective, results from not spelling out (from not narrating) one's engagement in the world; or, better, self-deception arises from spelling out one's engagement such that one avows neither one's fears, anxieties, or insecurities; nor one's actions; nor the consequences of one's actions. Stern, building on Fingarette's analysis of self-deception, argues that weak dissociation entails narrative rigidity, which means that individuals organize their experiences so that their actions and their consequences are narrowly spelled out, by omitting actions and consequences that do not "fit" a dominant, rigid story.[61] Inflexible narration, in other words, means that ideas, meanings, values, and affects that are unconsciously perceived to contradict the dominant-conscious narrative are excluded or unformulated and, therefore, outside awareness. In weak dissociation, Stern argues, we spell out only what "we believe we can tolerate, or that furthers our purpose, or that promises a feeling of safety, satisfaction, and the good things in life; we dissociate the meanings that we believe we will not be able to tolerate, that frighten us and seem to threaten the fulfillment of our deepest intentions."[62]

Western religious and political anthropologies are stories we tell about ourselves and the world to rigidly secure our sense of existential significance. The realities of existential insignificance and impermanence give rise to intolerable anxiety (annihilation anxiety), which threatens to expose and heighten our insecurities. All of this is defended against through weak dissociation or rigid narrations—the dogmas we hold about our superiority and the inferiority of other species. Our instrumental actions toward other species and the Earth are justified and legitimated by these narratives, which further function to "prove" our significance.

This weak dissociation also functions psychosocially by reducing or obstructing empathy for the lives of other species. To have empathy, one must recognize the singularity of another being. When our stories keep telling us that other species do not possess singularity, there is no possibility for

---

60. Fingarette, *Self-Deception*, 62.
61. Stern, *Unformulated Experience*.
62. Stern, *Unformulated Experience*.

empathy. Weak dissociation's obstruction of empathy accompanies another psychosocial function, the absence of remorse for our destructive actions. The resulting lack of empathy and remorse in weak dissociation are evident in Abrahamic scriptures. Indeed, all of this is evident in the stories about God. For instance, many religious and irreligious people are no doubt familiar with the exodus story, wherein the Israelites are oppressed by Pharaoh. To convince Pharaoh to let the Israelites go, God sends a fifth plague that decimates horses, donkeys, camels, herds of cattle, and flocks of sheep (Exod 9:1–4). This "miracle" reveals the significance of the Israelites and the absolute insignificance of these animals. In fact, God kills many innocent Egyptians (why not just take out the Egyptian leadership?) and orders the Israelites to ethnically cleanse the promised land. There are in these stories no hints of empathy for the horrific sufferings and deaths of other species and Othered persons, and there are absolutely no hints of remorse. Since it is believed that God acts and orders the Israelites to kill the inhabitants of the promised land, why would any Israelite have any empathy or a sense of remorse? I have chosen the exodus and conquest stories because they have been used repeatedly throughout history to justify, for instance, the ethnic cleansing of indigenous peoples by ostensibly good Christian Europeans. These are excellent examples of weak dissociation, wherein the significance of the storytellers is ontologically affirmed, while Others' significance is disavowed. What cannot be tolerated is not simply existential insignificance but also the horrors that result from our securing the ontological rift over and against the singularities of other species (and Othered human beings).

The resulting lack of remorse and empathy that attends weak dissociation represents not simply our alienation from other species, but our self-alienation. The rigid narrations that secure my sense of existential significance and permanence insure that I am not in touch with the reality of my existential insignificance and impermanence. Self-empathy cannot take place, because I am not aware of my anxiety, fear, and insecurity. This unawareness keeps me from empathizing with someone else's existential fears. Indeed, when I encounter from someone else existential anxiety related to insignificance and impermanence, I am likely to be motivated to avoid that person or try to convince (evangelize) them to adopt my "truths" or my hopes; these events I have seen play out many times when good Christian people encounter those who are dying and who are not "believers." In such encounters what comes to the fore is not only intrapsychic alienation but also self-other alienation.

Closely associated with weak dissociation are the defenses of rationalization and moralization. There are times when, despite our best efforts, we cannot ignore the suffering of other species—suffering that results from our instrumental use. While I no longer recall where I heard this, I once listened to a philosopher discuss the question of justice when it comes to killing other species for human use. He rightly decried factory farms and industrial slaughterhouses because in his view they treat animals unjustly. He argued, however, that if other sentient species are to be killed, the killing must be done "humanely" with minimal suffering. Of course, he continued, for species considered to lack sentience, wholesale killing is not just or unjust. The notion of justice does not apply to nonsentient species. These and other mental gymnastics represent the defensive operations of rationalization and moralization. Moreover, the rational schemas entailed in such views remain hierarchal, though now nonsentient species[63] are on the lowest rung of the ladder. Again, for those beings on the lowest rung, our rationalization and moralization also obstruct empathy and remorse we might feel toward them. In listening to this thoughtful man, I still detected lingering arrogance and omnipotent thinking so prevalent in Western ways of relating to other species and the Earth. How is it that human beings decide what is and what is not sentient? Why do we become the arbiters of what is existentially significant or inferior? What right do we have to create zones of nonjustice, denying the singularities of other species?

We do not have to turn to philosophers to note the rife presence of rationalization and moralization vis-à-vis other species. The fish and meat industries depend on all of us using these defenses. So, as I mentioned above, when I buy that pound of steak and a pound of tuna, I give no thought to the suffering these animals endured. Indeed, that I live thousands of miles from the meatpacking plant or the docks simply makes this easier. But let's imagine I read a story about the meat or fishing industry. I grudgingly admit that these animals suffer and that we should find ways to reduce their suffering, but in the end, I say, we have to eat. So, I am back at the grocery store to buy hamburger. This action is based on rationalization and moralization, which ranks the singularities of human beings on the highest end of the hierarchical valuation system. Moreover, both operations, like weak dissociation, undermine our capacities for empathy and remorse.

I want to extend this discussion to further demonstrate the pervasive psychosocial intractableness of the Western ontological rift. The particular polis in which we are born entails complex meaning and belief/value

---

63. It is certainly possible to contest the blanket assumption that "lower" animals are not sentient. Scientists are discovering all kinds of complex communications that take place outside human awareness or observation vis-à-vis other species, including nonanimal species. But even if we knew definitively that an animal was nonsentient, that is not in itself a legitimation for exploitation. It is simply category we use to rationalize and moralize our actions.

systems that we gradually internalize.[64] This internalization leads to the formation of what Lynne Layton[65] calls the normative unconscious, and to what Timothy J. Zeddies[66] calls "historical unconscious." Both the normative and the historical unconscious are imbricated with conscious political constructions of reality, yet they omit the present and past sufferings of marginalized Others (including the lives and sufferings of other species). For millennia, few Western philosophers, for instance, recognized the political agency of women, which meant that the polis's apparatuses attempted to debase women's self-esteem, self-confidence, and self-respect. Women, in other words, were (and continue to be, in some places) not deemed politically normative or relevant and, therefore, not or rarely remembered. Put another way, women and girls were not politically significant for millennia. Similarly, indigenous peoples and enslaved persons were not part of White European normative or historical consciousness. One might counter that indigenous peoples are in US history books, but they are supporting actors to the dominant story, as are enslaved people. In my view, the vitriol expressed by US conservatives about critical race theory reveals their anxiety that normative and historical constructions are under threat by people who want to raise to consciousness the significance of people of color.

Normative and historical unconsciousness are also present in relation to other species. The ontological rift, in other words, represents human beings as normative and creatures of and with history. As I mentioned above, other species are in the stories of Abrahamic scriptures, and they are often depicted in history books (e.g., George Washington on his horse). But they are not central to the story. Other species do not have a story or a history, because we see them as lacking agency and language. The ontological rift, then, accompanies the normative and historical unconscious, yet this is not the case in indigenous narratives where other species possess speech, insight, wisdom, and value, and are inextricably part of the people and their history.[67]

I want to linger here for a moment, because there is an interesting twist to this story. I imagine that many readers who have children or recall their own early childhood know that children's literature[68] reveals, like in-

64. Schafer, *Aspects of Internalization*.
65. Layton, *Toward a Social Psychoanalysis*.
66. Zeddies, "Behind, Beneath, Above, and Beyond."
67. Kohn, *How Forests Think*.
68. It is not only children's literature where we see animals being central to a story. Here is I am thinking of Jack London's stories *White Fang* and *Call of the Wild*. London demonstrates empathic imagination in telling these tales—an imagination that bridges, in part, the rift between human beings and other species.

digenous stories, that other species have language, agency, and memory. Illustrators and writers wonderfully animate them, giving them significance. In other words, other species are not relegated to the background or to an anonymous part of the anthropological landscape. They, like human beings, are central to children's stories, offering guidance, wisdom, playfulness, and other gifts. Other animals, then, are initially part of many children's worldview. Alienation is not yet present.

What happens then to these stories? As Western children grow up, they internalize the stories associated with the ontological rift, leaving these early stories to the unconscious or, if recalled or read, relegated to be the merely amusing or fanciful, though many adults may still enjoy these stories. The hugely popular comic strip, *Calvin and Hobbes*, is an example, which I return to in the last chapter. Calvin is a little boy whose best friend is Hobbes, a stuffed tiger. To Calvin, Hobbes is very much alive, and they go on adventures, comfort each other, feel remorse for harms, argue, and make up. When an adult is in the frame, Hobbes looks very much like a stuffed animal. Why do so many adults love these characters? I think one explanation is that they touch on unconscious memories we associate with our early imaginations, when we were connected to other animals who played significant roles in our lives. Adults reading this comic strip and other children's literature may see it as whimsical play of the imagination. But I am not so sure. I think we overlook truth or wisdom if we associate literature or comic strips for children as merely childish thoughts that have nothing to do with the real (adult) world. And I wonder if many Westerners (and anthropologists) do much the same thing when they listen to or read indigenous stories, wherein other species are animated and play significant roles in the normative and historical consciousness of indigenous people. Anthropologists of old often viewed indigenous people as primitive and uncivilized—as if civilization's ontological rift were the happy and inevitable goal of all human beings. They were deemed to be childlike because their world is animated. And as a result, we have overlooked the practical wisdom of seeing and relating to other species as unique, as inextricably a part of our lives, and as existentially significant as we are.

This reminds me of a comment Frank Linderman made. Linderman chronicled the life of the Crow chief Plenty Coups. Plenty Coups, a famous leader of the Crow people, remarked: "With all his wonderful powers, the white man is not wise. He is smart, but not wise."[69] Frank Linderman, who was a friend of Plenty Coups, said, "I am convinced that no white man has ever thoroughly known the Indian, and such a work as this must suffer

---

69. Quoted in Lear, *Radical Hope*, 139.

because of the widely different views of life held by the two races ... I have studied the Indian for more than forty years, not coldly, but with sympathy; yet even now I do not feel that I know much about him."[70] Linderman spent four decades of his life trying to understand indigenous people he encountered but in the end felt distant and knew mostly a sense of alienation from indigenous people. My interpretation of Linderman's effort and account is that his lack of understanding manifests civilization's ontological rift with its attending alienation. Linderman, despite his commendable sympathy, remained alienated from indigenous people because he was unconsciously operating out of the ontological rift. The White man may be smart, but he is not wise, for practical wisdom entails the absence of the ontological rift; wisdom does not entail merely crossing it: if we leave it behind, we see and treat other species as integral to our lives, to our dwelling together in the polis. The wisdom of early childhood and the wisdom of indigenous peoples point to the truth that life is interconnected and that other-than-human species and Othered human beings all depend on one another and the Earth to survive and thrive. All living beings share in existential insignificance and impermanence. This wisdom is lost when we internalize the stories, practices, and psychosocial defenses associated with the ontological rift, becoming alienated from "Nature" and other species.

Perhaps Linderman, despite his affection for Plenty Coups and other indigenous people, could not face the fact that White civilization carried existential deceptions while indigenous peoples carry a truth that threatens to expose and undermine Westerners' assumptive worlds—worlds dependent on the ontological rift. Perhaps, this unconscious threat gave rise to attempts to destroy indigenous peoples and their cultures. And maybe the reason we bifurcate childhood from adulthood—seeing childhood as something to leave behind (when in fact it never leaves us) and shaming people who apparently do not—is that the wisdom and truth of childhood threaten our Western adult assumptive world, where civilization, sovereignty, and the ontological rift dominate.

In summary, a number of intersubjective defensive operations maintain the ontological rift and protect us from experiencing our alienation from Nature and our fears and insecurities about the truths of existential insignificance and impermanence. By depicting the various psychosocial defenses that are part of the assumptive world of many Western persons, I intended to highlight the seemingly insurmountable challenges of getting beyond the ontological rift, its attributes and ways of life. I also posit the possibility that raising this to consciousness will invite people to change—not

---

70. Quoted in Lear, *Radical Hope*, 1–2.

simply to choose to bridge the ontological rift but to make it inoperative. The first step, however, is to become cognizant of the rift and its consequences. The next step, the focus of the last chapter, is to imagine apparatuses that facilitate our respect for the singularities of other species and of the Earth.

Conclusion

A colleague, in a fit of frustration, said church members were like termites on a ship made of wood. He was not, in my view, demeaning, but pointing to the tragic aspects of life in the church. I think the analogy is fitting when we consider climate change. Termites have no clue that the food source they are gobbling up will cause the ship to become structurally unsound, and leave the inhabitants to perish when the ship inevitably sinks. I believe there is some truth to this analogy when it comes to Western assumptive worldviews implicated in the climate emergency. As human beings, many of us are tragically unaware that our behaviors, which emerge out of apparatuses of the ontological rift, are leading to climate disaster. In this chapter, I wished to delve more deeply, not only into what this chasm is, but also into its psychosocial features—defenses that operate to maintain the ontological rift and that keep us from seeing the truths we come to know in early childhood, truths that indigenous peoples know. My hope is that this chapter has allowed readers to more deeply appreciate the intractableness of Western assumptive worldviews and the attending challenges and obstacles we face in overcoming them.

Of course, we are not termites, who possess their own singularity. Human beings, while finite and shaped by their cultures, have some capacities for critical self-awareness and limited freedom to change. Part of the thrust of this book and, in particular, of this chapter is to be clear about what those limits are—limits associated with the apparatuses that produce and maintain the ontological rift. A question may arise as to how we are to bridge or overcome this chasm we have created. Is there a remedy, or are there multiple remedies, so that the ship does not sink? Or, to return to the burning house metaphor of Chapter 1, can we rebuild our ways of dwelling without the architectural problem of civilization's ontological rift? Before offering some ideas about this, I need to tell one more part of the story.

4

The Emergence of a Philosophical/ Theological Explanation and "Remedy" for the Ontological Rift/Alienation

Sin and Salvation

The state necessarily introduces estrangement into social existence.[1]

The political body of the West hides a dangerous pathology.[2]

If there is one thing "civilized" human beings have in common with their so-called primitive relatives it is the desire and need to comprehend and respond to suffering—physical, mental, and spiritual. Understandably, people, whether "civilized" or not, relied and rely on narratives and rituals not only to make sense of a dis-ease but also to develop remedies. Andrew Scull, for instance, indicates that ancient Greek stories tended to view a malady such as epilepsy as a sacred disease, in the sense of attributing its cause to the gods.[3] Spiritual diagnoses are also evident in scripture, such as when Jesus commands the demons tormenting a man into

1. Kovel, *Radical Spirit*, 213.
2. Kishik, *Power of Life*, 25.
3. Scull, *Madness in Civilization*, 20–25.

a herd of pigs (Mark 5:1–13). Relying on religious narratives to understand what we would today call psychological illnesses, continued for millennia. In the fall of 1671, for instance, "Elizabeth Knapp suddenly clutched her legs and throat and cried out in pain. For days she wept, laughed and gestured absurdly, cast herself at the fire, confessed sins, suffered hallucinations, fell into fits, confessed to a compact with the devil, denied any compact with the devil, skipped about the house, roared, yelled, barked like a dog, bleated like a calf, and stared vacantly into space."[4] Without doubt, those closest to Elizabeth would have been deeply distressed and perplexed to see her suffering and would have hoped to find a remedy. Reverend Samuel Willard was called to help diagnose and treat her, using scripture as an interpretive framework and rational argument as a method of cure. Not surprisingly, his efforts failed, though to his credit, "he called on the townsfolk to be compassionate."[5]

Of course, not all diagnoses relied solely on religious explanations for suffering. Other interpretive frameworks were used. Ancient Greek physicians sought "empirical" evidence in their attempts to understand the etiologies of diseases such as epilepsy, melancholia, and what today is diagnosed as schizophrenia.[6] In the West, as Christianity declined, the attempt to provide empirical diagnoses and cures led, in many cases, to a plethora of interpretations and approaches that today seem farfetched, destructive, misogynistic, racist, classist,[7] and utter failures.[8] Indeed, Sandor Gilman and others have demonstrated how the medical field in the nineteenth and twentieth centuries relied on sexist and racist representations of patients when providing "empirical" depictions of disease, which shaped the kinds of "cures" offered.[9] It was not an accident that diagnoses of hysterical neuroses were focused on women and centered on a feature of women's bodies (wandering womb) in the depiction of the condition. The remedies, including Freud's introduction of psychoanalysis, utterly failed to uncover the real sources of suffering—sources located in the apparatuses of social, political, and economic patriarchy. And lest we in contemporary times believe we have moved beyond this, arriving at state-of-the-art diagnoses and remedies, we need only be reminded (1) that racism and sexism continue in the

---

4. Holifield, *History of Pastoral Care*, 42.
5. Holifield, *History of Pastoral Care*, 44.
6. Scull, *Madness in Civilization*, 26–27.
7. Doerner, *Madmen and the Bourgeoisie*.
8. See, Jodelet *Madness and Social Representation*; Porter, ed., *Faber Book of Madness*; Porter, *Social History of Madness*; Ussher, *Madness of Women*.
9. Gilman, *Difference and Pathology*; Gilman, *Picturing Health and Illness*; Gilman, *Disease and Representation*.

medical profession and (2) that the current *Diagnostic Statistical Manual* (*DSM*) is a cultural, political, and economic document that is not universal, definitive, or necessarily effective.[10]

While there have been a great deal of misdiagnoses and failed remedies throughout history, the point here is that human beings feel compelled to understand and respond when we encounter persons in distress (or those who transgress social-cultural norms[11]). Over the years, I have seen numerous therapists and ministers who, when faced with people in distress, rely on their respective interpretive frameworks to make quick diagnoses in order to relieve themselves of the anxiety of not-knowing. And often enough, patients feel a sense of relief when they are given a definitive diagnosis, even if it is incorrect. I think it is fair to say that all human beings, as meaning-making creatures, seek to understand our distress with the aim of alleviation and, if not alleviation, some solace in the midst of suffering. In one sense, then, this book is an attempt to grasp the forms of life that are implicated in the maladies many of us in the West have created vis-à-vis other human beings and other species—the ontological rift. The story I have told is that the etiology of the ontological rift between human beings and other species has been located in the marriage of civilization and sovereignty, giving rise to destructive relations between Western societies, Othered human beings, other-than-human species, and the Earth. In this chapter, I continue this story by arguing that the apparatuses producing the ontological rift contribute to conscious and unconscious experiences and relations of existential alienation. These relations and experiences—produced by apparatuses of civilization and sovereignty—give rise to the need to explain, philosophically and theologically, this alienation and to offer remedies. What I will argue is that (Western) philosophical and theological explanations for experiences of alienation and their attending remedies function to distract and mystify the real sources of alienation, while perpetuating, if not reproducing, sovereignty, the ontological rift between human beings and Nature, and alienation. That is, they exacerbate exactly what they claim to alleviate. Put another way, Western philosophies and Israelite traditions[12] emerged during the rise of both civilization and the belief that sovereignty is necessary for

---

10. Villarosa, *Under the Skin*; Pollock, *Sickening*; Cushman, *Constructing the Self*; Kovel, *White Racism*; Kovel, *Radical Spirit*.

11. There are numerous occasions when people are "diagnosed" because they are transgressing societal or religious norms. In the first iteration of the *DSM*, gays and lesbians were pathologized.

12. When I use the term "traditions," I am referring to varied narratives and ritual performances, which, in the story I am relating, produce and enact the ontological rift, giving it a sense of ontological reality.

human dwelling. These accompanied the ontological rift and experiences of alienation. Abrahamic religions and Western philosophical-theological traditions have provided explanations for experiences of alienation, which include remedies that have obscured the real sources of our collective disease. This discouraging depiction of religion and philosophy is necessary for moving to corrective lenses and possible remedies that are the topic of the next chapter.

I begin by discussing alienation as a central theme in Western philosophical and theological anthropologies. Indeed, these anthropologies indicate that alienation is an existential or ontological fact. At the same time, these philosophical and theological explanations of the sources and experiences of alienation have engendered various remedies, which mystify the real human sources of alienation. So, for instance, I will show that notions of sin and salvation central to the Abrahamic traditions have served to explain and provide a spiritual remedy for alienation while leaving in place and unquestioned apparatuses of civilization's sovereignty that produce and reinforce alienation. I will also note that literature can also function, in part, as an apparatus for the ontological rift, portraying both its inevitability as well as methods for its mitigation—methods that obscure the human-made, human-caused experiences of alienation. The irony and tragedy present in Western constructions of the ontological rift and experiences of alienation is that many people believe both the rift and the state of alienation are inevitable existential features of human existence, even though they are both merely constructions of many, but not all, human beings and societies. Finally, in the concluding section of this chapter I address the psychosocial cognitive operations that function to maintain anthropologies of the ontological rift.

I must offer a number of caveats before setting out on another chapter of the story I am telling. First, I am not suggesting that all philosophies and theologies have somehow missed the mark (or truth) and that I am now offering the answer. A great deal of practical wisdom is to be found in Abrahamic traditions and Western philosophies. The story I present here is that climate change has increasingly revealed a beam in our Western eyes. For as Plenty Coups observed about White people, "With all his wonderful powers, the white man is not wise. He is smart, but not wise."[13] If we become aware of this beam, then we are invited to reimagine political philosophies and theologies that foster forms of life that nurture respect for all human beings, other species, and the Earth—a respect that gives rise to

---

13. Quoted in Lear, *Radical Hope*, 139.

sustainable living.[14] Second, in the following argument, I am not asserting that experiences of alienation are unique to those who are subject to Western philosophical and religious apparatuses. Nor am I saying that existential alienation is simply and solely the result of the rise of civilization and attending ideas of sovereignty. It is certainly plausible that human beings, whether considered "civilized" or "primitive," experience, at times, alienation in relation to other human beings or other species. Indeed, numerous stories from indigenous people, stories that do not assume the ontological rift, depict varied experiences of alienation.[15] Nevertheless, while it is one thing to say that human beings sometimes experience alienation, it is altogether another to ontologize alienation by making it foundational to philosophical or theological anthropologies. In my view, this is a logical mistake: a person takes note of (or people in a society observe) a common feature of human experience and then elevates this feature to ontological status, which the Abrahamic traditions have done with (God's) sovereignty and its corollary, human alienation. Third, when I suggest that the apparatuses of the ontological rift mystify the real sources of alienation (namely, sovereignty and its attributes), I am not in any way implying some sort of conspiracy among Western religious, political, and economic elites to establish and maintain their privileges, power, and prestige. I am arguing that the rise of civilization and the belief in the necessity of sovereignty for human dwelling produced experiences and relations of alienation, which philosophies and theologies ontologized. Ontologizing sovereignty has also meant ontologizing alienation, which has functioned to make alienation anthropologically normative. At the same time, the real sources of alienation (namely, the apparatuses of sovereignty) have been mystified. Fourth, in discussing the focus on sin and salvation in Abrahamic religions, I recognize that entire books could be devoted to the varied histories of the terms "sin" and "salvation" and their complexities. I do not believe getting lost in definitions is necessary as I continue to tell a story in this chapter. Exhaustively defining terms would take me far afield. Instead, I will simply opt to make some general comments about and associations with the concepts of sin and salvation as they pertain to alienation. Finally, in critiquing sin and salvation, I am not suggesting that the concepts, in the Anthropocene Age, are no longer relevant precisely because they are implicated in the mystification of the real sources of alienation and (Western) human destructiveness. In critiquing Abrahamic traditions, I hope to create spaces (1) to reimagine Western

14. See McKinnon, *Climate Change and Political Theory*; Nussbaum, *Justice for Animals*.

15. See Kerven, *Native American Myths*; Erdoes and Ortiz, eds., *American Indian Myths*; Deloria, *God Is Red*.

religions that are tied to the rise of civilization and sovereignty, and (2) to foster new forms of living that radically respect other species and the Earth, while also accepting human existential insignificance and impermanence. To recall Clayton Crockett, "We need to experiment radically with new ways of thinking and living, because the current paradigm is in a state of exhaustion, depletion, and death."[16]

Alienation: Meanings, Sources, and Remedies

Merriam-Webster's online dictionary indicates that the term "alienation" has etymological roots in the Romance languages. In Middle English, *alienacioun* referred to the "transference of property rights," "derangement," or "estrangement," and was borrowed from the Anglo-French *alienaciun* and *alienation*, which in turn was taken from Latin *aliēnātiōn-, aliēnātiō* (meaning either "transference of ownership," or "estrangement, hostility."[17]) The definition of "alienation" today generally encompasses estrangement, whether psychological (e.g., having to do with affections, thoughts, embodiment), social (e.g., having to do with behaviors), or ecological (having to do with relations between culture and nature). Nevertheless, alienation does not necessarily mean separation or isolation. That is, one can be estranged from one's partner while remaining in relation to the person. Or we may be alienated from nature or from other species, yet not separated or isolated from them. Even when we consider the ultimate theological form of alienation (i.e., hell), those who dwell in hell are estranged from God, yet there continues to be a relation between them and the residents of heaven, since those in hell continue to suffer alienation from God (the ultimate portrayal of ontological alienation) whereas those in heaven experience communion with God (the opposite of ontological alienation). Given this brief depiction of alienation, in this section I offer illustrations of alienation taken from philosophy, theology, and literature with the aims of (1) identifying varied types of alienation, (2) demonstrating its pervasiveness, and (3) depicting its social-political functions vis-à-vis sovereignty and the ontological rift.

Since the European philosophical tradition, for Whitehead, "consists of a series of footnotes to Plato,"[18] I begin with Plato's allegory of the cave in the *Republic*. Socrates offers his companions "a parable of education and

---

16. Crockett, *Radical Political Theology*, 165.

17. *Merriam-Webster*, s.v. "alienation (*n.*)," https://www.merriam-webster.com/dictionary/alienation/.

18. Whitehead, *Process and Reality*, 39.

ignorance as a picture of the condition of our nature."[19] "Imagine mankind," Socrates continues, "as dwelling in an underground cave with a long entrance open to the light across the whole width of the cave; in this they have been from childhood, with necks and legs fettered, so they have to stay where they are. They cannot move their heads around because of the fetters, and they can only look forward, but the light comes to them from fire burning behind them higher up at a distance. Between the fire and the prisoners is a road above their level, and along it imagine a low wall has been built, as puppet showmen have screens in front of their people over which they work their puppets."[20] As the dialogue continues, it becomes clear that the prisoners take the shadows on the wall in front of them to be reality or truth.

Socrates then asks his friends to imagine what would happen if one of these prisoners was released from the chains. In turning her neck, she would be hurt or dazed by the firelight. Socrates then asked, "What do you think [she] would say, if someone told [her] that what [she] saw before was foolery, but now [she] saw more rightly, being a bit nearer reality and turned towards what was a little more real?"[21] This is only the first step, and it is important to stress that Socrates is saying she is not yet seeing reality or truth. The light from the fire is not the sun, not the ideal form. "Then suppose," he continues, "[she] were compelled to look towards the real light," which was painful, causing her to flee. Socrates continues by suggesting that "someone should drag [her] by force, up the rough ascent . . . until he could drag [her] out into the light."[22] Later in this conversation, Socrates has his friends imagine what this free person, who now sees reality, would do, perhaps returning to the cave to tell her comrades about the truth and that they are seeing illusions or images that are not real. Rather than celebrating and showing gratitude to the released prisoner for freeing them to see reality, those who remain captives to the shadows ridicule and then kill her.[23]

A great deal has been written about this allegory, and it is not necessary to cover all of the territory. Instead, I am more interested in highlighting several features vis-à-vis alienation. First, the allegory is a key feature of Plato's philosophical anthropology and reveals that he understands the fundamental element of human life to be alienation. Note first the inherent hierarchical schema in the allegory. The ignorant, which apparently is most of humanity, live at the lowest reaches of the cave where there are only

19. Rouse, trans., *Great Dialogues of Plato*, 312.
20. Rouse, trans., *Great Dialogues of Plato*, 312.
21. Rouse, trans., *Great Dialogues of Plato*, 313.
22. Rouse, trans., *Great Dialogues of Plato*, 313.
23. Rouse, trans., *Great Dialogues of Plato*, 315.

illusions, while the enlightened few, having first seen the firelight are now, after being forced, above ground to see the truth.[24] For Plato, human beings are born into the world of illusions, and it is only through a painful series of awakenings, often by force, that a rare few see and contemplate the light/truth. This hierarchical epistemological ladder is also represented in Plato's view of the ideal form of the Good.[25] For Plato, there are two realms, "the Realm of Being inhabited by perfect and unchanging things, and the Realm of Becoming, which is the world offered to us by our senses, the world of imperfect and temporary things."[26] Ideal forms are eternal and perfect, while "the world of sense-experience is merely shadow."[27] Human beings, then, are alienated or estranged from ideal forms, dwelling in an imperfect world of illusions at the bottom of the cave. At best, a few can manage the ascent to truth, but none ever attain or experience the Ideal Form of Truth.

Another feature of Plato's epistemology is its hierarchical-binary valuation. The Ideal Forms are superior to the inferior Realm of Becoming. Reason is superior to nonreason. Truth is superior to belief.[28] One might recall from Chapter 1 that one attribute of sovereignty is this hierarchical-binary valuation that legitimates separation into classes, which is also evident in Plato's political schema wherein philosopher-kings are rulers.[29] Ideally, philosopher-kings have been trained to contemplate the good, which, to return to the cave allegory, means they are the rare few who can see the light of Truth, even if it is not the Ideal Form itself.

There are three related points here. First, even philosopher-kings are estranged from the Ideal Forms, though they reside on the top tier of the epistemological ladder. To put it another way, philosophers are not chained to their seats staring at shadows on the cave wall and believing the shadows are reality. This sets them apart (in a class) from other human beings, who reside at the bottom of the cave (and so are inferior). Second,

---

24. An interesting aspect of this allegory is the presence of "showmen" who manipulate puppets so that they appear as shadows on the wall in front of the prisoners. Who are these "showmen"? They are not enlightened, and they serve only to keep prisoners captive to illusions. I can certainly think of examples of showmen who create and operate apparatuses that mystify the real sources of suffering. I can also imagine showmen as intrapsychic defenses against being disillusioned. I would also mention that Plato's character who is freed is questioned and dragged into the light. Who is doing the questioning and dragging? Perhaps they are prophets, like Tiresias, Nathan, and Martin Luther King Jr., or gadflies like Socrates, Nietzsche, and Freud.

25. Rouse, trans., *Great Dialogues of Plato*, 309.

26. Grayling, *History of Philosophy*, 69.

27. Grayling, *History of Philosophy*, 69.

28. Rouse, trans., *Great Dialogues of Plato*, 309.

29. Ryan, *On Politics*, 58–63.

epistemological alienation exists among and between human beings. Most human beings are duped, while the elite few bask in the sunshine of truth/reality. In brief, what we note here is the ontologizing of alienation vis-à-vis the Ideal Forms and creation. This parallels the relational and epistemological alienation manifested in political/class relations whereby some humans are constructed as superior while others are constructed as inferior. Third, while human beings are alienated from Ideal Forms, there is a remedy to our deepest experiences of being alienated and bound to illusions. This remedy, in Plato's allegory, is force. Consider how the person who is freed is forced to experience the light, and how, later, when the individual attempts to free her comrades, she is ridiculed and killed. The point here is that force and violence are inevitable existential features of alienated human existence.

In one sense, while Plato's anthropology ontologizes alienation, his political philosophy deals with what it means for human beings to dwell together and to dwell in this imperfect world. In a nonideal world, the reality of alienation means that dwelling here is impermanent and imperfect. Our true home is the world of Ideal Forms, and the presence of this ideal in Plato suggests that, for him, we return to this perfect, eternal world after death. Plato's dialogues, for instance, portray Socrates dwelling in Athens until he is charged with corrupting the youth and sentenced to death—the ultimate political act of alienation. Instead of heeding the call of his friends to escape, Socrates chooses death over exile, confident that the judges of the dead will deem him to have lived piously and well.[30] Socrates's decision implies that Plato leaves room for a place after death where Socrates would abide eternally with other pious people in a world of Ideal Forms. Plato's dialogues are also rife with the language of traveling or embarking, of our temporary home on earth, and of the more perfect world of Forms.[31] It is as if Plato's Socrates views life as moving from this inadequate world to an Edenic dwelling after death—at least for those who have lived well and piously (where living well and piously is the *means* of attaining dwelling vis-à-vis Ideal Forms). For those who were not pious or virtuous, the afterlife entails justified torment for their failings; hell is a dwelling of eternal alienation and suffering.

Plato's political philosophy is another example of a philosophical depiction of dwelling and its connection to forms of alienation that are given ontological and epistemological roots. Consider that non-Athenian citizens are constructed as barbarians, and that within the polis women are alienated

---

30. Rouse, trans., *Great Dialogues of Plato*, 517.
31. Rouse, trans., *Great Dialogues of Plato*, 460ff.

from the political sphere, even though they dwell in the city.[32] Although Aristotle's political philosophy differs from Plato's work, they share a hierarchical anthropology and epistemology such that human beings dwelling in this world are estranged in varying degrees from the Good or the first-mover (pure thought—God).[33]

As I have noted, Plato and Aristotle have had an enormous influence on Western philosophers and theologians. For this reason, I want to leap over the centuries to note the threads of ontological alienation that are present in the idea of our homelessness in this world, which has been a consistent theme in Western philosophies, despite numerous philosophical differences in varied depictions of what it means to dwell. In the early nineteenth century, Georg Hegel had a Platonic take on our existential homelessness, arguing that Socrates gave birth to the homeless spirit by liberating subjectivity (the independence of an individual's thought) through the Socratic method of questioning.[34] According to Hegel, human beings are existentially in chains until partially liberated by the Socratic method; this reading of Plato overlooks the inherent violence and force endemic in his allegory of the cave. Over a century after Hegel, two prominent philosophers, Martin Heidegger and Emmanuel Levinas, agreed about our existential homelessness but disagreed about its causes and implications. For Heidegger, human dwelling is entwined with existential homelessness. David Gauthier argues that Heidegger "interprets homelessness as a symptom of the abandonment [or forgetfulness] of Being by beings."[35] In Gauthier's view, Heidegger understood that while dwelling is an existential need[36] and the ground of ethics,[37] it nevertheless is accompanied by a sense of homelessness—a sense of being alienated from our true home. Phillip Tonner adds to this discussion, arguing that for Heidegger, "Dwelling is the constitutive state of a manner of existing that is at once engaged, embedded and bodily."[38] Part of this engaged, embedded, and embodied aspect of dwelling is the importance, for Heidegger, of place, identity, and tradition, which together *mitigate our estrangement or sense of existential homelessness.* Heidegger believed, Gauthier contends, that the challenge "is

---

32. To be fair, Plato, unlike Aristotle, believed women could be part of the guardian classes, though in reality women were excluded from the political sphere.
33. Grayling, *History of Philosophy*, 89.
34. Gauthier, *Martin Heidegger*, 3–5.
35. Gauthier, *Martin Heidegger*, 129.
36. Vogt, "Human Ecology," 243.
37. Wood, *Reoccupy Earth*, 56.
38. Tonner, *Dwelling*, 8.

to create a philosophy that will facilitate a return to rootedness to help man to become at home in the world."[39] "I know that everything essential and everything great," Heidegger writes, "originated from the fact that man had a home and was rooted in tradition."[40] Having a home and being rooted in tradition mitigate existential homelessness.

Critics of Heidegger, like Emmanuel Levinas, argue that his obdurate focus on place, identity, and tradition vis-à-vis existential homelessness fits well with the Nazis' racism, antisemitism, and German exceptionalism—realities of extreme alienation.[41] Phillip Tonner also criticizes the Heideggerian philosophical view that "only anatomically fully modern humans dwell,"[42] a perspective according to which "primitive" peoples were incapable of dwelling; this way of thinking embraces the hierarchy in Plato's allegory of the cave. More to the point, one can note here the alienation that is created between modern and so-called primitive or, perhaps, uncivilized peoples. Regardless, according to these scholars, Heidegger considered human dwelling to be fraught with alienation, and he believed the partial remedy to be rooted in identity, tradition, and place.

Emmanuel Levinas's philosophy is, in one sense, a corrective in response to Heidegger's philosophy of dwelling, though Levinas retains the thread of ontological estrangement. Levinas contends that Heidegger "effectively subordinates ethics to ontology,"[43] and it is ontology that tends to eliminate "the alterity, or otherness, of the comprehended being."[44] More pointedly, Gauthier states that in Levinas's view, "the Heideggerian project is ethically problematic because it is oblivious to the needs of strangers"[45]—not to mention the needs of other species vis-à-vis their dwelling. Contra Heidegger, Levinas believes, in part, that our refusal to be obliged to the Other, and not our forgetfulness of Being, is the reason humans experience homelessness.[46] The source and sense of homelessness, for Levinas, "provides the impetus for human fraternity"[47]—dwelling together. Gauthier notes that in Levinas's political philosophy "the home achieves its full dignity when

39. Gauthier, *Martin Heidegger*, 9.
40. Quoted in Gauthier, *Martin Heidegger*, 92.
41. Guess, *Changing the Subject*, 226–49.
42. Tonner, *Dwelling*, 9.
43. Gauthier, *Martin Heidegger*, 104.
44. Gauthier, *Martin Heidegger*, 105.
45. Gauthier, *Martin Heidegger*, 97.
46. Gauthier, *Martin Heidegger*, 113.
47. Gauthier, *Martin Heidegger*, 114.

the Other is welcomed."[48] In his book *Totality and Infinity*, Levinas states, "To dwell is not the simple fact of the anonymous reality of a being cast into existence, as a stone one casts behind oneself; it is a recollection, a coming to oneself, a retreat home with oneself as in a land of refuge, which answers to a hospitality, an expectancy, a human welcome."[49] Here is the apparent paradox of Levinas's view: the Other evokes a sense of homelessness, and this homelessness is mitigated by the infinite obligation to recognize and welcome Others in their singularity. For Levinas, dwelling is the existential foundation of being and becoming human. Nevertheless, both Heidegger and Levinas understood human beings to be existentially homeless, which for Heidegger suggests the need for roots (i.e., place) and identity, and for Levinas suggests the importance of hospitality toward strangers.

I suspect the idea that human beings are existentially homeless resonates with many people, especially those of us in the West who have grown up unwittingly internalizing the apparatuses that produce the ontological rift. The philosophers noted above, in part, function to provide reasons for our sense of alienation, which, at the same time, mystifies the sources of the ontological rift and our experiences of alienation or homelessness. As plausible as a philosophy centered on alienation is, an eco-philosophy that portrays human beings as being at home on this Earth—our only home—is equally plausible, in my view. We are not homeless, pining for a reunion with Ideal Forms, aching to know the Ground of Being, or longing for a future home with the gods. The Earth, for human beings and all other species, is our home. It is the foundation in which diverse forms of life emerge and are sustained. We are not destined to be alienated from it, though clearly we can experience a sense of alienation from the Earth and from one another. This experience is real, but the belief in existential alienation is an illusion. Our beingness, like the beingness of all other-than-human species, is of the Earth. In other words, the Earth, which is itself impermanent, is the very foundation of life, and I suspect that only a relatively small percentage of humans past and present have believed or currently believe that it is not our true and only home.

What is implied in the discussion above is another feature of philosophical anthropologies that foreground existential alienation. Bruno Latour, for one, argues that Western philosophies have for millennia differentiated culture from Nature.[50] He contends that ecology "is not the irruption of nature into the public space but the end of 'nature' as a concept

---

48. Gauthier, *Martin Heidegger*, 131.
49. Levinas, *Totality and Infinity*, 156.
50. Latour, *Facing Gaia*, 35.

THE EMERGENCE OF A PHILOSOPHICAL/THEOLOGICAL EXPLANATION   123

that would allow us to sum up our relations to the world and pacify them."[51] We have come to see Nature as something distinct from the human, and this distinction points to our alienation from Nature. Recall that in Chapter 1, I provided an example of this in Freud's work, which is simply a manifestation of the alienation from Nature that we in the West seem to take for granted. I noted that Freud wrote that "the principal task of civilization ... is to defend us against nature,"[52] which he viewed as a perennial task since he was under no illusion "that nature has already been vanquished."[53] It is "nature" we should fear, because of its cruelty and indifference. Here we see a vivid example of our alienation from Nature, which ironically Freud did not consider to be illusory. We are, however, discovering what a powerful and destructive illusion it truly is. It is an illusion because, as Latour argues, the distinction between Nature and humanity is merely a concept, a cognitive distinction, rather than a fact, though we accept it as a fact just as anyone sitting in the depth of Plato's cave would. "Culture," then, is an integral part of nature, just as ant or bee cultures are.

I wish to stress here that distinguishing between Nature and culture or between human beings and other species is not necessarily a problem or an indication of existential alienation. I agree with Charles Sanders Peirce that all living beings possess varying semiotic capacities.[54] As human beings, we differentiate between this and that object or this and that person as we navigate the world. Many indigenous peoples make all kinds of distinctions between human beings and other species without believing there is an ontological rift between Nature and culture, between human beings and other species. Put another way, the philosophies of indigenous peoples do not ontologize alienation and the difference between the human species and other species.

Let me return to Plato's allegory to highlight other related features of alienation manifested in Western philosophy. The poor bastards chained to their seats in the cave are obviously alienated from "Reality." This is an *epistemological alienation* that gives rise to interhuman and interspecies estrangement. Western epistemologies have fetishized Reason, arguing that human beings have the capacity for reason while other "lower" species do not. Other species are constructed as dumb brutes "lacking" reason. And as I discussed in previous chapters, this hierarchical valuation of reason has led to the justification of exploitation of other species or simply to overlooking

51. Latour, *Facing Gaia*, 36.
52. Freud, *Future of an Illusion*, 15.
53. Freud, *Future of an Illusion*, 15.
54. Peirce, *Peirce on Signs*.

them, as if they have little or no significance in relation to human dwelling. We seem unable to imagine that we are more like other species than we are different from them or that, just as we do, other species think as well.[55] In Western thinking, in other words, nonhuman existence is constructed in terms of lack and inferiority, leading to our estrangement from other species.

All of this does not imply that human beings do not have unique capacities, such as reason, self-reflection, and symbolization. Yet distinction and differentiation are not necessarily dependent on hierarchical valuation schemas. When they are, the end result is varying forms of misrecognition, and attending instrumental epistemologies result. By this I mean that human beings, who believe that human beings are superior to other species because of reason and symbolization, will fail to recognize and respect the singularities of other species and their semiotic ways of moving through the world, and this lack of recognition and respect for other species will serve as the "reasonable thinking" behind exploiting or ignoring them.

This epistemological alienation is also evident in varied forms of estrangement among human beings. Western philosophical traditions have largely relied on hierarchical valuation apparatuses that assume varying levels of the capacity for reason among human beings. Plato placed the guardian class (philosophers, some of whom could be women) at the top of the social-political scale. Aristotle and innumerable other Western philosophers constructed women (and Nature) as possessing less capacity for reason than men, which justified (and justifies) women's exclusion from adult male spaces. Add to this the long history of Western colonization, which constructed indigenous peoples as having childlike capacities for reason (necessitating in place of these "lesser" capacities the putative superior reasoning and attending forms of life of Western colonizers). Of course, this colonizing kind of reasoning also served to justify exploiting or exterminating native peoples and their cultures, and legitimated enslaving "primitive" peoples (Africans). Further evidence of this alienation, as I noted in the previous chapter, is seen in what Lynne Layton[56] calls the "normative unconscious" and Timothy J. Zeddies[57] names the "historical unconscious." Those who are seen as lacking reason (Othered human beings and other-than-human species) are not seen as normative, and they are excluded synchronically and diachronically. In other words, we know that

---

55. See Kohn, *How Forests Think*; Castro, *Cannibal Metaphysics*; Zúñiga, *Pluralist Politics*.

56. Layton, *Toward a Social Psychoanalysis*.

57. Zeddies, "Behind, Beneath, Above, and Beyond."

across history women, indigenous peoples, and other-than-human species have been constructed as nonnormative vis-à-vis men so that they are, more often than not, excluded from historical narratives that establish Western men (and societies) normative.

Let me circle back to Plato's allegory of the cave. In addition to picturing epistemological alienation from Truth or Reality, this allegory can also show a kind of intrapsychic alienation, which was picked up in some twentieth-century psychologies that I will touch on below. For now, one can view this allegory as representing our desire to hold on to our soporific illusions while ardently resisting the painful truth/light. The pain or suffering is having to give up or mourn our cherished illusions, which we believe to be reality. Each individual human psyche is structured like the cave, if you will. The highest part—reason—is capable of grasping the truth, but not in Ideal Form, which means we remain ontologically estranged from Ideal Forms. Our passions or emotions, from Plato's perspective, are easily yoked to false beliefs or perceptions—hence the need for reason to guide the horse/psyche.[58] Emotions are not necessarily estranged from reason (though they can be), but there is a constant struggle between the "lower" ("primitive") recesses of our psyche and our "higher" capacities such as reason, which is necessary for practical wisdom. So the struggle, according to the allegory, is fraught with the specter of alienation. Indeed, if we consider this allegory from a psychological perspective, the psyche is at war with itself. Recall that in returning to free one's comrades who are chained to their chairs, the one who has seen the light is shamed, killed, or both. Violence and shame, which are inherently alienating, are woven into the very structure of the Platonic psyche—epistemological alienation is psychological alienation.

But aren't shame and violence (which together characterize alienation) features of human existence? Yes and no. Yes, in the sense that human beings can experience shame and may act out violently. No, in the sense that it is, in my view, a category mistake to then say that these are foundational features of the psyche. Shame and violence emerge as a result of human-constructed apparatuses that produce and maintain hierarchical valuations of and beliefs in superiority and inferiority, which are existential illusions.[59] There is nothing in nature that supports these beliefs, and, if anything, the Anthropocene Age, as I have noted in previous chapters, has belied these illusions. So, the problem with Plato's cave allegory is that it functions as an apparatus that confirms intrapsychic alienation as an existential fact. If

---

58. Sorabji, *Emotion and Peace of Mind*, 21–22.

59. Psychological alienation can also emerge as a result of varied forms of trauma perpetrated by other human beings. This "fact" does not then mean that human beings are therefore psychologically alienated. See Meares, *Intimacy and Alienation*.

we peruse Western history, we find countless examples of one group humiliating, exploiting, and subjugating other groups, whether within society or against other peoples. We then seem to conclude that humiliation and political violence (i.e., alienation) are inevitable intrapsychic, interhuman, and interspecies realities. I wonder if Western psyches have projected onto Othered human beings and other-than-human species their individual and collective unconscious fear of their own shame and insecurity. Put another way, the realities of existential impermanence and insignificance are constructed around valuations of superiority and inferiority, which means Othered persons and species are deemed inferior. In Plato's allegory, from an intrapsychic perspective, the eternal Ideal Forms (permanence and significance) remain partially accessible through our capacities for reason and contemplation, which are superior to the inferior illusions at the base of our psyches—illusions that we, individually and collectively, will hold on to by way of shame and violence.

Before moving to the Abrahamic traditions, I must summarize the main points here. First, Western philosophical traditions tend to see alienation as a central feature of human existence. Ontological alienation is the sense of being estranged from Ideal Forms or from the gods. This ontological alienation is further manifested by our sense that our dwelling on earth is inferior to the dwelling that awaits us after death, if we have lived piously. This earth, if you will, is not our true home. Our true home is Being's Ideal Forms. Closely associated with this sense of homelessness on Earth is our alienation from Nature. Differentiating between Nature and Culture depends on hierarchical valuations that place nonhuman species lower on the significance scale and set Nature itself in opposition to Culture. Ontological alienation joins up with epistemological alienation, which means that reason becomes superior to inferior forms of cognition. And epistemological alienation gives rise to interspecies, interhuman, and intrapsychic alienation. Western philosophical traditions have, for the most part, explained alienation or estrangement in different ways, offering various remedies for it, namely, contemplation, piety, rootedness, and hospitality. What Western philosophies leave in place are the various apparatuses that produce and maintain the ontological rift and experiences of alienation related to its maintenance, while, at the same time, mystifying the sources of alienation, namely, apparatuses of sovereignty and the ontological rift. As I stressed above, it is one thing to argue that human beings, at different times and for different reasons, have experiences of estrangement; it is another leap to argue philosophically that alienation is an ontological or existential ground of human life.

Recall that in Chapter 1 I argued that Western philosophies, Judaic scriptures, and later Abrahamic traditions emerged within and spoke into the context of spreading civilization. These philosophies and scriptures originated at the same time that apparatuses began to bolster the idea that sovereignty was existentially necessary for human belonging. Like Western philosophies, the Abrahamic traditions ontologize alienation. In Genesis, Yahweh creates the world, and Adam and Eve, as the story goes, violate the one commandment given to them (Gen 3:10–19). Their punishment is being expelled from Eden, and this exile symbolizes their estrangement from God and their conflict with Nature.

In the discussion above, I addressed the theme of existential homelessness as it is found in Western political philosophies. The same theme is also evident in Abrahamic scriptures and theologies. In Judeo-Christian scriptures, the Hebrew word for God is *Makom*, which means place.[60] Although God may mean "place," there are in Judeo-Christian scriptures many stories of homelessness, homesickness, dwelling, and belonging—of searching for and finding home, and of all the ambiguity in that process. Abraham is called a wandering Aramean (Deut 26:5); Joseph is unhoused by being sold into slavery by his brothers (Gen 37:25–28); Israelites are aliens in Egypt and Babylon, and they come to dwell in the promised land by violently unhousing its residents (see the book of Joshua). In Christian scripture, Jesus leaves home and gathers his disciples to do the work of God. Jesus claims, "The foxes have holes and the birds of the air have nests, but the Son of Man has nowhere to lay his head" (Luke 9:58). In John's Gospel, Jesus says "in his Father's house there are many dwellings," thus indicating to his disciples that while they have left their homes, their real home is with God (John 14:2).

One of the central figures of Western Christian theology is Saint Augustine of Hippo, who similarly and understandably took up this idea of ontological estrangement and homelessness. In *The City of God*, Augustine echoes the idea that our true home is not the Earth.[61] In Augustine's theology, Adam and Eve were expelled from their perfect home because of disobedience, which left their descendants to live lives of restlessness—a restlessness or homesickness that is unresolved until one resides in God.[62] This tension between home and homelessness, not dissimilar to Plato's rendition of Socrates, is amplified when Augustine, in the very opening lines of his *Confessions*, states, "you have made us for yourself, and our hearts are

60. Casey, *Fate of Place*, 17.
61. Augustine, *City of God*.
62. Augustine, *Confessions*, 333.

restless until they can find peace in you."⁶³ Much of subsequent Christian political theology reflects the tension between our material dwelling on the Earth and spiritual dwelling with God.

In biblical literature, estrangement from God is manifested in numerous stories of human beings missing the mark, whether individually or as a group. Cain murders Abel (Gen 4), the Israelites disobey God's commands with regard to gathering manna (Exod 16), God is infuriated when the Israelites construct and worship a golden calf (Exod 24), Samuel warns Israel of the dangers of human kingship (1 Sam 8:11–17), King David has his general killed so he can marry Bathsheba (2 Sam 11), the prophet Amos rails against the political elites and the people who have violated the covenant. These are just some of the stories that portray human beings missing the mark (Hebrew, *chatá*; Greek, *hamartia*) when it comes to heeding the sovereign God's commands.⁶⁴ Missing the mark stems from the first couple's disobedience, reinforcing the view that human beings are alienated from God, and that this alienation is exacerbated by sin.

In these and other biblical stories, estrangement from God is also joined to estrangement between human beings, whether that means between those within the Israelite community or those without. The story of the tower of Babel offers an explanation for human division and alienation, the source of which is the hubris of trying to be like God (Gen 11). In the exodus story Egyptians (human beings in positions of power) exploit and oppress the Israelites. Alienation here is "caused" by oppression, but alienation is also evident first in God's command that the Israelites kill Egyptians (and nonhuman species) and later in God's command that the Israelites ethnically cleanse the promised land. Christian scriptures continue the theme of the seemingly inevitable existential estrangement of and between human beings. King Herod (Matt 2), after listening to the wise men, seeks to emulate King Laius, from the Oedipus story, by removing a future threat to his rule. The Roman soldiers, acting on behalf of the emperor, torture and execute people, including Jesus. Jesus is the Christ who defeats sin and death, through his suffering, death, and resurrection. The book of Revelation is a cosmic story of alienation, wherein the forces of evil, which include other human beings, are violently defeated by God and righteous humans.

Existential estrangement is also manifested in relation to other-than-human species in the Bible. Eden marks a place and time when human beings and other species live in harmony—a place and time where there is no alienation. Adam and Eve are blamed for their disobedience (sin), and the

---

63. Augustine, *Confessions*, 17.
64. Farley, "Sin."

consequences mean they are expelled from this idyllic place. Unfortunately, other species (not just the serpent) are apparently expelled as well, which hardly seems fair or just. Add to this God's punishment of Adam and Eve, wherein there is perpetual enmity (alienation) between women and serpents (Gen 3:14–15). As I mentioned previously, other-than-human species are constructed as not having souls, which I take to mean they are excluded from the kingdom of God and, therefore, denied ontological significance or permanence. One cannot get more alienated than that.

The concept of sin is a theological diagnosis of the existential, ontological condition of human beings. The varied stories of alienation in the Bible provide an etiology not only for alienation but also the diverse forms of suffering associated with it. Of course, not all suffering is necessarily the result of sin, unless we anchor the origin of suffering in Adam and Eve's eating the forbidden fruit and so failing to obey God. If we link the reason for suffering with the story of Adam and Eve, we are in the territory of the idea of original sin. Original sin is a theological version of ontogeny recapitulating phylogeny. All human beings are born into sin, which means that alienation is present at birth. Even if one believes that infants, because they lack the capacities for willing and reason, are incapable of sin, they nevertheless are thrown into a fallen world where they will inevitably sin.

Of course, every diagnosis comes with a prescribed remedy or remedies. The Israelites frequently sin, and for them the remedies are confessing the sin, asking for forgiveness, committing to return to the covenant, offering the occasional animal sacrifice, and witnessing ritual sacrifices and scapegoating. These remedies do not get rid of alienation, but alienation is ameliorated. For Christians, the antidote for sin is found in salvation offered by and through Christ's suffering, death, and resurrection. Wolfhart Pannenberg's notion of prolepsis indicates that the kingdom of God (a state without alienation) is partially experienced and realized in the present.[65] This suggests that salvation is never fully realized here and now. We remain caught in the grip of sin, though by believing in Jesus Christ, participating in worship and other sacraments, confessing our sins, seeking to atone for our sins, and pursuing Christian virtues, we have hope for our eventual union with God in God's kingdom, once we have shed this mortal coil. What is also interesting and relevant are Christian beliefs in heaven and hell. For those who are saved and enter heaven after death, alienation is overcome and they are in union with God. All the rest are estranged from God for eternity, which means that alienation remains and is never overcome. Like Western philosophical apparatuses, Abrahamic traditions diagnose the

---

65. Pannenberg, *Theology and the Kingdom of God*.

human condition as ontological alienation, and this view comes with varied remedies. In the story I am telling here, the diagnosis and remedies function to mystify the real sources of alienation, namely, the human construction of apparatuses that produce sovereignty and the ontological rift.

Alienation, the Ontological Rift, and Literature

I have been focused on providing generalizations about explanations and remedies for existential alienation evident in Western philosophical and theological apparatuses. I contend that these proffered remedies mystify the real sources of alienation, leaving in place and unquestioned the ontological rift and beliefs in existential alienation. Nevertheless, it is not only Western philosophies and theologies that have operated to produce, maintain, and mystify the ontological rift and sources of alienation. I suggest that literature can also function as an apparatus. While it would be interesting and informative to delve into Western literature to explore how human alienation from other species is portrayed, it is not possible to do so.[66] Still, as a single example, I will summarize and examine the plot of Jack London's *Call of the Wild* to illustrate how the ontological rift's alienation pervades literature. This work functions, in part, as an apparatus that confirms both the ontological rift and existential experiences of alienation, as well as hints at the remedy. I have also chosen it because London imagines the inner life of a dog (Buck) and the dog's relation to Nature,[67] civilization (the ontological rift), and Othered human beings (i.e., indigenous peoples). Finally, while I argue that *The Call of the Wild* reveals the ontological rift and experiences of alienation, it also manifests moments of inoperative love—a remedy that I will bring forward in the last chapter.

London's story begins in Santa Clara, California. Buck lives with Judge Miller and, as London narrates, "Buck was neither house-dog nor kennel-dog. The whole realm was his."[68] In this bucolic "civilized" setting, there is an air of foreboding. Unbeknownst to Buck, "men, groping in the

---

66. Edward Said and Stuart Hall, in different ways and contexts, examine Western literature's representations of Oriental peoples and indigenous peoples. This approach could also be taken in how other species are represented in literature, such as in scripture. Said, *Orientalism*; Said, *Culture and Imperialism*; Hall, ed., *Representation*; Hall, *Cultural Studies*.

67. I would like to point out that while novels can function as apparatuses that portray the ontological rift as reality, there are stories from children's literature where there is no ontological rift and no sovereignty. I will attend to this in the next chapter when I address the absence of the ontological rift in early psychosocial development.

68. London, *Call of the Wild*, 762.

THE EMERGENCE OF A PHILOSOPHICAL/THEOLOGICAL EXPLANATION 131

Arctic, had found yellow metal [and] these men wanted dogs."[69] One of the judge's laborers, Manuel, while the family is away from the house, sells Buck to a man who transports dogs to the Alaskan territory. Buck had trusted Manuel, accepting "the rope in quiet dignity," unaware of Manuel's treachery.[70] When Buck growls after being handed over, the man tightens the rope, leaving Buck unconscious. Buck is then thrown into the back of a carriage. In captivity and on the long trek to Alaska, Buck is brutally beaten, painfully learning that the man with the club is the lawgiver.[71] Buck's first day in Alaska "was like a nightmare. Every hour was filled with shock and surprise. He had been suddenly jerked from the heart of civilization and flung into the heart of things primordial . . . All was confusion and action, and every moment life and limb were in peril."[72] In the weeks and months ahead, Buck would be used to pull a sled with other dogs, finding ways to survive brutal treatment, and would compete with other dogs on the team for scarce resources.

In the narrative, London juxtaposes Nature and civilization. When Buck lives with the judge, Buck is in the midst of civilization and he is domesticated. Buck trusts the judge and Manuel. We might think that Buck at this point feels no sense of alienation, because he is ensconced in the seemingly loving relationships of this family. But Manuel's decision to sell Buck reveals the alienation already present by way of the ontological rift. For Manuel, Buck is a mere animal to be used and sold. And for the buyer Buck's use value lies in his being sold in Alaska to those seeking gold. It is his ill-treatment at the hands of Manuel and other men that Buck experiences as profound alienation. In addition, Buck later realizes that the judge and the family did not really love him but rather cared for Buck vis-à-vis Buck's utility.

As London's story continues, Buck is purchased by a man named Hal and then is beaten to make him submit to the demands of his ostensibly civilized "owner." Hal provides minimal care for Buck and the other dogs with the aim of using them to obtain profit. To survive, Buck performs. During this period, Buck is alienated from Hal and the other dogs with whom he competes for survival. On one occasion, after an exhausting, cruel trip, Buck **is** physically spent. Hal is having none of it: "Get up there, Buck! Hi! Get up there! Mush on!"[73] London writes, "This was the first time Buck had

69. London, *Call of the Wild*, 761.
70. London, *Call of the Wild*, 763.
71. London, *Call of the Wild*, 768.
72. London, *Call of the Wild*, 770.
73. London, *Call of the Wild*, 805.

failed."⁷⁴ Hal then proceeds to beat Buck mercilessly and only stops because John Thornton, a wiser, more compassionate prospector, intervenes, saying, "If you strike that dog again, I will kill you."⁷⁵ From Hal's instrumental epistemological perspective, because Buck has failed to perform, he is not due even minimal care and can therefore be beaten and discarded as insignificant and useless. Torture and deprivation give rise to experiences of alienation, and I suggest that all of this is connected to the ontological rift between those who see themselves as civilized (superior and entitled) and those deemed to be from Nature and therefore inferior—fit to be used and, when their use value is exhausted, fit only to die or be killed.

Infuriated, John Thornton knocks Hal's knife away and cuts the straps that tether Buck to Hal's sled. Hal, having "no fight left in him," departs with his sister across the ice-covered river.⁷⁶ John "knelt beside [Buck] and with rough, kindly hands searched for broken bones. By the time his search had disclosed nothing more than many bruises and a state of terrible starvation, the sled was a quarter of a mile away."⁷⁷ Here is where an interesting turn in the story begins. John, like Hal and Manuel, is civilized, though he represents something different. John begins to take care of Buck. As Buck's wounds heal and he puts on weight, he discovers, to his surprise, that the other "dogs manifested no jealousy toward him. They seemed to share the kindness and largesse of John Thornton."⁷⁸ Thornton genuinely cares for the dogs in his company, and this care means that Buck and his mates do not have to compete for sustenance to survive. Indeed, survival is not the primary focus, as Buck begins to thrive under the ministrations of John Thornton. As London writes, "Buck romped through his convalescence and into a new existence."⁷⁹ "Love," London continues, "genuine passionate love, was his for the first time. This he had never experienced at Judge Miller's down in the sun-kissed Santa Clara Valley. With the Judge's sons, hunting and tramping, it had been a working partnership . . . But love that was feverish and burning, that was adoration, that was madness, it had taken John Thornton to arouse."⁸⁰ Put differently, Buck had experienced a sense of significance when he lived with the judge, but later, after experiencing the unconditional love of John Thornton, Buck realizes that his earlier

74. London, *Call of the Wild*, 806.
75. London, *Call of the Wild*, 806.
76. London, *Call of the Wild*, 807.
77. London, *Call of the Wild*, 807.
78. London, *Call of the Wild*, 808.
79. London, *Call of the Wild*, 808.
80. London, *Call of the Wild*, 770.

experience of significance vis-à-vis the judge and his family had been based on a "working partnership" and "a sort of pompous guardianship."[81] Buck, then, recognizes that other "men saw to the welfare of their dogs from a sense of duty and business expediency," but John "saw to the welfare of his as if they were his own children."[82] The mention of "children" suggests a kind of relation marked by the recognition of Buck's singularity, accompanied by a kind of care devoid of instrumental epistemologies, beliefs in superiority and inferiority, and relations of dominion/subjugation. More positively, John cares for Buck without any idea or aim that Buck would work for him; Buck is valued in himself and not for his use value. Buck, for instance, is free to remain in the camp or leave, which he eventually does.

John's love for Buck does not mean that for London there was an absence of alienation vis-à-vis Nature. London writes that "in spite of this great love he bore John Thornton, which seemed to bespeak the soft civilizing influence, the strain of the primitive, which Northland had aroused in him, remained alive and active."[83] During a stretch of London's story, Buck goes back and forth, from the civilized world of John (and company) to the wilds of Alaska and back again. He is torn between living and roaming with other dogs in the wilds and spending time with John. This ends when Buck returns one day to find John and his companion dead—killed by men from the Yeehat tribe.[84] The story closes with Buck fully back into Nature, away from civilization.

I think that, for London, Buck's true nature is to be in Nature. Although, care and love can go a long way toward establishing a relationship between a "civilized" man, like John, and Buck, in the end, civilization and Nature, for London, are separate and in conflict. Civilization entails domesticating Nature, like the judge did to Buck. Civilization also entails exploiting Nature, whether that means raping the land for profit or using other species and discarding them when they have lost their use-value. Let me add that London's story shows the power of unconditional love. John's love for Buck not only heals him; John's love frees Buck to get in touch with his Nature. Yet, in the end, love is not the remedy for overcoming the ontological divide between civilization and Nature. To be sure, love is preferable to pompous guardianship (from the judge) and to maltreatment (at the hands of those who lust after profit), but the end of the story reveals London's view that Buck's true nature is found in the wild and not in civilization. While

---

81. London, *Call of the Wild*, 808.
82. London, *Call of the Wild*, 809.
83. London, *Call of the Wild*, 810.
84. London, *Call of the Wild*, 828–29.

in Nature, Buck is alienated from civilization and its goods (and evils). London's story illustrates the presence in literature of the ontological rift and the forms of alienation that accompany this rupture. In addition, this novel—and, I contend, numerous others—represents and so instantiates the ontological rift and resulting types of alienation. That is, *The Call of the Wild* seems to tell the reader that the rift is a fact of life and can be mitigated (though not overcome) through care and love. Like Western philosophical and theological apparatuses of the abyssal rupture, novels can also serve to mystify the sources of our alienation, offering "remedies" that treat the symptom, not the source.

More needs to be said about mystification of the real sources of alienation, but first let me summarize this part of the story I am telling. Prior to the rise of civilization and the idea of sovereignty, I think it is safe to say that human beings had notions of the spirit world—a world without sovereignty and the attributes of civilization. Civilization and its apparatuses gave rise to experiences of human alienation, which were then ontologically explained either by concepts such as sin or by diverse stories enacted in rituals—or both. Hand in hand with concepts and stories naming the sources of suffering came remedies (e.g., salvation). The explanations and remedies, which leave intact the sources of alienation and the ontological rift, have functioned and still function to distract seekers from understanding the real sources of their disquiet (human constructions of civilization and sovereignty). We are alienated from the Ideal Forms, though contemplation and piety can bring us further into the light. From another angle, sin and salvation become anthropological dogmas, unquestionable facts of our estrangement from God.[85] Sin evokes the pain and suffering of ontological alienation, while salvation is the soporific for the realities of existential insignificance and impermanence. Civilization and Nature in Jack London's novel are not simply distinct but are in perennial conflict. Climate change, in fact, reveals how destructive civilization and sovereignty have been and continue to be. Civilization and sovereignty undergird Western philosophical and Abrahamic traditions, which have ontologized alienation while obscuring the real sources of destruction by humans vis-à-vis Othered human beings, other-than-human species, and the Earth. If we are to find ways to reimagine Western philosophy and Abrahamic scriptures in

---

85. Let me stress that I am not saying that notions of sin and salvation are without value or meaning. If sin is missing the mark that gives rise to varied forms of alienation, then we can with some confidence say that most cultural anthropologies have similar views. I am arguing that ontologizing sin and salvation, especially yoking them to the attributes of civilization and sovereignty, raises significant problems and should be eschewed.

order to create forms of living grounded in respect for all species and the Earth, we must critically reexamine anthropologies and the ways they mystify the real sources of our destruction. Such reexamination creates space to reimagine remedies—remedies that are clear-eyed about the sources of destruction—and to embrace forms of life founded on care and respect for all: such embrace will indeed accept human existential insignificance and impermanence. All of this is a topic for the next chapter.

Further Thoughts on the Psychosocial Dynamics of Mystification

Above I have made the claim that Western philosophical and Abrahamic traditions have mystified the real social-political sources of alienation without explaining the psychosocial dynamics of mystification. In this section, I rely on psychoanalytic concepts to further our understanding of the dynamics and power of mystification. Of course, I recognize that it is possible to make use of other theories and concepts from the human sciences to explicate mystification, but I believe that psychoanalytic concepts are particularly apt for demonstrating the intersubjective cognitive operations that keep the machines of Western civilization and sovereignty running.

Philosopher Herbert Fingarette analyzed the dynamics and sources of routine self-deception.[86] Fingarette viewed self-deception in this way: "it is when we judge that there is a purposeful discrepancy between the way the individual really is engaged in the world and the story he tells himself that we have the complex but common form of self-deception in which we are interested."[87] According to Fingarette, this self-deception results from not spelling out (not narrating) one's own engagement in the world; or, better, such self-deception results from spelling out one's engagement in such a way that one does not avow one's actions or their consequences.[88] Psychoanalyst Donnel Stern, building on Fingarette's analysis of self-deception, used the term "weak dissociation" to refer to a kind of narrative rigidity whereby individuals organize their experiences so that their actions and the consequences of those actions are narrowly spelled out; actions and consequences are omitted that do not "fit" the dominant, rigid story.[89] In inflex-

---

86. Fingarette, *Self-Deception*.
87. Fingarette, *Self-Deception*, 62.
88. Fingarette focuses on narrating experience vis-à-vis self-deception. I would include performative actions such as rituals, which reinforce self-deception or weak dissociation.
89. Stern, *Unformulated Experience*.

ible narration, ideas, meanings, values, and affects that are unconsciously (according to the normative unconscious) perceived to contradict the dominant-conscious narrative are excluded or unformulated and, therefore, remain outside of individuals' awareness. In weak dissociation, Stern argues, we spell out only what "we believe we can tolerate, or [what] furthers our purpose, or [what] promises a feeling of safety, satisfaction, and the good things in life; we dissociate the meanings that we believe we will not be able to tolerate, that frighten us and seem to threaten the fulfillment of our deepest intentions."[90] As a result "of so insistently turning our attention elsewhere . . . we never even notice alternative understandings. Focal attention under these conditions is controlled by the intention to enforce narrative rigidity."[91]

Weak dissociation explains, in part, how Western philosophies and religions have elevated their stories to anthropological truths, so that they serve as apparatuses that have deceived most of us into rigidly believing that human beings are superior (to other species) and that alienation, whether in relation to God or Nature, is an existential fact. Put another way, for millennia we in the West have spelled out our engagement in the world in ways that disavow the singularities of other species (and of some human beings). Indeed, in our inflexible, yet often creative, spelling out, we accept the truth of the ontological rift and its attending zone of nonjustice—a zone where the idea of justice has no relevance vis-à-vis other-than-human species and the Earth. The dynamics of weak dissociation help explain why the real sources of alienation are mystified, as well as why we have, more often than not, shown no accountability or remorse for the sufferings and needs of other species.

There is more to this story. Stern says we spell out only what we can tolerate, which suggests that the intersubjective operation of weak dissociation functions to keep out what is intolerable. To identify what is intolerable, screened by the apparatuses of mystification, I want to take a brief detour. Sigmund Freud, not without some grandiosity, argued that there have been three blows to human narcissism.[92] The first shock came from Copernicus, when human beings learned that we are not the center of the universe. The second jolt was delivered by Darwin, when we learned that human beings are part of evolution, like all other living creatures. We are animals as well. Freud added to the list, contending that human "megalomania will have suffered its third and most wounding blow from psychological research of the

---

90. Stern, *Unformulated Experience*, 128.
91. Stern, *Unformulated Experience*, 132.
92. Freud, *General Theory of Neurosis*.

present time which seeks to prove to the ego that it is not even master in its own house."[93] First of all, I think there is little evidence that the "shocks" Freud enumerated had any short- or long-term impact on Western narcissism. Western religions continued to spell out the view that human beings are ontologically special, even while we are alienated from God and Nature by virtue of original sin. And for those secular folks, like Freud, there was always science and capitalism to assure us of our prowess, specialness, and difference from Nature. If anything, the shocks Freud listed demonstrated the resilience of Western apparatuses, which continually affirm the existential significance of human beings. Indeed, the human sciences, as evident in Freud's anthropology, function as apparatuses of weak dissociation. Nevertheless, while Copernicus, Darwin, and Freud may have "shocked" Western consciousness, Westerners, by and large, continued to hold to forms of life that disavow the singularities of other species, which has been a key factor in our destructive behaviors toward other species and the Earth.

A much more psychological and spiritual shock is realizing that we are in the midst of the Anthropocene Age. We may have found ways to deal with the shocks that Copernicus, Darwin, and Freud ushered in, but the revelations associated with climate change are not so easily warded off. What Western weak dissociation has screened so effectively for millennia is the existential truth of human insignificance and impermanence. It is too painful and frightening to look behind the curtains of superiority and specialness to glimpse the fragile, insignificant, and impermanent creatures we are. Like the Wizard of Oz behind his curtain, we hide behind our apparatuses, and it is a small animal of climate change that pulls back the scrim of our deception. Still, we want to hold tightly to philosophical and religious stories that affirm, not only our singularity, but the possibility of ontological permanence. For those who are not religious, nationalism can serve to affirm significance and continuing being: I will die but my country will live on. Or others may work diligently to engineer ways to live on other orbs, believing science will be our savior as we become an interplanetary species; all the while these efforts contribute to mystifying the real sources of our alienation. Implicit here is the continuity of the human species, as well as a disregard of other species. We can imagine the end of this world but not the end of humanity, a state that only evidences our powers of mystification and of weak dissociation. Yet, the event of climate change can, for many people, undermine weak dissociation, raising to consciousness our existential insignificance and impermanence. When mystification recedes, we may accept

---

93. Freud, *General Theory of Neurosis*, 285.

the fact that we will go the way of the dinosaurs, whether by our own hands or in the inevitability of cosmic time.

Stern recognizes that the intersubjective defensive operation of weak dissociation can be breached, but we are creatures with a wide array of collective psychological defenses. When confronted by the realities of the Anthropocene Age, we nevertheless rely on various forms of denial and rationalization to maintain our beliefs and forms of life, even as we rocket toward our extinction and the extinction of millions of other species. Economists Gernot Wagner and Martin L. Weitzman believe that capitalism or the market fuels creativity and innovation, which can be harnessed to reduce greenhouse gas emissions (through carbon credits, offsets, geoengineering, and so forth).[94] Michael Northcott points out that scientists such as Paul Crutzen call "for a significant ramping up of research and development by scientists and technologists of the technical means for intentional intervention in the Earth System, including active geoengineering of the atmosphere."[95] Understandably, these scientists and others want to save humanity, but not by reimagining ways of living that are free of the very apparatuses implicated in our current dilemma. Indeed, these calls represent intersubjective cognitive operations (i.e., rationalization and denial) that continue to mystify the real sources of our struggles and, in turn, make it difficult "to experiment radically with new ways of thinking and living."[96]

Conclusion

Above I alluded to the movie *The Wizard of Oz*. I remember as a child watching that film every fall, for reasons I cannot recall. In one sense, it is a story of alienation. Dorothy finds herself in a strange land and seeks to return home to her aunt and uncle. The good witch tells her that she must go to the city of Oz and seek help, a remedy for her alienation. After various ordeals, she and her companions arrive at Oz and are confronted by a very powerful visage who shows little empathy or interest in Dorothy's estrangement. Then, Dorothy's dog, Toto, pulls back the curtain, revealing an aged man pulling the levers that created the fiction of the all-powerful Oz. Like all happy endings, each character has their wish fulfilled, and Dorothy wakes up at home surrounded by loved ones. I think that Westerners have created and maintained fictions to explain our alienation as existential or ontological truths. These fictions offer remedies that only serve to maintain

---

94. Wagner and Weitzman, *Climate Shock*.
95. Northcott, "On Going Gently," 24.
96. Crockett, *Radical Political Theology*, 165.

the apparatuses of the Great Oz (sovereignty and the ontological rift). But unlike in the movie (where even though the remedies are exposed as frauds, they still turn out to be remedies), the remedies we have devised are not real remedies: they are curtains screening the apparatuses of the ontological rift. We in the West are like the Great Oz; we believe we are powerful and significant as we pull the levers of capitalism, nationalism, and religion. It is the Anthropocene Age that pulls back our curtain, revealing our fragile finitude and our existential insignificance and impermanence. But unlike the "wizard" in the story, who readily admits he is a charlatan, we are not likely to act so beneficently when exposed. In real life, individuals and groups who seek to establish dominance over other human beings (and over other species like the lion, tin man, and scarecrow) are very reluctant to give up their power—to face their limitations, to accept accountability, and to give in to remorse for their destructive actions. Our reluctance keeps us from acknowledging the ontological rift as well as the pseudoremedies for our alienation. This is not a counsel for despair. Instead, it is a needed step to reimagine forms of life without the ontological rift and its attending alienation. Whether this will be an adequate response to the climate emergency is not the main point. Rather, reimaging ways of living that do not include the apparatuses of the ontological rift and its mystifications entails facing the categorical demand to care for all life and its source—the Earth—and to accept our existential insignificance and impermanence, which bind us to all living creatures.

5

A Coming Radical Jesus for the Anthropocene

Nihilism is an attitude in which everything, human life above all, is without essential meaning or value.[1]

There is no sense in anything I do, if the house burns down. And yet it is exactly while the house is burning that one must carry on as always, must do everything with care and precision, perhaps even more diligently—even if no one notices. Perhaps life will disappear from Earth leaving no memory of what was done, for better or for worse. But you must carry on as before.[2]

This is our defiance—to practice love even in hopelessness.[3]

It is not clear whether the passage into the profane is a simple abandonment of theology, that is, just completely forgetting all about it, or rather, that it is a new promised Epicureanism requiring an overcoming of the theological legacy together with its anthropological pessimism.[4]

---

1. Brown, *Nihilistic Times*, 21.
2. Agamben, *When the House Burns Down*, 1.
3. Kaur, *See No Stranger*, 241.
4. Zawisza and Hagedorn, "Faith in the World," 25.

> If God exists he isn't just churches and mathematics.
> He is the forest. He's the desert.
> He's the ice caps, that are dying.
> He's the ghetto and the Museum of Fine Arts.[5]

In a *Star Trek: The Next Generation* episode called "True Q" (season 6, episode 6),[6] Amanda is a young woman assigned to the *Enterprise* to conduct research, which she loves. While on the ship, Amanda begins to have experiences that trouble her. Sometimes what she imagines in her head happens in reality. Enter Q, a nearly omnipotent being. He appears on the *Enterprise* to deal with this young woman, who apparently is a member of Q's people. Amanda is torn between remaining a limited human being and finishing her internship on the *Enterprise* or becoming a being like Q. At one point in the episode, while on the bridge with Captain Picard, Amanda listens to the distress of lieutenant commander Geordi La Forge. Geordi is on the surface of the planet the *Enterprise* is orbiting, trying to help engineers keep the planet from an impending climate catastrophe. The planet's dominant species had for centuries polluted their world, and the present generation is desperately attempting to use science to prevent the total collapse of the global environment. As Amanda and the crew listen, it appears that climate collapse is unstoppable. At this point, unbeknownst to the captain, Amanda decides to become a Q and use her powers to save the planet. The viewer sees the planet's atmosphere miraculously, more accurately magically, cleansed and life restored. Who needs engineers to save a world when one has a Q?

Many of us love a happy ending, where people and a planet are saved from extinction. The entertainment industry is rife with magical heroes with superpowers who come to the rescue of "damsels" in distress, beleaguered peoples, and other species (sometimes aliens: note *Avatar*). It may be that this genre of movies, TV shows, and graphic novels is a form of escapism from the grim realities of our lives and, in particular, the dire present and future realities of the climate emergency. It may also be that in an increasingly secular society these stories function to reassure us of our existential significance and continuity or to distract us from our existential insignificance and impermanence, while keeping in place the attributes of

---

5. Oliver, *Devotions*, 87.
6. Scheerer, dir., "True Q."

sovereignty and the ontological rift. Today, I suspect many of us wish for a Q to save us from ourselves.

Is Amanda, as a Q, a stand-in for Jesus *qua* savior, as she saves the people from the consequences of their generational environmental sins? If so, this seems to trivialize Jesus and the idea of salvation, attributing both to magical thinking. While, in my view, there is a great deal of magical thinking in all religions, magical thinking does not result in ways of living that have practical methods, aims, and results. Amanda saves the people, though we can surmise there is no change in how they live, which parallels the escapist entertainment that many of us enjoy. I appreciate and enjoy *Star Trek* and other science fiction movies and TV shows, though I can say with certainty that none of them has led to changes in my way of living. This is not supposed to be the case with Jesus, though many people, past and present, profess, with great piety and self-righteousness, to follow him only to continue being spiteful, cruel, miserly, bigoted, and passionately indifferent. Add to this all the professed Christian conversions throughout the last two millennia and the fact that nothing seems to have changed, especially in our relationships with one another, with other species, or with the Earth. I am reminded of Søren Kierkegaard, who surveyed the landscape of Christian Europe and asked whether a Christian could be found in all of Christendom.[7] Despite this sad fact, the question of the relevance and meaning of Jesus for Christians pervades every age. This is especially the case when we are confronted with looming climate catastrophes and the possible extinction of not only of humans but millions of other species.[8]

The previous chapters have set out to analyze and describe what has been and what is wrong with Western forms of living, rooted in philosophical and theological anthropologies that have emerged against the background of apparatuses of sovereignty and the ontological rift. In the previous chapter, I argued that the "diagnosis" of the human condition vis-à-vis Western philosophies and theologies—a very large claim, I realize, but part of the story I am telling—attends remedies that mystify the real sources of our distress, keeping the apparatuses of civilization, sovereignty, and the ontological rift in place. In other words, the forms of life associated with the ontological rift and sovereignty continue unchanged, and I argue these forms of life are untenable given the trajectory of climate change. The analysis of the previous four chapters creates a space to reimagine ways of

---

7. Kierkegaard, *Concluding Unscientific Postscript*.

8. Famed biologist E. O. Wilson predicts that half of the known species will become extinct by the end of this century as a result of climate change and other human-caused environmental degradations (Wilson, *Future of Life*).

living that render inoperative[9] the apparatuses of sovereignty and the ontological rift. That is, these new ways of living generate relations wherein the singularities of other species, other human beings, and the Earth are respected and nurtured.[10] If this is to be the case, then we need to develop anthropologies—psychological, theological, and philosophical—and practices that further ways of living that foster respect and nurture of human beings, other species, and the Earth. Yet, developing nurturing, respectful anthropologies will not happen by magic in the Anthropocene Age. More specifically, developing anthropologies friendly to nonhuman species and the Earth must include reimaging the Jesus of scripture and tradition, reconceptualizing traditional theological concepts like sin and salvation, and revitalizing religious practices and rituals. In other words, forming these new anthropologies entails telling a story of a radical coming[11] Jesus who renders inoperative the apparatuses of sovereignty and the ontological rift, and who thereby creates spaces for diverse forms of living that respect and care[12] for the singularities of other species and the Earth.

9. For Agamben, "inoperativity" means to deactivate the functioning of apparatuses, which does not mean that these apparatuses cease operating or do not continue to have effects. More will be explained about this term below. See Prozorov, *Agamben and Politics*, 31–34.

10. Genny Rowley uses the term "intersystemic care" to address how individuals and communities can care for human beings, other species, and Earth. There are many points of agreement between her notion and my notion of "anarchic care." The difference, however, is that anarchic care, I argue, renders inoperative sovereignty and its damaging iterations. Rowley, "Practicing Hope"; Rowley, "Intersystemic Care," 119–20.

11. "Coming" refers to the potential or possibility of not the person of Jesus, but of forms of living that render inoperative the apparatuses of the ontological rift and sovereignty.

12. Numerous philosophers and pastoral theologians have mined the depths of the concept of care. It is not possible to explicate the notion of care, because it will distract me from the topic of this chapter. However, I can return to a brief definition of care offered in the Introduction, as well as identify some of the scholars who have sought to define and describe the attributes of care. Care is everything we do to help individuals, families, communities, and societies to (1) meet vital biological, psychosocial, and existential or spiritual needs of individuals, families, and communities; (2) develop or maintain basic capabilities with the aim of human flourishing and the flourishing of other species [since we are dependent on a biodiverse Earth], (3) facilitate participation in the polis's space of appearances, and (4) maintain a habitable environment for all. I add to this definition that care as a political-ecological concept involves shared critical and constructive reflection on how the structures (and their accompanying narratives and practices) of the state, governing authorities, and nonstate organizations (e.g., businesses, labor unions, religious and secular communities, and so forth) and actors meet or fail to meet the four features of this definition of care. See Bubeck, *Care, Gender, and Justice*; the Care Collective (Chatzidakis, et al.), *Care Manifesto*; Engster, *Heart of Justice*; Hamington, *Embodied Care*; Hamington and Flower, eds., *Care Ethics*. Held, *Ethics*

It is important to clarify what I mean by "radical" since it shapes the method used in making my argument. The adjective or noun "radical" comes from the Latin *radix*, which means "root," or the late Latin *radicalis*, pertaining to having roots. The adjective can mean far-reaching, fundamental, absolute, or thorough-going change. In the context of politics and religion, "radical" can refer to revisionist, reformist, or revolutionary changes. While I think what I am proposing in this chapter is revisionist, the primary meaning of the term "radical" is "roots" or "pertaining to roots." This shapes how I will proceed. That is, I begin with a depiction of psychosocial developmental perspective, because psychosocial development pertains to the *roots* of human subjectivity and relations. In particular, I will argue that good-enough parental care, while influenced by societal apparatuses of sovereignty and the ontological rift, is anarchic.[13] Anarchic care renders inoperative the apparatuses of sovereignty and the attending ontological rift. I also emend psychoanalytic developmental perspectives to depict epistemologies and relations that are free of the ontological rift, though, these epistemologies are later largely repressed in favor of epistemologies associated with beliefs in superiority and inferiority, and relations of subordination and subjugation. This is, however, not the case for many indigenous peoples, a claim that requires further elaboration. Nevertheless, I contend that anarchic care and the attending capacity to exercise impotentiality with regard to the apparatuses of the rift are possible in adult lives, and I will provide illustrations of this. Once this root has been articulated, I turn to the part of the story where I reimagine a radical Jesus who is a paradigm of forms of living related to a nonsovereign God—a God in which there is no ontological rift.[14]

---

of Care; Helsel, *Pastoral Power*; LaMothe, *Care of Souls*; Oliner and Oliner, *Toward a Caring Society*; Ramsay, "Compassionate Resistance"; Robinson, *Globalizing Care*; Robinson, *Ethics of Care*; Rogers-Vaughn, *Caring for Souls*; Rumscheidt, *No Room for Grace*; Sevenhuijsen, *Citizenship*; Tronto, *Moral Boundaries*; Tronto, *Caring Democracy*.

13. Anarchy simply means without rulers or without a sovereign. The term struck fear in Thomas Hobbes, who associated anarchy with chaos and mob rule (which is not, by definition, anarchy). Not surprisingly, Hobbes was part of and served the sovereign class. In the nineteenth century, Pierre-Joseph Proudhon embraced the idea of anarchy, though it continues today to be associated with the chaos and violence of mob rule, which invites wondering if this covertly functions to reinforce the belief in the necessity of the sovereign and sovereign classes. I am using "anarchy" to refer to relations where sovereignty and its apparatuses do not operate.

14. Rafael Zawisza argues that Hannah Arendt, influenced by Christian theologies, "hoped that through mutual pledges it would be possible to enforce 'the consistent abolition of sovereignty within the body politic.'" Arendt is not the only political philosopher to indicate that sovereignty is not necessary for political belonging. In his discussion of the works of Spinoza, David Kishik argues that the sovereign "state . . is not a *necessary* condition" for political belonging, a point addressed in the philosophy

I make two other points before continuing. To begin with psychosocial development, to my mind, means that the care provided to Jesus growing up, while obviously different in many ways from parental care in present-day Western cultures, has parallels with care any good-enough parent offers. Yes, we know little of Jesus' childhood, but we can safely presume that he (or more accurately the Jesus of my story) received a considerable amount of care from his parents and others in order to become a well-functioning adult. Put another way, good-enough parental care founds subjectivity and psychosocial development, and the experience of parental care connects us to the Jesus of scripture and to other human beings from other cultures and times. By turning to a developmental perspective before discussing "Jesus," I am also staking a claim that good-enough parental care—whether we are considering indigenous peoples past or present, Jesus, or some other human being who lived before the rise of civilization—is not determined primarily by the apparatuses of the ontological rift and sovereignty, though, as I will show, these apparatuses can influence, but do not determine, parental care. This claim indicates the existential possibility of forms of living that render inoperative those apparatuses, which means that answers to the climate emergency are not external to those of us in the West; rather, the seeds are within our own early experiences of care and potential in our own subjectivity.

Since I am wading into deep and problematic waters when mentioning and discussing Jesus, I need to explain how I approach and use "Jesus." Greek philosopher Xenophanes wrote, "if oxen and horses or lions had hands, and could paint with their hands, and produce works of art as [humans] do, horses would paint the forms of the gods like horses, and oxen like oxen."[15] We can say the same for our diverse depictions or theological interpretations of Jesus, which range from a very conservative Jesus supporting the market society[16] or US imperialism[17] to a revolutionary Jesus who undermines capitalistic-imperialistic, and patriarchal regimes,[18] and

---

of Giorgio Agamben (Zawisza, "Between Adamite Dreams and Original Sin," 103). See also Kishik, *Power of Life*, 39; Agamben, *Coming Community*.

15. Grayling, *History of Philosophy*, 26.

16. See Cox, *Market as God*; MacDonald, *Thieves in the Temple*; Novak, *Toward a Theology of the Corporation*.

17. McDougall, *Jesus Was an Airborne Ranger*.

18. See Cone, *Black Theology of Liberation*; Cone, *Cross and the Lynching Tree*; Crossan, *Jesus*; Crossan, *God and Empire*; Cupitt, *Radical Theology*; Gutiérrez, *Theology of Liberation*; Horsley, *Jesus and Empire*; Horsley, *Covenant Economics*; Horsley, *Jesus and the Powers*; Moltmann, *Gospel of Liberation*; Reuther, *Sexism and God Talk*; Schüssler Fiorenza, *Discipleship of Equals*; Segundo, *Liberation of Theology*.

who supports queer theology.[19] Not surprisingly, whether they are scripture scholars, theologians, ministers or laypeople, those who paint pictures of Jesus are all arguing for the real Jesus. While I will use scripture and the insights of scripture scholars in my portrayal of Jesus, I make no claim that my depiction of Jesus is the real Jesus. I am also not interested in the perennial preoccupation for the search for the real or historical Jesus or in questions about the relationship in Jesus of the human and the divine natures. I am not concerned with creeds, doctrines, and dogmas, which tend to function as apparatuses of the status quo and often foster exclusion and division. Instead, I am playing with "Jesus" as a paradigm for imagining forms of living free of the ontological rift and sovereignty. I am, in other words, telling you a story or a constructive fabulation about a human being named Jesus—a fictional story that makes no claim to the Truth or historical events,[20] but that perhaps articulates a smaller, more radical truth of anarchic knowing and compassionate relating to other species in terms of their singularities. Let me add that the Jesus of my story has nothing to say about the afterlife[21] and, indeed, is not interested in it. Instead, the focus is on the here and now of anarchic care for all living species and the Earth upon which life depends. This is a "Jesus" who (1) accepts the *temporal constructed significance* of all creatures,[22] (2) embraces both the existential insignificance and

---

19. Tonstad, *Queer Theology*.

20. Vine Deloria argues that part of the problem with Christianity is its focus on history divorced from land and, in particular, its focus on the events of creation and the life of Jesus. "Changing the conception of religious reality from a temporal to a special framework involves surrendering the place of teaching and preaching as elements of religion... A religion defined according to temporal considerations is continually placed on the defensive in maintaining its control over the interpretation of historical events" (Deloria, *God Is Red*, 67–68). In this vein, I am not interested in the historical figure of Jesus. Instead, I am trying to portray the idea of a form of life that renders inoperative the apparatuses of sovereignty and those that produce and maintain the ontological rift.

21. Of course, human beings are concerned about the "afterlife" as it pertains to caring about the lives of those who will continue to exist and thrive after we are dead. But the afterlife associated with the idea of eternal existence of a soul is not relevant in my telling of this story.

22. A question may arise regarding the ethical parameters for using and killing other species. I will not address this, except to say that recognizing and caring for the singularities of other species does not preclude killing or using them per se. These instances require moral considerations that take into account not only the animal being used or killed and its implications for other species. Consider, for instance, that mosquitoes carry various illnesses, some of them deadly to human beings. Surely we want to find ways to protect human beings from these diseases, which may entail limiting mosquito populations. However, attempts to eradicate them would impact other species who depend on mosquitos as a food source. For more in-depth discussions, see Korsgaard, *Fellow Creatures*; Nussbaum, *Justice for Animals*; Singer, *Animal Liberation*.

impermanence vis-à-vis all life, and (3) lives out the categorical demand to care for the world and its diverse inhabitants.[23] In addition, the Jesus of my story can be any gender and ethnicity, because my story is about imagining forms of human life that manifest anarchic care for all species and therefore are not bound to a specific culture or a particular gender. My story also suggests that "Jesus" is not bound to a religious tradition, secular tradition, or particular age. Let me stress, in my constructive fabulation, there is no anonymous Christian, whether that refers to a person from another religion or a loving and compassionate person who is atheistic, humanistic, or agnostic. The *Jesus in my story refers to ways of living* that can be glimpsed, beyond Christianity, in other religions, spiritualities, and secular philosophies (e.g., indigenous philosophies and religions), whether these are connected to "civilization" or not.

Readers will recognize that I have not and will not refer to Jesus as the Christ. The "Jesus" of my story is not concerned about being anointed the Son of God or being seen as the savior for depraved humanity to live eternally in a kingdom of God—a kingdom devoid of other species. The Jesus of my fabulation is not interested in being worshiped, adored or loved, or ensconced in creeds; neither is he interested in Jesus-and-me religious experiences. Rather, the Jesus I am telling about is simply a human being living with and caring for other human beings, other species, and the Earth—a Jesus living out the categorical demand to respect and care for all life. In other words, the Jesus of my story is quite ordinary, even as "Jesus" is being transgressive toward political and religious authorities and their varied apparatuses of sovereignty and the ontological rift. Treating Jesus as simply human facilitates our ability to see "Jesus" (or, more accurately, forms of life) in ordinary human beings, past and present, who seek to care for other human beings, other species, and the Earth in the here and now. Further, if the future figures in this story, it is because ordinary human beings are justly concerned in the present for the future flourishing of non-existents—human and other-than-human.

My depiction of Jesus may raise other questions: Is my proposed notion of Jesus heretical? Why use Jesus at all? As to the issue of heresy, there is a long, sordid history of people having been accused of and killed for contradicting orthodox religious beliefs. We know that an assembly of male citizens accused Socrates of heresy, impiety, and corrupting the minds of the youth, which ended in his being sentenced to death.[24] A cursory scan

23. Agata Bielek-Robson examines the work of Hannah Arendt and depicts a shift from loving the God of theology to love of the world. This is, in many ways, the form of life I am addressing here (Bielek-Robson, "Amor Mundi").

24. Rouse, trans., *Great Dialogues of Plato*.

of Western history regarding heresy reveals not reconciliation, mercy, and love, but alienation, violence, and coercive conformity.[25] In the early centuries of the Christian religion, people of rival sects were lynched or massacred.[26] Religious leaders like Archbishop Nestorius, who remarked to Emperor Theodosius II, "Give me the earth purged of heretics and I will give you heaven in return,"[27] were not above seeking God's blessing for and help to annihilate nonbelievers and, worse, heretics. Beloved Saint Augustine predicted everlasting torment—a permanent ontological rift—for those he deemed to be heretical.[28] Perhaps more apt to the topic in this chapter, as Rafael Zawisza notes, "In the history of Christianity various groups called Adamites were accused of heresy because they contested the necessity of hierarchical order."[29] In brief, religious and secular leaders and followers across the centuries, ensconced in the safety of their theological and philosophical fortresses and canons, have happily washed heretics' blood from their hands as they have sought the seductions of a "pure" faith and absolute Truth. In all of this, the accusation of heresy is a tactic of the apparatuses, which are aimed at preserving, through forms of sovereign violence and social shame, not orthodox beliefs or Truths per se, but forms of living that are linked to the ontological rift and sovereignty. Heresy is about sovereign power, privilege, position, and prestige. Of course, someone may accuse me of heresy or corrupting the youth, but the story of Jesus in this chapter is about forms of life that recognize and care for the singularities of all life. I am, in other words, not proposing an unorthodox or orthodox view. These terms—"heresy," "orthodoxy," "unorthodoxy"—simply do not apply in my constructive fabulation. Applying any of these terms to my depiction of Jesus would be analogous to accusing an indigenous person of heresy or of being unorthodox because the stories she is telling about the wise spider. She knows it is fiction that bears practical wisdom.

This moves me to the question of why to use "Jesus" at all. I have a couple of responses to that question. First, having been a Western Christian for most of my life and working as a pastoral theologian for decades, I have some familiarity with scriptures and traditions that attempt to portray the real Jesus. While there are innumerable depictions and interpretations of Jesus, I think it is clear that a core feature of the stories about Jesus is that he acts transgressively vis-à-vis the religious establishment and Rome. I do not

---

25. Tanner, *Church in the Later Middle Ages*.
26. Tanner, *Church in the Later Middle Ages*, 210.
27. De St. Croix, *Christian Persecution*, 207.
28. De St. Croix, *Christian Persecution*, 209.
29. Zawisza, "Between Adamite Dreams and Original Sin," 103.

think this is somehow unique to Jesus and his ministry. There are plenty of examples, throughout history and from around the world, of human beings transgressing the dominant religious, political, and economic apparatuses of their cultures and times (e.g., Buddha, Shotoku Taishi, Mary Wollstonecraft, Patrice Lumumba, Desmond Tutu, Sojourner Truth, Emma Goldman, Lucretia Mott, and Rosa Parks, to name a few). "Jesus," then, becomes a paradigm of radical transgression—transgression rooted in care and justice for those who have been marginalized, repressed, and oppressed, which includes other species and the Earth. Put another way, Jesus was not an apologist for religious authorities, business leaders, or Roman occupiers; rather, as I indicate below, he was someone concerned about the marginalized and oppressed—those who were forced to scratch out existence (bare life)[30] in the shadows of Roman and religious sovereign authorities. Second, I hope to shake up Christian establishments with their sedimented creeds, rituals of worship, and ossified forms of Christian living that are captive to the ontological rift and the varied notions and practices of sovereignty. In my imagination, if "Jesus" were to come in our time, they would not want to be praised, idolized, idealized, or worshiped; neither would they ascribe to the ontological belief in a sovereign creator. Instead, *they would invite practices that embody forms of living that respect and care for the singularities of all human beings, other species, and the Earth*—forms of life that transgress the apparatuses of the ontological rift and sovereignty.

The Developmental Roots of Anarchic Care and Epistemologies Lacking the Ontological Rift

Human beings are altricial creatures, by which I mean we are born undeveloped, needing considerable amounts of consistent care in order to mature into adults. I think it is safe to say this is a truism that pertains to all human beings across the world and time—including in the ages before the emergence of civilization. Of course, what care has looked like varies widely according to culture and historical era. While I acknowledge diversity in care, I will be making some generalizations about care and development. This is a continuation of the story I am telling that while not subscribing to universal, timeless truth, reveals some truths that may resonate with readers. Let me add two other reasons for beginning with a psychosocial developmental perspective. The roots of subjectivity lie in our early relationships with

---

30. Agamben uses the term "bare life" to refer to persons "caught up in the sovereign ban ... stripped of all protections and abandoned to the force of law." See Prozorov, *Agamben and Politics*, 102.

caregivers. Indeed, human subjectivity is potential at birth and becomes actual (dynamically understood) as a result of parental care.[31] The absence of care is death. Distorted care leads to distortions in subjectivity. Second, as I will attempt to demonstrate, early relationships and forms of knowing and relating are absent from the apparatuses of the ontological rift and sovereignty, which does not mean these apparatuses do not continue to have an impact on these significant early relationships. I suggest only that parental care is the existential root (radical) that remains, even as children later begin to internalize the symbol systems associated with the apparatuses of the ontological rift and sovereignty. If care is not part of the apparatuses of the ontological rift and sovereignty, then anarchic care is a universal feature (albeit one subject to significant variation) of human existence, whether in so-called civilized societies or in indigenous societies. From a diachronic perspective, we can imagine that the root of Jesus' subjectivity lay in the anarchic care from his parents, which is why I begin here.

There are numerous developmental theories, but I will restrict myself to psychoanalytic perspectives, mainly because I am more familiar with them and not because they are necessarily better or superior. Indeed, as I have argued in an earlier chapter, Freud's developmental view functions, in part, as an apparatus of the ontological rift and sovereignty. To avoid this, I make use of emended views of prominent psychoanalytic theorists—theorists who have significant influence in psychoanalytic and other circles. More particularly, I reframe Christopher Bollas's and Donald Winnicott's psychosocial development perspectives, arguing that (1) the rift is absent vis-à-vis good-enough parental anarchic care and (2) early semiotic processes are ways of knowing the world (epistemologies) that represent rudimentary interspecific perspectivism (a multiplicity of points of view) and multinaturalism (innumerable species means there are innumerable

---

31. It may be helpful to say a bit more about actuality and potentiality. Aristotle posited a relation between potentiality (*dynamis*) and actualization (*energeia*). For Giorgio Agamben, the Western philosophical tradition has largely "subordinated potentiality to actuality: so, we begin with the actual, speaking humans and their political and artistic productions, and we see potentiality at present as a capacity or skill that is defined by the final action. We see potentiality as secondary or accidental" (Colebrook and Maxwell, *Agamben*, 188). From Agamben's perspective, there are two features of Aristotle's views. First, "the very essence of humanity lies in a potentiality that is expressed when it does not unfold into actuality" (Colebrook and Maxwell, *Agamben*, 189). A second key idea here is "that potentiality is not exhausted in its own actualization" (Ugilt, *Giorgio Agamben*, 25). In other words, potentiality is what marks all living beings, but human beings have the capacity not to actualize potential (impotentiality) *and* even in actualizing potentiality, never exhaust it. For Agamben, to move from potentiality to actuality means the individual must undergo a change. In my view, undergoing a change vis-à-vis potential to actual subjectivity depends on good-enough parental care.

natures—not one Nature).³² Interspecific perspectivism and multinaturalism are generally abandoned³³ when children internalize and transition to Western apparatuses and their epistemologies of the rift, though some indigenous peoples retain these two epistemological features.³⁴ I suggest, however, that there is evidence that the rift does not necessarily have the last word in adult life. There are instances, though not enough, where adults engage with one another and with other-than-human species out of interspecific perspectivism and multinaturalism.³⁵

Let me begin this developmental story with Christopher Bollas, who uses the concept "unthought knowns" to refer to "that which is known, but not yet thought,"³⁶ which "constitutes the core of one's being."³⁷ The origins of these unthought knowns, for Bollas, can be found in the earliest period of psychosocial development, when the good-enough parent is not an object in the sense of being differentiated from another object or (more accurately) being represented symbolically. More positively, the parent-object is represented semiotically vis-à-vis the infant. In Bollas's perspective, a parent, as "object," because of their caring attunements, "alters the infant's

---

32. In explicating perspectivism and multinaturalism, anthropologist Eduardo Viveiros de Castro contends that "virtually all peoples of the New World share a conception of the world as composed of a multiplicity of points of view. Every existent is a center of intentionality apprehending other existents according to their respective characteristics and powers" (Castro, *Cannibal Metaphysics*, 55). He states further that "Multiplicity can be taken as a kind of plurality [and] Amazonian multinaturalism affirms not so much a variety of natures as the naturalness of variation—variation as nature" (Castro, *Cannibal Metaphysics*, 74). What this means is that indigenous peoples Viveiros de Castro encountered viewed other species as possessing selves—actual or potential—and that these selves have their own perspectives and ways of knowing.

33. My partner recently came across an intriguing article from *The New York Times*. The writer was talking about how her daughter (age eleven) had decided to get rid of her stuffed animals. Her mother was puzzled because these stuffed animals had been important to her daughter. Her daughter replied, "They never really did come alive, I know that, but in my imagination they did." She turned to me with white-hot anger. "My imagination is gone and you never told me this would happen" (Egan, "'No Love Is Ever Wasted'"). In my view, this illustrates how the internalization of Western epistemologies leads to a loss of imagination that believes in the singularities of other beings, real and imagined.

34. See Castro, *Cannibal Metaphysics*; Kohn, *How Forests Think*.

35. Roger Berkowitz explores Hannah Arendt's political philosophy, pointing out that Arendt advocated for an openness to infinite number of standpoints in political life, because it enables persons to look upon the same world from the standpoints of others. This is a kind of interspecific perspectivism that, for Arendt, is necessary for political life—a political life that includes other species. See Berkowitz, "Actions," 175, 178.

36. Bollas, *Shadow of the Object*, 4.

37. Bollas, *Shadow of the Object*, 60.

environment to meet [the infant's] needs."[38] This parent-infant interaction, in other words, is *a process* that alters the infant's experience or subjectivity.[39] We might think of the process of care as presymbolic Representations of Interactions that have been Generalized (RIGs).[40]

When referring to these early experiences, Bollas understandably points out that they are prerepresentational or presymbolic, which, I argue, points to a type of knowing and relating. As Bollas notes, the "object is 'known' not so much by putting it into an object-representation, but as a recurrent experience of being."[41] These experiences of being or of unthought knowns as core experiences of being, Bollas contends, "are fundamentally wordless occasions" and are "notable for the density of the subject's feelings and the fundamentally non-representational knowledge of being embraced by the aesthetic object."[42] Bollas points to a kind of semiotic knowledge the infant has that is distinct from the knowledge associated with later semiotic forms that are part of the capacities for symbolization. It is, then, not quite accurate to say the parent is not an object vis-à-vis the infant. We must ask what kind of object the parent is, because this early form of knowing presupposes a rudimentary semiotic ability to differentiate between objects. This "aesthetic object" refers, as I understand it, to semiotic organizations of experiences of the process of being-with-parent caregiving (RIGs).

Before remarking more upon the parent's anarchic care during infancy, I must say more about the wordless core of one's being. First, I suggest that good-enough parent-infant interactions or processes lead to the infant's presymbolic and preconscious organizations of self-respect, self-confidence, and self-esteem in relation to an envirosomatic caring and the aesthetic parent-object. Presymbolic senses of self-esteem, self-respect, and self-confidence are features of the unthought known and the foundation of the infant's nascent agency or ego. The infant's budding agency entails being able to surrender to the parent's ministrations, which include "beliefs" that the self-world or environment is safe or trustworthy, as well as a wordless hope that the parent-object will respond to the infant's cries or assertions.[43] So an infant may surrender to varied contexts (e.g., to the crib) or to objects or persons (e.g., to a blanket, to nonparent figures). Second, I contend that the core of one's being includes semiotic knowing that is quite fluid in the

---

38. Bollas, *Shadow of the Object*, 15.
39. Bollas, *Shadow of the Object*, 13–15.
40. Stern, *Interpersonal World*.
41. Bollas, *Shadow of the Object*, 13.
42. Bollas, *Shadow of the Object*, 31.
43. See Erikson, *Childhood and Society*.

sense that it engages diverse "objects" (relations and contexts) that become (1) part of self-world and (2) objects to trust and hope in. Put another way, infants, while possessing a rudimentary ability to differentiate, have a kind of cognitive flexibility or plasticity, viewing objects and contexts as extensions of the self, yet distinct. The infant, then, attributes a rudimentary selfhood to these objects.[44] This early epistemological plasticity will be important as infants begin to develop semiotic capacities associated with symbolism (i.e., language, narratives, and rituals).

This is an important point. I am suggesting that infants' "method" of knowing and relating to the world entails attributing selfhood to the environment and its objects. Typically, this period of development is seen as narcissistic because each infant engages the parents only in terms of the infant's self. Of course, infants have neither the capacity to recognize other persons nor the ability to take the Other's perspective. But what I am positing is that early forms of knowing entail ascribing selfhood to the environment and its objects. To put this wordless experience into words as best we can, infants possess nascent selves and "believe" that other objects possess selves like but not identical to them. If infants viewed everything as identical to themselves, then they would have no capacity for differentiation or negation (not-me). Bollas's research into emerging capacities in infants for differentiation and negation (not-me) indicates to me that there are rudimentary distinctions between selves and objects, but these "objects" are perceived to be selves as well.

Bollas argues that these early unthought knowns are evident in adult life, such as in surrendering to music or to religious ritual, for instance. His argument is that core experiences of early infancy continue to be part of our subjectivity, our adult-symbolic ways of knowing and relating, though we are not conscious that these adult experiences are linked to early wordless experiences. I think Bollas would agree that I-Thou experiences fall under the category of wordless experiences of infancy that reverberate in adult experience. The "Thou" in I-Thou experiences can include inanimate objects, other-than-human species, or landscapes, for example. In these experiences, early semiotic organizations are present within more complex

---

44. This perspective alters how we might think about narcissism vis-à-vis the first stage of life. Typically, narcissism is understood as a sense that the world-environment exists to meet my needs. I think this is one way to construct narcissism, but it suggests a way of knowing and relating that does not quite fit with what I am suggesting. Instead, the narcissism, if you will, of early infancy is a kind of rudimentary knowing wherein the self is part of the world, and the objects within the world of objects are selves as well—existents. An adult illustration of this is Martin Buber's I-Thou relations, though this represents other complexities. Put another way, I-Thou relations represent the presence of unthought knowns. Buber, *I and Thou*.

symbolic organizations: while there is differentiation, there is also the belief that the Thou is a part of the self, though distinct. Indeed, in some I-Thou experiences, the Thou is believed to possess its own singularity, which is connected to an early sense of knowing, wherein other objects are believed to possess a self connected to but distinct from the infant's self.

From my perspective, the unthought known represents early semiotic knowing that is devoid of the ontological rift and sovereignty and their attributes. The infant, while possessing a rudimentary capacity for valuation, is not yet able to hold the idea or belief that she is superior to the inferior object—a valuation associated with later cognitive operations of negation and objectification. Similarly, early differentiation is not accompanied by cognitive distinctions between self (later, human nature) and "Nature." There is, in other words, no concept of "Nature" for the infant. There are only semiotic organizations of self-environment(s)—multinatures vis-à-vis objects-self-contexts. In other words, for the infant, self and environment are intertwined, and discrete environmental objects possess selves. This is a presymbolic knowing that comprises rudimentary interspecific perspectivism and multinaturalism.

This early type of knowing and relating has environmental and evolutionary relevance. Infants, of course, cannot survive on their own, but, as philosopher John Macmurray writes, the infant "is, in fact, 'adapted', so to speak paradoxically, to being unadapted, 'adapted to complete dependence' . . . He can only live through other people."[45] In their unadapted, dependent-vulnerable state, infants possess an impulse or motivation to communicate—"the impulse to communicate is [their] sole adaptation to the world."[46] This impulse to communicate includes cognitive semiotic plasticity that enables infants to adapt to varied objects or contexts, organizing experiences presymbolically. The relevance here is that the embodied self is embedded in the world, and there is no distinction between self and Nature or World. This accompanies a degree of flexibility for the infant in knowing and communicating vis-a-vis multiple context-objects. Flexible adaptation to varied contexts that are extensions of a sense of self is environmentally (and, therefore, evolutionary) relevant for infants especially and for all humans in general. Indigenous persons have been able to survive and flourish in very diverse habitats in which their senses of embodied selves are embedded. Unfortunately, this cognitive flexibility, when in thrall to the attributes of the ontological rift, is diminished by rigid, instrumental-objectifying epistemologies of civilization that are undermining the habitats of millions

---

45. Macmurray, *Persons in Relation*, 8, 51.
46. Macmurray, *Persons in Relation*, 60.

of species, including human beings. Put another way, the epistemologies associated with the ontological rift undermine interspecific perspectivism and multinaturalism, which are necessary in order to perceive and respect the singularities of other species.

There is more to say here, but I want to turn briefly to parental ministrations during infancy. While the apparatuses of sovereignty and the ontological rift shape adult knowing and relating, I contend that they are not operative in good-enough parental care of children. The parents' good-enough care is anarchic in that the issue of sovereignty or ruling over their subordinate children is inoperative. Good-enough parents do not believe they are superior to their infants, nor do good-enough parents engage their children out of instrumental knowing and relating. And while object or instrumental knowing is present, it is subordinate to personal knowing—recognizing and treating the infant as a unique, valued, inviolable, agentic subject.[47] This personal knowing of parental care, which is a complement of an infant's impulse to communicate, provides what is due an infant, whether meeting material or psychological needs. Put another way, good-enough care lacks the instrumental epistemologies associated with the ontological rift, and this lack is crucial vis-à-vis infants and their early semiotic organizations of experience—unthought knowns. Let me offer an illustration. Activist Ruby Sales recalls her childhood and the love of her parents:

> I grew up in the heart of Southern apartheid. And I'm not saying that I didn't realize that it existed, but our parents were spiritual geniuses who created a world and a language where the notion that I was inadequate or inferior or less-than never touched my consciousness. I grew up believing that I was a first-class human being and a first-class person, and our parents were spiritual geniuses who were able to shape a counterculture of black folk religion that raised us from disposability to being essential players in society.[48]

Sales's parents experienced and suffered from the apparatuses of racism (White sovereignty and a type of ontological rift wherein African Americans are constructed as inferior and where instrumental epistemologies objectify them). Yet, their anarchic care for Sales and her siblings rendered these apparatuses inoperative, creating spaces for her to experience a

---

47. See Macmurray, *Persons in Relation*.

48. Sales, "Where Does It Hurt?" I would also point to the works of other African Americans whose parents desperately tried to care for them in the midst of a racist society. See Coates, *Between the World and Me*; Hinds, *Gift Grows in the Ghetto*; Laymon, *Heavy*; X, *Autobiography*.

deep wordless rapport with her parents and to obtain presymbolic and later symbolic senses of self-esteem, self-respect, and self-confidence. Of course, Sales's self-awareness represents complex symbolic, autobiographical organizations of known experiences, but I suggest these are also connected to unthought knowns or core experiences of being rooted in early childhood—experiences not determined by the ontological rift and its apparatuses.

Giorgio Agamben's work about the capacity for human impotentiality yields another key point about the anarchic care of Ruby Sales's parents vis-à-vis the ontological rift of racism. Agamben writes:

> *Other living beings are capable only of their specific potentiality; they can only do this or that. But human beings are the animals who are capable of their own impotentiality. The greatness of human potentiality is measured by the abyss of human impotentiality.* Here it is possible to see how the root of freedom is to be found in the abyss of potentiality. To be free is not simply to have the power to do this or that thing, nor is it simply to have the power to refuse to do this or that thing. To be free is . . . *to be capable of one's own impotentiality.*[49]

To illustrate this complex discussion, Agamben turns to Herman Melville's "Bartleby, the Scrivener." When Bartleby is told by his boss to do something, Bartleby replies, "I prefer not to." For Agamben, Bartleby is choosing to *not actualize his potentiality* with regard to the demands made by his boss, who represents the realities of the larger capitalist apparatuses. Bartleby's *preferring not* means these apparatuses are rendered inoperative. For Agamben, "inoperativity" means to deactivate the functioning of the apparatuses, which does not mean that these apparatuses cease operating or do not continue to have effects.[50]

Given this, I understand the anarchic care of Ruby Sales's parents to be a case where they exercised their capacity for impotentiality vis-à-vis racist apparatuses, their attending instrumental epistemologies, and beliefs in superiority and inferiority. They "preferred not" to live out of these apparatuses in caring for their children. As Ruby makes clear, her parents may have deactivated the apparatuses of racism in caring for their children, but these apparatuses of the ontological rift continued to have their negative effects. Yet, in exercising their capacity for impotentiality (freedom), Ruby's parents created a space wherein the potentialities (and capacity for impotentiality) of their children (e.g., senses of embedded-embodied self-respect, self-confidence, and self-esteem) could flourish.

49. Agamben, *Potentialities*, 182–83 (italics original).
50. Prozorov, *Agamben and Politics*, 31–34.

Before moving on, I raise an important aspect of impotentiality and anarchic care vis-à-vis Sales's parents and others who were and continue to be marginalized and oppressed. Anarchic care and impotentiality represent varied forms of resistance to those apparatuses that aim to diminish or humiliate persons. Such resistance may be observed in routine situations (as when Sales experienced the care of her parents or when resistance is public, in protests, boycotts, and the like). The civil rights movement of the 1950s and sixties and the current Poor People's Campaign begun in 2018 by William Barber II and Liz Theoharis are two examples of public resistance, and what distinguishes these from violent revolutions is that these acts of impotentiality manifest the means of care and nonviolent justice toward opponents.[51] That is, impotentiality of nonviolent resistance renders the apparatuses of political violence inoperative, though, as I have stressed above, these apparatuses do continue to have negative effects, as civil rights activists know well.[52]

To return to the task at hand, I have been focusing on early childhood and the absence of the ontological rift, both with regard to good-enough parental attunements and the infant's semiotic organizations of experiences that represent embodied-embedded senses of self-esteem, self-confidence, and self-respect. The rudimentary self is embodied and embedded in and indistinguishable from the environment-objects. I now turn to D. W. Winnicott's work to depict the transition to symbolic-semiotic organizations of experience and their attending changes in knowing and relating. In one sense, Winnicott's view of transitional phenomena is closely related to Bollas's view of unthought knowns. Winnicott writes that transitional phenomena represent "separation that is not separation but a form of union."[53] The infant is beginning to further differentiate between self, parent, and other objects. The first transitional object, let's say a cherished blanket, represents the parent-infant caring process. The earliest selection of a transitional object, in other words, is in "accordance with its consistency, texture, size, volume, shape, and odor,"[54] as well as the parent's "technique of mothering"—the caregiver's handling, holding, comforting, and consoling of the infant.[55] That is, because it represents the parent-infant caring interactions, the object provides the infant the solace necessary to manage the task of differentiation. Differentiation involves becoming more distinct from the

51. LaMothe, "Pastoral Theology."
52. See Mantena, "Showdown for Nonviolence."
53. Winnicott, *Playing and Reality*, 98.
54. Kestenberg and Weinstein, "Transitional Objects," 89.
55. Winnicott, *Playing and Reality*, 11.

parent-object,[56] as well as engaging other objects in the environment. For Winnicott, in possessing the transitional object, the infant both retains and partially hands over a belief in his or her own omnipotence to recognize and use external objects.[57] There is, for Winnicott, a paradoxical interplay of the internal and external. The object is "not an internal object—it is a possession. Yet it is not (for the infant) an external object either."[58]

I offer some extensions of Winnicott here. First, the possession of this early transitional object (e.g., a blanket) precedes the infant's capacities for symbolization. Second, the object represents not only the technique or process of parental care but also the infant's embodied-embedded semiotic senses of self-esteem, self-respect, and self-confidence. The transition that the infant makes to the transitional object represents a developing ability to differentiate and to link these senses of self with other "chosen" objects. Third, the period when the transitional object is central is a time when a nascent capacity for impotentiality makes its appearance. Selecting the transitional object, not only provides solace for the infant in the face of separation, but allows infants to exercise their burgeoning capacity to "prefer not" to engage with parents. At the same time, the object represents the technique of parental care. Fourth, the selection of the first transitional object indicates epistemological plasticity, even as it represents a narrowing to select a particular object. In other words, I suggest that the infant continues to experience objects-contexts as connected to the self and as having selves. This is difficult to depict, but imagine that the object is seen as part of the self, but as having a self that is distinct from the infant-self. The world of objects-contexts is a world of selves, even as the infant appends a sense of self to a particular object—exercising an epistemology of rudimentary interspecific perspectivism and multinaturalism. This will become clearer when I depict secondary transitional objects.

Winnicott does not clearly differentiate between the transitional objects that precede symbolization and those that he viewed as part of adult life, but there are significant cognitive and relational differences between a transitional object of early childhood and one taken from and representing the cultural field in adulthood. A child selects and uses as a secondary transitional object a cultural object. This object not only represents the technique of parental care; it also represents the child's entry into and use of the cultural-symbolic world. As Paul Pruyser posits, "the transitional object may be the first means for articulating that aspect of selfhood that is social

---

56. Winnicott, *Playing and Reality*, 3–4.
57. Winnicott, *Playing and Reality*, 9–11.
58. Winnicott, *Playing and Reality*, 9.

and public."⁵⁹ Put another way, the second transitional object functions as a bridge from the idiosyncratic world of parent-infant interactions to the more expansive sociocultural world. By calling the object a bridge, I mean that through using the object the child is learning to incorporate and make use of shared language, narratives, and practices. The object provides a safe place (because the child believes it is under his or her omnipotent control) for the child to assimilate, accommodate, and use larger shared cultural meanings and values, albeit with a child's unique constructions.

One might immediately note that through this second transitional object the child is internalizing the cultural meanings, beliefs, and values associated with sovereignty and the ontological rift. I suggest this is not quite the case. Indeed, I argue that this second transitional object is more of a liminal object-space, representing features not associated with the ontological rift or sovereignty. A playful illustration will help here. Bill Waterson's popular and humorous adult cartoon *Calvin and Hobbes* portrays stories of a child, Calvin, and his stuffed tiger, Hobbes. Whenever Calvin and Hobbes are together, Hobbes is alive, animated, and engaging in work, play, and arguments with Calvin—albeit in Calvin's imagination. When an adult is present, Hobbes is portrayed as a mere stuffed toy. In one sense, parents/adults are unable to see and relate to Hobbes other than as an inanimate toy. Hobbes is a cultural object (a toy), but he is also a tiger—representing the "animal" world. Calvin constructs Hobbes as possessing a unique self/agent.⁶⁰ Together in their play, they engage other unique selves—animated objects. According to anthropologist Eduardo Kohn, "Nonhuman selves [like Hobbes] have ontologically unique properties associated with their constitutively semiotic nature," even if this exists solely in Calvin's imagination.⁶¹ *Calvin and Hobbes* represents a type of epistemology that is interspecific perspectivist and multinaturalist—an epistemology and form of relating devoid of beliefs and values associated with sovereignty and the rift. Calvin, in other words, can imaginatively view Hobbes and other animate objects as possessing unique selves and perspectives, which also means that there are many natures or forms of living. In addition, the playful interactions between Calvin and Hobbes are not characterized by ruling or subordination/

---

59. Pruyser, *Play of the Imagination*, 59.

60. Referring to indigenous epistemologies, Castro contends that "all existents are not necessarily *de facto* persons [though] there is *de jure* nothing to prevent any species or mode of being from having that status . . . All animals and cosmic constituents are potentially and virtually persons . . . This is not a simple logical possibility but an ontological potentiality" (Castro, *Cannibal Metaphysics*, 109). In my discussion of *Calvin and Hobbes*, Hobbes, for Calvin, is a person.

61. Kohn, *How Forests Think*, 91.

subjugation or by beliefs in superiority and inferiority. Furthermore, their interactions can be viewed as a process wherein Calvin is expanding and deepening his capacity for impotentiality. That is, in playing with Hobbes, Calvin can "prefer not" to abide by the expectations, meanings, beliefs, and values of the adult world, and he can exercise impotentiality in relation to Hobbes. (And in Calvin's imagination Hobbes can make the same choice for impotentiality.) Indeed, the cartoon portrays numerous transgressive moments—moments that can be understood as instances when the creator himself, not to mention his characters, exercises the capacity for impotentiality. I think one of the reasons for the popularity of this comic strip is that it reminds adults of a time in childhood when the world was animated and we possessed more imaginative flexibility or plasticity.

I have offered one illustration, but if we turn to children's literature we see a similar thing taking place. Often other species are animated, possessing unique selves and perspectives, and this can be the case for inanimate objects. These illustrated stories are written by adults who use their imaginations to create these worlds; the creation of such worlds signifies a type of complex integration of presymbolic and symbolic epistemologies, an integration that makes use of interspecific perspectivism and multinaturalism. Many of us enjoy children's stories, but when it comes to the stories of indigenous peoples, in which, often, inanimate objects and other-than-human species are also animated and understood as possessing selves, Westerners or those caught up in the apparatuses of sovereignty and the ontological rift tend to construct these stories as primitive or childish, failing to recognize and appreciate the local knowledge and wisdom embedded in them.

While Winnicott believed that transitional phenomena occur in adulthood (e.g., in science, religion, and art), early transitional objects fade as a child increasingly internalizes cultural objects and practices. Hobbes, in Winnicott's view, "is not forgotten and it is not mourned. [Such an object] loses meaning, and this is because the transitional phenomena have become diffused, have become spread out . . . over the whole cultural field."[62] The cultural field of Western philosophies and sciences possesses apparatuses of sovereignty and the ontological rift, which children increasingly internalize as they grow toward adulthood. Hobbes loses meaning, value, and self; Hobbes's loss of singularity goes largely unnoticed as Calvin learns to take on the epistemologies of sovereignty and the ontological rift. Nature becomes monolithic, impersonal, and dominant to Calvin, rather than multiple, personal, and anarchic. Other-than-human species are constructed as lacking selves and are depersonalized, making them available for

---

62. Winnicott, "Transitional Objects," 91.

remorseless exploitation. Owing to a loss of interspecific perspectivism and multinaturalism, human beings (if they are not Othered) possess selves or souls, while other animals do not. This loss of singularity or personhood for nonhumans accompanies the rise of beliefs in human superiority, dominion, and privilege, and in the inferiority of other animals—beliefs associated with instrumental epistemologies and with relations devoid of interspecific perspectivism and multinaturalism.

Yet not all of these early experiences and ways of knowing are lost. Writer Kerry Egan's daughter truly grieved the realization that her stuffed animals were not alive, yet "The night we put them away, Mary went back to retrieve one to sleep with. Over the years, a few more have re-emerged to sit on her bed, where she holds them at night. They may no longer come alive, but the memory of the life they once lived and the love she once poured into them still exists. The love that she, or anyone, pours into the world will always exist."[63] This kind of enlivening love is still present for many adults. Grown-up authors of children's literature animate other species and inanimate objects in their work. Pet owners love their companion animals, believing them to have personalities, and some adults (scientists and others) believe in the singularities of other species and the concomitant obligation to treat them justly.[64] Yet, the Western apparatuses of sovereignty and the rift dominate the cultural fields of capitalism, nationalism, and imperialism, which crowd out, shame, and minimize forms of knowing and relating that attribute singularity to other species. The results of depriving both Othered humans and other-than-human species of singularity have proven and are proving to be incredibly destructive to these beings and to the Earth.

In summary, I have extended Bollas's concepts of unthought knowns and core experiences to refer to presymbolic epistemologies that compose organizations of experience. Early forms of knowing and relating are understood as embodied-embedded senses of self-environment, which accompany rudimentary belief in the selves of other objects-environments. Parents' good-enough anarchic care provides infants with senses of self-respect, self-esteem, and self-confidence (early agency), which are extended to objects. I suggest that this early form of knowing, devoid of the knowing associated with sovereignty and the ontological rift, represents rudimentary epistemologies and relations characterized by interspecific perspectivism and multinaturalism. Also, I argue that good-enough parental anarchic care represents an exercise of impotentiality with regard to both sovereignty

---

63. Egan, "'No Love Is Ever Wasted.'"

64. See Korsgaard, *Fellow Creatures*; Nussbaum, *Justice for Animals*; Singer, *Animal Liberation*.

and the rift. That good-enough parental care appears to close to universal (though subject to variation) among humans indicates that deactivating the ontological rift and its instrumental epistemologies is possible, even given prevalence of the rift in Western societies. I have borrowed Winnicott's notion of transitional objects to portray the movement away from this early presymbolic form of knowing. Here I indicate that the secondary transitional object helps a child's movement toward internalizing and making use of increasingly complex symbol systems, though the child (and the object) still retain the earlier rudimentary knowing characterized by interspecific perspectivism and multinaturalism. I argue further that the secondary transitional object is not mourned because the child adopts the apparatuses of the rift, leaving in the background and splitting off those epistemologies associated with interspecific perspectivism and multinaturalism. Evidence for the presence of these early forms of knowing are available and present in adult life, though they tend to be marginal.

A Fabulation: The Coming Jesus

The shift from a developmental perspective to Jesus will likely appear logically disconnected or irrelevant, especially since we have no data about the parental care given to Jesus. While there are significant differences between our present age and the historical context in which Jesus grew up, there are also similarities. Jesus was born in the cradle of Western civilization with its apparatuses of political-theological sovereignty and the ontological rift. I also believe it is safe to posit that Jesus' parents provided sufficient care, perhaps we could say anarchic or inoperative care, in the midst of the oppressive and marginalizing apparatuses of the Roman Empire. Jesus, in other words, was a product of good-enough care, which was evident in his abilities to engage and care for diverse people, to effectively deal with conflictual situations, and to forgive his enemies. In this section, I begin by sketching the social-cultural and political context of Jesus' day, making use of various scripture scholars. These scholars have a particular angle that I find helpful in imaginatively depicting the coming radical Jesus for the Anthropocene without claiming that their views represent the "real" Jesus. Within this discussion about the Jesus of scripture, I will make use of Jacob Taubes's work and Giorgio Agamben's notions of inoperativity and impotentiality as they pertain to Roman and Jewish forms of sovereignty. All this will serve as a foundation for my constructive fabulation of Jesus, who represents radical forms of living (1) that render inoperative (by exercising impotentiality) the apparatuses of sovereignty and the ontological rift; (2) that recognize, respect, and care for the singularities of all living beings, through epistemologies marked by interspecific perspectivism and multinaturalism; (3) that embrace the existential insignificance and impermanence of living beings;[65] and (4) that live out of the categorical demand to care for life and the Earth, even in the face of hopelessness.

Before starting, I want to offer some preliminary thoughts and qualifications. In earlier chapters, I claimed that Western political philosophies and theologies emerged in conjunction with the emergence of civilization, serving as apparatuses that essentialize civilization and the idea that sovereignty is existentially and ontologically necessary for human belonging. The historical Jesus was born into a time when human beings, at least, were thoroughly dependent on the apparatuses of sovereignty and on the ontological rift to found their forms of living. Indeed, as I noted in previous chapters, the Torah is full of references to God's sovereignty and its apparent necessity for the survival and flourishing of the Israelites. Nevertheless, as I have argued above, these apparatuses do not determine us, because good-enough parental care is anarchic, and early relations of care are largely free of the ontological rift. When we consider scripture, then, it is important to note that Jesus could not have been entirely free of the narratives and rituals that grounded varied forms of living associated with sovereignty and the ontological rift. Nevertheless, in the story I am telling there are glimpses of inoperativity vis-à-vis apparatuses of sovereignty in Jesus' life and ministry. However, I am less confident about inoperativity with regard to the apparatuses of the ontological rift, since there is no evidence that Jesus believed that other species have souls or are citizens of the kingdom of God. The "coming Jesus," though, will represent forms of life that render inoperative the ontological rift and sovereignty, and will affirm the singularities of all living beings.

For the last three or four decades, a number of scripture scholars have delved more deeply into the political, social, economic, and cultural milieus of Jesus' time. This represented a shift away from questions and debates about the humanity and divinity of Jesus and toward questions about how the context in which Jesus was born and lived shaped his ministry. For instance, John Dominic Crossan has argued that Jesus, born in the midst of Roman Imperialism, was a revolutionary.[66] In his view, Jesus was not a

---

65. I am stating that human beings are capable of recognizing the synchronic significance of all living beings. In time, our care for living beings means each living being is significant, because we are constructing them as such. This does not mean all living beings have existential or ontological significance beyond our caring for them. This means embracing our collective existential insignificance and impermanence.

66. Crossan, *Jesus*; Crossan, *God and Empire*.

revolutionary who aimed to overthrow Roman authorities and their cruel disciplinary regimes that demanded submission. Rather, Jesus pointed to a kingdom ruled by love. Don Cupitt viewed Jesus similarly, though more as a "moral liberator who saves us, not from our sins, but from the very concept of sin. He saves us from the government of our life by religious law."[67] Cupitt, like Crossan, also argues that "early Christianity had repudiated the Emperor cult," but that later "conciliar Christianity came increasingly to be modeled on the Emperor cult."[68] Theologians of varied persuasions have similarly interpreted scriptural references to Jesus as indicating a liberative praxis.[69] Other scholars, while acknowledging the liberating features of Jesus' ministry, focus on the economic suffering of the peoples of Palestine. Richard Horsley discusses the powers of empire, the powers of a covenant community, and the power of hope for those who suffer under the boot of oppressive economic apparatuses.[70] Horsley also depicts the political-economic project of Jesus, as he faced the apparatuses of Rome's Imperium.[71] Delving into the economics of this period, scripture scholar Douglas Oakman contends that Jesus was involved in peasant resistance vis-à-vis Rome and Jewish political-religious leaders.[72] Unfortunately, as Oakman notes, "While Jesus' historical resistance to imperial realities left its traces in early traditions, it is also true that later scribes shifted from Jesus' focus on political relations to theology . . . In this sense, the New Testament made an early contribution to obscuring Jesus' peasant resistance."[73] This view is also held by Don Cupitt, who argues that "with the rise of supernatural Christological doctrines, the moral teaching of Jesus was increasingly revised, and even reversed in meaning, by his professed followers."[74]

Oakman and Cupitt contend that New Testament writers (and others) operated, in part, to obscure Jesus' resistance and moral teaching. It is important to linger here. Those who transgress the ethos of dominant political-economic elites are often marginalized, oppressed, and killed by sovereign classes. If the transgressor becomes popular after death, these very same elites (consciously or unconsciously) work to fit the individual

---

67. Cupitt, *Ethics in the Last Days*, 29.
68. Cupitt, *Radical Theology*, 101.
69. Cone, *Black Theology of Liberation*; Gutiérrez, *Theology of Liberation*; Horsley, *Jesus and Empire*; Howard-Brook, *"Come Out My People!"*; Moltmann, *Gospel of Liberation*; Reuther, *Sexism and God Talk*; Segundo, *Liberation of Theology*.
70. Horsley, *Jesus and the Powers*.
71. Horsley, *You Shall Not Bow Down*.
72. Oakman, *Radical Jesus*.
73. Oakman, *Radical Jesus*, 15.
74. Cupitt, *Ethics in the Last Days*, 26.

into public narratives and rituals that obscure the transgressive message or, worse, that support the status quo. Consider how Martin Luther King Jr. was fictionalized after his murder such that the radical nature of his message and his critique of political, economic, and military apparatuses of the US Empire have been obscured.[75] We now have a Martin Luther King Jr. Day, streets named after him, statues, museums, and celebrations that, more often than not, conceal just how dangerous his message was to the forces of the status quo. A different example is the commercialization of Che Guevara (on T-shirts, coffee mugs, and the like). It makes sense that the early radical message of Jesus the peasant would have been absorbed into the dominant meaning-making apparatuses of the time, and that the more radical and transgressive tilt of Jesus' ministry came to be buried, especially when the educated elites began writing about Jesus. In a very short time, Jesus becomes linked to the sovereign God and the kingdom of God. Of course, it is possible that Jesus, having grown up in a religious milieu in which the sovereignty of God was espoused, accepted this, and it may have been part of his message. Fair enough; but I believe it is more likely that sovereign classes would have interpreted the messages of Jesus in such a way as to leave untouched and unquestioned their sovereignty and its necessity for political belonging.

It is not simply the New Testament authors[76] who, as Oakman claims, obscured the peasant Jesus. Theologians and other religious leaders buried and bury the transgressive Jesus under mountains of writings that obsessively focus on defining his natures. (This preoccupation reminds me of Jonathan Swift's *Gulliver's Travels*, wherein Gulliver is astounded by the angry and violent arguments within different communities about which end of an egg to break.) Add to this the theologians and liturgists after Constantine, who worked diligently to write, sing about, and worship Christ's sovereignty (and their own). Moreover, numerous theologians and religious leaders proclaimed and celebrated the sovereignty of Christ while evangelizing and ethnically cleansing indigenous populations. But, as Oakman and Cupitt posit, the transgressive spirit of Jesus could not be completely obscured by the New Testament authors or later theologians, which, I believe,

---

75. Shelby and Terry, eds., *To Shape a New World*.

76. Oakman rightly points out that these writers were already part of the elite classes because they were educated. Only a very tiny percentage of the population had the education to read and write. Understandably, whether conscious or not, these writers would have framed Jesus and his ministry from the dominant interpretive frameworks of their time. These frameworks, I contend, functioned as apparatuses of sovereignty and the ontological rift (Oakman, *Radical Jesus*, 91).

is evident in the recent work of scripture scholars like Oakman and Horsley and in numerous liberation theologians.

Scripture scholars and theologians are not alone in pointing to the transgressive traces evident in scripture. Philosopher Jacob Taubes turns to the writings of Paul,[77] arguing that his theology contains a radical message. Commenting on Taubes's work, Wolf-Daniel Hartwich, Aleida Assmann, and Jan Assmann write that Paul's Epistle to the Romans was "directed against Rome and relativizes Rome's world imperialism . . . and directed against Jerusalem in that it relativizes the limits of Israel's self-definition, which are founded on *nomos* and *ethnos*."[78] Stated differently, Jesus "frees himself from the determination of *ethnic* ties and the Roman idea of empire," as a condition of belonging vis-à-vis the *ecclesia* or polis.[79] *Nomos* and *ethnos* are intertwined with and dependent on sovereignty, whether we are talking about Roman sovereignty or the patriarchal form of sovereignty manifested in Jewish forms of leadership in that period (e.g., Herod as a client king and the sovereign classes of Pharisees and Sadducees).

Hartwich et al. explain further that Paul, from Taubes's perspective, "doesn't oppose a political theology of the Torah to the Roman *nomos* of the earth in order to establish a new national form of rule. He fundamentally negated the law as a force of political order. With this, *legitimacy is denied to all sovereigns of this world, be they imperatorial or theocratic*."[80] The Epistle, then, makes inoperative "the function of the law as ordering power, be it in the context of political order, church order, or a natural order."[81] The messiah, in other words, can neither represent nor legitimate institutions of earthly sovereignty and the use of political violence to establish belonging/identity. Instead, the messiah "can only make them irrelevant (inoperative) and ultimately replace them."[82] Nevertheless, Hartwich et al. stress that the "position of Paul doesn't imply any positive political form,"[83] though the principles of belonging are identified, namely, anarchic relations of care, inclusion, mercy, compassion, and forgiveness.

Glimpses of this radical inoperativity or impotentiality vis-à-vis human and divine sovereignty can be seen in the early Christian communities. The *ecclesia* does not rely on sovereignty and political violence to establish

---

77. Taubes, *Political Theology of Paul*.
78. Hartwich et al., Afterword, 117.
79. Hartwich et al., Afterword, 119 (italics added).
80. Hartwich, et al., Afterword, 121 (italics on *nomos* original; other italics added).
81. Hartwich et al., Afterword, 122.
82. Hartwich et al., Afterword, 142.
83. Hartwich et al., Afterword, 121.

belonging and cooperation.[84] Hartwich et al. contend that the "*ecclesia* understands itself, not as an autarchic polis that separates itself militantly from other communities, but as a new universal world order."[85] "The new political order," they continue, "is constituted by love in its two forms: love of neighbor (inward love) and love of enemy (outward love)."[86] Put differently, the *ecclesia* renders inoperative sovereignty as necessary for organizing the community, which, in turn, means that subordination and subjugation, as well as beliefs in inferiority and superiority, are also rendered inoperative. This inoperative-anarchic love also creates political spaces to include Othered persons (and other species). A hint of this is in Galatians (3:28), where we read, "There is no longer Jew or Greek, there is no longer slave or free, there is no longer male and female; for all of you are one in Christ."

Philosopher Giorgio Agamben, who is familiar with both Taubes's work and scripture, provides a philosophical view of this form of political belonging without sovereignty. In the coming community, Agamben argues, human beings can "co-belong without any representable condition of belonging," "without affirming identity."[87] According to Agamben, "What the State (or sovereign) cannot tolerate in any way is that the singularities form a community without affirming an identity, that human beings co-belong without any representable condition of belonging."[88] Using Agamben's notion of inoperativity, which I will explain in detail below, identity that is rooted in and dependent on sovereign apparatuses (Jewish or Roman in the case of Paul) is deactivated with regard to who belongs and who merits recognition and care. Taubes and Agamben, then, envision political belonging that does not depend on belief in the necessity of human or divine sovereignty. This is glimpsed in the life of a radical Jesus wherein he exercises his impotentiality toward the sovereign apparatuses of the Roman Imperium and the Jewish client-state.

Two other philosophers, Jeffery Robbins and John Caputo, show that there is an argument to be made that Pauline literature supports a

---

84. In Acts (5:1–11), Ananias and his wife, Sapphira, both die after being confronted about lying to Peter and the community regarding the sale of their property. It is not at all clear that Peter commanded this. The only detail is they died at his feet, giving no explanation as to how. What is interesting here is the underlying violence that is obviously connected to God, and this violence strikes fear into community members. This functions the same way as sovereign's exercise of political violence, which may be a vestige of the power associated with rulers.

85. Hartwich et al., Afterword, 130 (italics added).

86. Hartwich et al., Afterword.

87. Agamben, *Coming Community*, 5.

88. Agamben, *Coming Community*, 5.

nonsovereign God.[89] Robbins writes, "The crucified body of Jesus proposes not that we keep theology out of politics but that we think theology otherwise, by another paradigm, another theology, requiring us to think God otherwise, as a power of powerlessness, as opposed to the theology of omnipotence that underlies sovereignty."[90] Caputo makes a case for the weakness of God—for a God without sovereignty or the unconditional without sovereignty.[91] While I am sympathetic to Caputo's argument regarding "weak" theology and the nonsovereignty of God, I take issue with the adjectives "weak" and "strong" for a couple of reasons. First and foremost, Caputo's use of the word "weak" to name a theology of God's nonsovereignty suggests that "weak" and "strong" are opposed, that they are binary. To be sure, Caputo, relying on Paul's letters, points to the paradox that Paul lays out of the strength or power of weakness. This is a helpful rhetorical device, but one I wish to dispense with because of the negative connotation of weakness, especially in a militaristic, imperial nation like the United States. Second and more importantly, the adjective "weak" is woefully inadequate as a descriptor for the theology Caputo is constructing. In defining the adjective "weak," dictionaries use phrases like "liable to yield, break, or collapse under pressure," "lacking in bodily strength," "lacking force, potency or efficacy," and "deficient in mental power."[92] The definition and synonyms of "weak," then, are not fitting when one considers Jesus' ministry and death. For Caputo, Jesus "is the parable" of the kingdom of God, wherein the "power of the kingdom is the powerless power" that transforms people. Obviously, in relying on Paul, Caputo is saying that the life, ministry, and death of Jesus Christ are key in a weak theology. Yet, if we follow this, are we saying Jesus showed mental deficiency in forgiving his tormentors? Did Jesus lack force and potency in his ministry and in enduring torture and the cross? Did Jesus collapse under the pressure of imperial authorities? The answers, of course, are a resounding no. But this does not mean I am endorsing the idea of Jesus being strong, at least in the sense of a "strong theology" that emphasizes a sovereign God's dominance,

---

89. There are other philosophers, influenced by Abrahamic traditions, who similarly argue for nonsovereignty of God. For instance, Rafael Zawisza argues that Hannah Arendt "sees the greatest mistake of traditional metaphysics as being its vision of God, which she regards as a false premise. Consequently, this conception of God creates, quite logically, the only imagined relation of human beings to God, namely one of obedience, subservience, order, and hierarchy" (Zawisza, "Between Adamite Dreams and Original Sin," 92–93).

90. Robbins, *Radical Democracy*, 173.

91. Caputo, *Weakness of God*, 26.

92. Dictionary.com, s.v. "weak" *(adj.)*, https://www.dictionary.com/browse/weak/.

omnipotence, and subjugation of unequals. To affirm such a theology would be to trap oneself in a binary complementarity, which would reinforce human constructions of sovereignty. Instead of "weak," I prefer the term "vulnerable," which I do not place in a complementary relation with invulnerability. To do that would be to again juxtapose strength and weakness. Vulnerability, in terms of Jesus' ministry, is not in a complementary relation with the invulnerability of God. Rather, it represents the capacity to be open to caring for marginalized and oppressed Others, as well as those responsible for their suffering.

To play with this further, the coming Jesus is vulnerable in the sense of being open to the needs and sufferings of all living beings (and their needs for an environment where they can survive and flourish). His openness and exposure attend exercising his capacity for inoperativity in two senses. First, vulnerability as openness means rendering inoperative apparatuses of civilization and sovereignty that create the ontological rift and its illusions of human ontological significance and permanence. When the illusion of human ontological significance and permanence crumble, space opens for recognizing and responding to the singularities of other species and Othered human beings. Second, Jesus' vulnerability as openness attends inoperative-anarchic care, by which I mean care that, in spite of the apparatuses, provides a relation and behavior that facilitates actualizing the potentialities of all living beings. Third, Jesus' vulnerability as openness allows forms that recognize and care for and about the singularities of other species (and Othered human beings); such recognition and care require epistemologies that embrace an interspecific perspectivism and multinaturalism. Other species, in other words, have selves that are unique, and our awareness of this uniqueness carries with it the categorical demand to respect and care for them. Fourth and relatedly, Jesus' vulnerability as openness exudes anarchic care that accepts the existential reality and necessity of political plurality, not simply the plurality of human beings and their ways of belonging, but also the plurality of living nonhuman beings whose flourishing is necessary for political belonging.[93]

Let me return to scripture to further illustrate Jesus' transgressive message and his inoperativity/impotentiality vis-à-vis the political realities dependent on sovereignty and the ontological rift. In Paul's Epistle to the Philippians, we read that Jesus, "though he was in the form of God, did not regard equality with God as something to be exploited, but emptied [*kenosis*] himself, taking the form of a slave, being born in human likeness. And

---

93. Hannah Arendt, in her political philosophy, argues that the existential foundation of political life is plurality. While she is focusing on plurality with regard to human beings, I would extend this to other species. Arendt, *Human Condition*.

being found in human form, He humbled himself and became obedient to the point of death—even death on a cross" (2:6-8). There are two features here. First, kenosis can be imaginatively understood as Jesus exercising his capacity for impotentiality and so rendering inoperative divine sovereignty. This suggests the possibility of anarchic relations—relations not dependent on the ruler for organizing society. Second, to take on the form of the slave is to be captive to the apparatuses of human sovereignty that produce, legitimize, and maintain slavery. Yet, in emptying himself and taking on the form of an enslaved person, Jesus is already indicating that he is not captive to or determined by these apparatuses, whether they are Roman or Jewish. A paradigmatic illustration of this is found in Jesus' forgiving his tormentors (Luke 23:34). The Roman Empire, with its particular brand of brutal sovereignty, relied on varied means of public torture to terrorize colonized peoples, with the aim of coercing them to submit to their subjugated status.[94] When Jesus is tortured and put to death by those acting on behalf of the sovereign, Jesus forgives his Roman tormentors. Jesus' forgiveness was an act of care that instantiated impotentiality, rendering inoperative the apparatuses of Roman sovereignty and creating the possibility for repair, though there is no evidence to suggest the Roman guards responded. The act of forgiveness is not an act of an enslaved person or an act dependent on a sovereign God. Rather, it is a radical act of inoperative-anarchic care that in the moment renders the apparatuses of Imperial and Jewish sovereignty inoperative, yet these very apparatuses continued. Jesus was executed and the Roman Imperium continued for centuries.

Jesus' radical anarchic care demonstrated in this act of forgiveness reminds me of Dostoevsky's *The Brothers Karamazov*. In this novel, the Grand Inquisitor, who, in my view, represents the apparatuses of sovereignty and the sovereign classes, interrogates Jesus. The narrator says, "When the Inquisitor ceased speaking he waited some time for his Prisoner [Jesus] to answer him. [The Prisoner's] silence weighed down upon him. He saw that the Prisoner had listened intently all the time, looking gently in his face and evidently not wishing to reply. The old man longed for Him to say something, however bitter and terrible. But He suddenly approached the old man in silence and softly kissed him on his bloodless aged lips. That was all His answer. The old man shuddered."[95] The kiss represents a moment of radical inoperative care, wherein Jesus renders inoperative the rubrics of and relations between sovereign torturer and victim. Jesus is a victim of torture but is not defined by it, which creates a space for him to act in a caring way. This act invites the

94. See Crossan, *God and Empire*.
95. Dostoevsky, *Brothers Karamazov*, 654.

possibility of something new. The narrator adds, "The kiss glows in his heart, but the old man adheres to his idea."[96] The Grand Inquisitor has an experience and feels the possibility of something different, but he, like the imperial guards, ignores it so that he can adhere to his idea, his sovereign role.

The story I am telling of the coming Jesus represents a form of life wherein people exercise their capacity for impotentiality vis-à-vis the apparatuses of civilization and sovereignty. In rendering these apparatuses inoperative, as well as their relations of subordination/subjugation and illusions of superiority and inferiority, a space opens to recognize, respect, and care for the singularities of other species and Othered human beings. Such care necessarily encompasses a recognition that all species are unique (a recognition that becomes possible if one holds to interspecific perspectivism, multinaturalism, and pluralism) and dependent on the Earth for their existence and flourishing; thus, acts of inoperative/anarchic care show respect and love for the Earth and its inhabitants. In addition, in my story, the coming Jesus accepts existential insignificance and impermanence of all life—all the while in the present attributing significance to all beings by recognizing and respecting their transient singularities.

All this suggests that there is no need for either salvation or the ontological rift, and both are present in the ideas of heaven and hell. That I want to dispense with the idea of salvation does not mean that I believe human beings do not "sin" or miss the mark; but I do believe there is no original sin that emerges out of human disobedience to a sovereign God, and so there is no inevitable human alienation from God and Nature.[97] The idea of original sin, then, is associated with the human fabrication of the apparatuses that produce and maintain ontological sovereignty and rift, ideas by which we (or those of us captive to the rift) alienate ourselves from Othered human beings, other species, and the Earth. Consider the Adam and Eve myth, an origin story that is the basis of the idea of original sin. Their sin is disobedience against a sovereign God. Their story blames human beings in all ages for the evils of the world, which emerge from our inherent disposition to disobey the sovereign God. It should not be too difficult to see that this myth is an origin story for sovereignty and the rift, which means the story and its attending theologies operate as apparatuses that essentialize and ontologize sovereignty in human life and relations to the world. In contrast, any cursory reading of indigenous stories reveals an absence of

---

96. Dostoevsky, *Brothers Karamazov*, 655.

97. Rafael Zawisza argues that Arendt's philosophy rejects or overcomes the idea of original sin, focusing instead on the centrality of natality, plurality, and nonsovereign relations (Zawisza, "Between Adamite Dreams and Original Sin," 91).

origin stories preoccupied with God's sovereignty or the sovereignty of human beings.

If we reject creation stories that instantiate sovereignty and instead focus on creation as caring actions, then with the coming Jesus there is no original sin and, therefore, no need for salvation.[98] To reframe this, the coming Jesus represents a "salvific" form of living in the sense that inoperative anarchic care *in the here and now* makes possible relations with other species and other human beings that operate without the rift. Perhaps it would be better to say that the coming Jesus' anarchic, inoperative care represents a form of living that is redemptive in the sense that it deactivates the ontological rift so that we can embrace the categorical command to care for all species.

Unfortunately, I am not confident that notions of salvation and redemption can be effectively reframed, because they are so deeply ensconced in scripture and theologies that are dependent on notions of a sovereign God, of human souls, and of eternity and/or the kingdom of God. These notions are inextricably tied to social, political, and economic apparatuses that produce both the ontological rift and various instrumental epistemologies. So the coming Jesus I envision represents forms of life that are focused on anarchic care in the present—care that necessarily recognizes the singularities of all species and makes use of epistemologies that manifest interspecific perspectivism and multinaturalism. This care in the present has a future orientation in the sense that caring in the present will allow for non-existents to exist in the future. Salvation, redemption, and the kingdom of God are simply inoperative when it comes to the categorical command to care for human beings, other species, and the Earth.

To continue with the story, the coming Jesus is not focused on loving or worshiping God—sovereign or otherwise—but on loving the world—the Earth and all its inhabitants. Similarly, this coming Jesus, in loving the world, has no interest in being worshiped or in Jesus-and-me relationships. Rather, the coming Jesus is interested in inviting people to develop unique anarchic caring relations with the world. In other words, the coming Jesus represents a form of life to be lived and practiced in all of its innumerable cultural and historical iterations, which means that the coming Jesus himself becomes inoperative with regard to religious ceremonies, narratives, or creeds. The focus of the coming Jesus is instead on practices of care (1) that render inoperative apparatuses of sovereignty and the ontological rift, (2) that recognize and respect the singularities of all living beings, which

---

98. See Kerven, *Native American Myths*; Erdoes and Ortiz, eds., *American Indian Myths*; Deloria, *God Is Red*.

requires epistemologies marked by interspecific perspectivism and multinaturalism, and (3) that embrace the existential insignificance and impermanence of all living beings.

The Coming Jesus: What Hope Is There in the Anthropocene?

Jesus of the New Testament appeared during a particular period and specific location of imperial suffering. The coming Jesus for today refers to forms of living that are necessary given the realities of the Anthropocene Era with its widespread sufferings and extinctions. There is no particular place, because the Earth itself is involved. As I mentioned above, the coming Jesus does not refer to a person or to the advent of a savior or redeemer, but rather to diverse forms of living that manifest anarchic care. The absence of a savior, from within or without, means facing the dire realities of climate change that many of us experience and are contributing to. If we take away the idea of salvation and the kingdom of God, given the Anthropocene and the specter of extinction, are we left without hope? And if there is a good possibility that humans and millions of other species will become extinct,[99]

99. There are scholars from various disciplines who advocate for a posthuman world. For instance, David Benatar argues that coming into existence results in harm to the earth and that "Creating new people is thus morally problematic." For Benatar, imagining a future Earth without humanity includes the possibility of the Earth eventual healing from the harms we have done. Similarly, Australian philosopher Patricia McCormack argues for a radical compassion which has as its ends "the end of identity, the end of religion, the end of self-serving political movements, the end of human life, the end of the anthropocentric world—ultimately the end of humans' violent occupation of the Earth." Adam Kirsch identifies two different, yet related, responses to the climate emergency, namely, antihumanism and transhumanism. Antihumanism thinkers embrace the idea of human extinction, which, like Benatar, will result in the eventual repair of a biodiverse Earth. Transhumanists envision a future where nanotechnology and geoengineering result in human beings escaping vulnerability and dependency, whether that means becoming an interplanetary species or becoming nearly immortal. Kirsch believes that while these responses are different, they share a common vision, which is that they represent a world where human beings are absent. These are thoughtful scholars, and I think they share a deep sensitivity regarding the sufferings and extinctions of other-than-human species, which result from human actions. I also suspect that these and similar works stem from their experiences of eco-remorse—a remorse not only for their contributions to destruction but our collective acts of degrading planet Earth. Eco-remorse can lead people to imagine, if not desire, the hastened end to humanity as a solution to an ailing Earth. I am not unsympathetic to their views and certainly can appreciate McCormack's view of radical compassion. However, I find these responses to eco-remorse troubling for two reasons. First, these authors use the collective term "humanity" when making their arguments about the degradation of the environment and human narcissism, anthropocentrism, and exceptionalism. What is

does that mean we are to despair? In other words, what does the coming Jesus or forms of living that embrace and live out anarchic care have to do with hope? I have written about this elsewhere,[100] but it is essential to return to the issue of hope and hopelessness because of the importance of hope for us living in the Anthropocene. I briefly consider hope as it is ensconced in theological traditions before moving to a view of anarchic care that is not contingent on a particular future vision or hope.

Generally speaking, hopes are founded in the past and expressed in the present toward an uncertain or unclear yet possible, future.[101] Hope, John Caputo writes, "is the affirmation of the future,"[102] though it is a future that cannot be determined, even as we act toward that future in the present. As Edward Farley notes, "hope has the character of both waiting and acting."[103] The Israelites cried out to God about their present suffering at the hands of Pharaoh in the hope of God's present consolation and future liberation. They would not have cried out if they had not had a past relationship with and memories of Yahweh, which gave rise to their hope that God would hear and respond to their cries. While the past and present were clearer, the future was not. Once liberated, they were still uncertain of the future, which gave rise to anxiety and the occasional grumble. For some Christian theologians, including Wolfart Pannenberg,[104] hope entails a present reality of God's future kingdom. The presence of God among us, while partially realized, is connected to the future kingdom where we will experience the fullness of communion with God. The future reality reaches back into the present albeit partial in its fullness. For Henriksen, Christian "hope opens up the future in—and of—the present world."[105]

---

ignored are indigenous peoples and their voices, stories, and rituals—stories and rituals that do not affirm or promote human dominion, exceptionalism, or a rift between human beings and "Nature." In my view, these scholars are addressing the apparatuses of Western civilizations and Abrahamic religious traditions, which together function to promote and maintain anthropocentrism, human sovereignty over "Nature," and instrumental epistemologies of extraction and exploitation. Second, experiences of remorse do not always lead to constructive actions, though I am interested in depicting changes that are constructive in the sense of genuinely seeking to repent and repair relations. Wishing or desiring the extinction of all human beings is not in my view a morally beneficial response to eco-remorse. Benatar, *Better Never to Have Been*, vii; Kirsch, *Revolt against Humanity*; McCormack, *Ahuman Manifesto*, 7.

100. LaMothe, *Radical Political Theology*, 263–94.
101. See Whitehead, *Redeeming Fear*, 96.
102. Caputo, *Hoping against Hope*, 141.
103. Farley, *Deep Symbols*, 100.
104. Pannenberg, *Theology and the Kingdom of God*.
105. Henriksen, "Hope," 130.

The idea of hope is deeply embedded in scriptures and theologies. Indeed, theologian Jason Whitehead writes, "Without hope, the possibilities of love and grace as practical acts of faith lose their flavor and meaning. Hope reveals our sense that the world can be a better place, that people can relate more meaningfully, and that God is present, active, and caring."[106] Jürgen Moltmann is, in one sense, a theologian of hope. He understands hope as the passion for the possible. Using Paul Tillich's view of faith as ultimate concern, Moltmann believes that "without hope for the ultimate" human beings turn violent.[107] Add to this systematic theologian Edward Farley's view that human action is contingent on hope, and we begin to see that for many theologians, "hope" is a fundamental reality of human existence and Christianity. It is not an accident that these theologians consider hope to be essential to action, because in the Christian traditions hope is considered an existential virtue.

Hope is challenged when it comes to the Anthropocene Age, though theologians such as Catherine Keller cannot imagine life without it. She remarks, "To come to our end without hope, is this not the future we fear?"[108] "Does this hopelessness," she continues, "not lead many politically responsible and ecologically sensitive thinkers to abandon hope as nothing but cruel optimism?"[109] Her answer is to opt for a fibrous hope that does not entail a "heavenly happy ending"[110] but faces squarely the challenges of the Anthropocene Age. Keller and others see the problems of hope in terms of wishful thinking, false optimism, or enervating despair. But I think they are unnecessarily essentializing hope as well as overlooking some of the problems with the Abrahamic foundations of hope.

Consider, first, the fact that Christianity (to select but one religion of civilization) is intertwined with apparatuses of the ontological rift and sovereignty. Given this state of being so intertwined with sovereignty and the rift, Christianity's vision and the hope that emerges from it are skewed. Christians act toward a vision (e.g., the kingdom of God) that excludes other species, or if other species are included, they are welcome only for the benefit of human beings, for their use value. There are innumerable historical examples of Christian hope that were (and are) profoundly exclusionary. Such visions give rise to brutal forms of political violence and the exploitation of Othered human beings, other-than-human species, and

---

106. Whitehead, *Redeeming Fear*, 37.
107. Moltmann, *Living God*, 180.
108. Keller, *Political Theology of the Earth*, 173.
109. Keller, *Political Theology of the Earth*, 173–74.
110. Keller, *Political Theology of the Earth*, 175.

the Earth. As theologian Miguel De La Torre points out, hope is often "responsible for maintaining oppressive structures,"[111] which include Christian apparatuses. He goes on to claim that hope, "as a middle-class privilege, soothes the conscience of those complicit with oppressive structures, lulling them to do nothing except to look forward to salvific futures."[112] In their hoping, members of the middle-class numb "themselves to the pain of the oppressed."[113] Critiquing Moltmann's theology of hope, De La Torre highlights how Christian hope is imbricated with the notion of conquering,[114] or, as I put it in previous chapters, with the apparatuses of civilization and sovereignty. If there is any question about the intersection of hope, privilege, power, and violence, one need only peruse Christian history and the long, bloody trail of hopeful Christians realizing their visions of what they believed to be God's promises. Indeed, Henriksen's rosy portrayal of "Christian hope as an activity-shaped and faith-based hope that expresses itself in love for all humankind"[115] is more in line with wishful thinking in light of over two thousand years of Christian history that reveals what self-identified Christians have done and are doing to other human beings and other species. Of course, there have been individuals and communities that have loved strangers and enemies, but they pale in comparison to the innumerable instances of hate, oppression, and marginalization perpetrated by "good" Christians who possess exclusionary visions of the good. For De La Torre, "To hope is to bury one's head in the sands of peace, making us useless to meet the inevitable struggle that is coming."[116] Instead, he wants "nothing to do with Christian hope, the protagonist of too many atrocities conducted in its name." "Do not shower me with reminders of God's future promises," he continues, "show me God's present grace through your loving mercy. Do not tempt me with riches of some afterlife; convince me of your sacrificial *agape* in the here and now. In the midst of unfathomable sufferings, the earth's marginalized no longer need pious pontifications about rewards of the hereafter. Nor do they need their oppressors providing the answers for their salvation."[117]

111. De La Torre, *Embracing Hopelessness*, xiv.
112. De La Torre, *Embracing Hopelessness*, 5.
113. De La Torre, *Embracing Hopelessness*, 5.
114. De La Torre, *Embracing Hopelessness*, 45. Many Christians in the US have supported the numerous wars of conquest in the nineteenth, twentieth, and twenty-first centuries without apparent recognition that the central figure of Christian faith was tortured and murdered by the Roman Empire.
115. Henriksen, "Hope," 127.
116. De La Torre, *Embracing Hopelessness*, 96.
117. De La Torre, *Embracing Hopelessness*, 96.

A second problem with Christianity's preoccupation with hope as a theological virtue is binary thinking. By this I mean the tendency to believe that the absence of hope necessarily means despair and the absence of vision needed to act. The reality is that life is much more complicated than binary thinking. I will explain this further below, but for now let me simply say that persons can act in the present, possess a vision, but not have hope. Third and relatedly, binary thinking about hope reveals a deep and pervasive fear and anxiety about hopelessness, which is evident, in my view, in Catherine Keller's theology. She asserts that fear and anxiety stifle the imagination and the possibility of acting toward a future when one is without hope.

Let me return to the idea of a coming Jesus and attending forms of living and relating. I am sure most theologians would say that the Jesus of scripture likely had hope, but I am not so sure. Jesus, as Oakman, Horsley, and others point out, was a peasant, and the peasant classes were exploited by members of the sovereign classes—both Roman and Jewish. As De La Torre makes clear, people of marginalized and oppressed classes do not have hope, if we understand hope to be related to the vision of the sovereign classes. In my story of the coming Jesus, his acts of anarchic care are grounded in the present and possess a vision of care and justice in the present and for the possibility of non-existent beings—human and other-than-human. This is a vision that is inclusive and eschews any idea of particular beings obtaining eternal life, because all life is existentially impermanent. The coming Jesus' acts of care are not contingent on hope, and there is no binary thinking that the absence of hope means despair. This does not mean that coming Jesus or persons who exhibit forms of living that embrace anarchic care do not have moments of feeling a sense of despair, but the action in the present is determined by the categorical demand and vision to care for other species, human beings, and the Earth upon which all life depends. Barry Lopez asks, given the present and future realities of climate change, "is it still possible to face the gathering darkness and say to the physical Earth, and to all its creatures, including ourselves, fiercely and without embarrassment, I love you, and to embrace fearlessly the burning world?"[118] His answer is that it "is more important to love than to be in power."[119] Valerie Kaur's answer is "to practice love even in hopelessness."[120]

Note that the emphasis here is on practice. The coming Jesus is about the practice of anarchic care that is not contingent on hope. If we accept that the coming Jesus represents forms of living that embrace and live out the

---

118. Lopez, *Embrace Fearlessly*, 122.
119. Lopez, *Embrace Fearlessly*, 121.
120. Kaur, *See No Stranger*, 241.

categorical command to practice anarchic care, then we need to narrate new stories, rituals, and political structures that encourage and facilitate forms (1) that render inoperative apparatuses of sovereignty and the ontological rift; (2) that recognize, respect, and care for the singularities of all living beings, which requires epistemologies marked by interspecific perspectivism and multinaturalism; and (3) that embrace the existential insignificance and impermanence of all living beings.

Lest we think this is some pie-in-the-sky perspective, there are communities (besides indigenous communities) around the world that in the diverse ways have sought to recognize and respect the singularities of other species and to care for the Earth. The Norwegian town of Longyearbyen, which has over fifty nationalities among its 2,500 residents, is a place where visitors do not need a visa. As one resident remarked, "All are guests," which he understood to mean guests of the island and its animal residents. As long as the guests stay in Longyearbyen, visitors' specific nationalities or identities are inoperative. This obviously does not mean that the residents and guests do not have identities, or that somehow they sacrifice them when they arrive.[121] Rather, these unique identities are not the condition of belonging, even as these identities are retained by individuals. Moreover, the town is "governed" by a community council that is not seen as sovereign or ruling over the residents.[122] This is a town that is inclusive—radically so—and reflects a kind of differentiated stance necessary for the existence of a radical community—whether secular or religious. I suspect also that the condition of belonging centers on hospitality, humility, respect, and care for others. There is also the German Kommune Niederkaufungen.[123] And there are religious and secular eco-villages emerging around the world.[124] Whether this will be enough is not the question, because that question makes care contingent on hope. The question is how to find ways to live that

---

121. "Longyearbyen" (https://en.visitsvalbard.com/visitor-information/destinations/longyearbyen/).

122. "Longyearbyen" (https://en.visitsvalbard.com/visitor-information/destinations/longyearbyen/).

123. English—Kommune Niederkaufungen (https://kommune-niederkaufungen.de/).

124. There are a number of readily available resources for faith communities as they deliberate on how to be more ecological in their dwelling: the Eco Church Christian environmental scheme for churches by A Rocha (https://ecochurch.arocha.org.uk/); the Interfaith Center for Sustainable Development (interfaithsustain.com/); and the Green Churches Network (https://greenchurches.ca/), to name a few. There are also secular ecovillages, including the Global Ecovillage Network: Community for a Regenerative World (https://ecovillage.org/).

embrace the categorical demand to care for creation and its inhabitants—an anarchic care that is not contingent on hope.

Conclusion

All stories told or lived come to an end, sinking beneath the waves of time. We may have some idea or even confidence about how our stories will end, but the endings are not as important as how our stories are lived. The crucifixion is a horrific end to the story of Jesus (or to the story of any other human being), but, in my telling of the story of the coming Jesus, this tragic end does not diminish the life lived even when we exclude the resurrection. In other words, we do not, in the story of this chapter, need a happy, glorious end of resurrection in order to find meaning and value in the life and service of this Jewish peasant. Instead, we look to forms of life that render inoperative the apparatuses of sovereignty and the epistemologies of the ontological rift—forms of life that foster practices of anarchic care. Human life and our stories will eventually end, but it is in present acts of caring for the singularities of all life where existential (temporal) significance, meaning, and purpose are found. Let me end with an excerpt from Barry Lopez's book: "Successfully locating the proper frame of mind and then acting is not, I think, about refusing to accommodate fear. It's about the cultivation of love."[125]

---

125. Lopez, *Embrace Fearlessly*, 200.

Bibliography

Agamben, Giorgio. *The Coming Community*. Translated by Michael Hardt. Theory Out of Bounds. Minneapolis: University of Minnesota Press, 2013.

———. *Creation and Anarchy: The Work of Art and the Religion of Capitalism*. Translated by Adam Kotsko. Meridian: Crossing Aesthetics. Stanford: Stanford University Press, 2019.

———. *Homo Sacer: Sovereign Power and Bare Life*. Translated by Daniel Heller-Roazen. Meridian: Crossing Aesthetics. Stanford: Stanford University Press, 1998.

———. *The Open: Man and Animal*. Translated by Kevin Attell. Meridian: Crossing Aesthetics. Stanford: Stanford University Press, 2004.

———. *Potentialities: Collected Essays in Philosophy*. Translated by Daniel Heller-Roazen. Meridian: Crossing Aesthetics. Stanford: Stanford University Press, 1999.

———. *State of Exception*. Translated by Kevin Attell. Chicago: University of Chicago Press, 2005.

———. *When the House Burns Down*. Translated by Kevin Attell. The Italian List. London: Seagull, 2022.

Ágoston, Csilla, et al. "Identifying Types of Eco-Anxiety, Eco-Guilt, Eco-Grief, and Eco-Coping in a Climate-Sensitive Population: A Qualitative Study." *International Journal of Environmental Research in Public Health* 19.4 (2022) 2461. https://doi.org/10.3390/ijerph19042461/.

Altman, Neil. "Black and White Thinking." *Psychoanalytic Dialogues* 10 (2000) 589–605.

American Psychiatric Association. *Diagnostic and Statistical Manual of Mental Disorders: DSM-5-TR*. 5th ed., text revision. Washington, DC: American Psychiatric Association Publishing, 2022

Anderson, Benedict. *Imagined Communities*. London: Verso, 1983.

Arendt, Hannah. *The Human Condition*. Chicago: University of Chicago Press, 1958.

———. *The Last Interview*. Brooklyn: Melville House, 2013.

———. *On Violence*. New York: Harvest/HBJ, 1970.

———. *The Origins of Totalitarianism*. New York: Harvest, 1994.

Ash, Gabriel. "The Empire's Coming Crisis." In *The Imperial Tense*, edited by Andrew J. Bacevich, 238–44. Chicago: Dee, 2003.

Auestad, Lene, ed. *Nationalism and the Body Politic*. New International Library of Group Analysis. London: Routledge, 2019.

Augustine. *City of God*. Translated by Henry Bettenson. 1972. Reprint, Penguin Classics. Harmondsworth, UK: Penguin, 1984.

———. *The Confessions of St. Augustine*. Translated by Rex Warren. A Mentor Book. New York: New American Library, 1963.

Bacevich, Andrew J. *American Empire*. Cambridge: Harvard University Press, 2002.

———, ed. *The Imperial Tense: Prospects and Problems of American Empire*. Chicago: Dee, 2003.

———. *The New American Militarism*. New York: Oxford University Press, 2005.

Barnett, Joshua Trey. *Mourning in the Anthropocene: Ecological Grief and Earthly Coexistence*. East Lansing: Michigan State University Press, 2022.

Baptist, Edward E. *The Half Has Never Been Told: Slavery and the Making of American Capitalism*. New York: Basic Books, 2014.

Barker, Ernest, trans. *The Politics of Aristotle*. 1958. Reprint, Oxford: Oxford University Press, 1971.

Barry, John M. *Roger Williams and the Creation of the American Soul*. New York: Viking, 2012.

Becker, Gary S. *The Economic Approach to Human Behavior*. Chicago: University of Chicago Press, 1978.

Bell, Daniel. *The Cultural Contradictions of Capitalism*. 20th anniversary ed. With a new afterword by the author. New York: Basic Books, 1996.

Benatar, David. *Better Never to Have Been: The Harm of Coming into Existence*. Oxford: Clarendon, 2008.

Bender, Peter. "The New Rome." In *Imperial Tense*, edited by Andrew J. Bacevich, 81–92. Chicago: Dee, 2003.

Berkowitz, Roger. "Actions That Deserved to Be Remembered: Transcendence and Immortality in a Secular World." In *"Faith in the World": Post-Secular Readings of Hannah Arendt*, edited by Rafael Zawisza and Ludger Hagedorn, 169–88. Frankfurt: Campus, 2021.

Bielek-Robson, Agata. "Amor Mundi: The Marrano Background of Hannah Arendt's Love for the World." In *"Faith in the World": Post-Secular Readings of Hannah Arendt*, edited by Rafael Zawisza and Ludger Hagedorn, 61–86. Frankfurt: Campus, 2021.

Birch, Kean. *A Research Agenda for Neoliberalism*. Elgar Research Agendas. Cheltenham, UK: Elgar, 2017.

Black, Daniel. *The Coming*. New York: St. Martin's, 2015.

Bodin, Jean. *On Sovereignty: Six Books on the Commonwealth*. Edited and translated by Julian H. Franklin. Cambridge Texts in the History of Political Thought. 1992. Reprint, n.p.: Seven Treasures, 2009.

Bollas, Christopher. *The Shadow of the Object*. New York: Columbia University Press, 1987.

Boorstin, Daniel. *The Image: A Guide to Pseudo-Events in America*. New York: Vintage, 1987.

Brown, Wendy. *Nihilistic Times*. Cambridge: Belknap, 2023.

———. *Undoing the Demos*. New York: Zone Books, distributed by MIT Press, 2015.

———. *Walled States, Waning Sovereignty*. New York: Zone Books, distributed by MIT Press, 2014.

———. "We Are All Democrats Now." In *Democracy in What State?*, by Giorgio Agamben et al., 44–57. New Directions. New York: Columbia University Press, 2012.
Bubeck, Diemut Elisabet. *Care, Gender, and Justice.* Oxford: Clarendon, 1995.
Buber, Martin. *I and Thou.* 2nd ed. New York: Scribner, 1958.
Camus, Albert. *The Plague.* Translated by Stuart Gilbert. Vintage International Series. New York: Vintage, 1991.
Caputo, John D. *Hoping against Hope: Confessions of a Postmodern Pilgrim.* Theology for the People. Minneapolis: Fortress, 2015.
———. *The Weakness of God: A Theology of the Event.* Indiana Series in the Philosophy of Religion. Bloomington: Indiana University Press, 2006.
The Care Collective (Chatzidakis, Andreas, et al.). *The Care Manifesto: The Politics of Interdependence.* London: Verso, 2020.
Carrette, Jeremy R., and Richard King. *Selling Spirituality: The Silent Takeover of Religion.* London: Routledge, 2004.
Casey, Edward S. *The Fate of Place: A Philosophical History.* 1st paperback ed. Berkeley: University of California Press, 1998.
Castro, Eduardo Viveiros de. *Cannibal Metaphysics.* Edited and translated by Peter Skafish. Univocal. Minneapolis: Minnesota University Press, 2017.
Chari, Anita. *A Political Economy of the Senses: Neoliberalism, Reification, Critique.* New Directions in Critical Theory. New York: Columbia University Press, 2015.
Chen, Patrick S. *Radical Love: An Introduction to Queer Theology.* New York: Seabury, 2011.
Chomsky, Noam. *Imperial Ambitions.* Interviews by David Barsamian. New York: Metropolitan, 2005.
Clinebell, Howard. *Ecotherapy: Healing Ourselves, Healing the Earth; A Guide to Ecologically Grounded Personality Theory, Spirituality, Therapy, and Education.* Minneapolis: Fortress, 1996.
Coates, Ta-Nehisi. *Between the World and Me.* New York: Spiegel & Grau, 2015.
Comtesse, Hannah, et al. "Ecological Grief as a Response to Environmental Change: A Mental Health Risk or Functional Response?" *International Journal of Environmental Research and Public Health* 18 (2021) 734.
Colebrook, Claire, and Jason Maxwell. *Agamben.* Key Contemporary Thinkers. Cambridge: Polity, 2016.
Cone, James. *A Black Theology of Liberation.* 1970. Reprint, Maryknoll, NY: Orbis, 2010.
———. *The Cross and the Lynching Tree.* Maryknoll, NY: Orbis, 2011.
Couldry, Nick. *Why Voice Matters: Culture and Politics after Neoliberalism.* London: Sage, 2010.
Cox, Harvey. *The Market as God.* Cambridge: Harvard University Press, 2016.
Crandon, Tara, et al. "A Social-Ecological Perspective on Climate Anxiety in Children and Adolescents." *Nature Climate Change* 12 (2022) 123–31.
Crawford, Neta C. *The Pentagon, Climate Change, and War: Charting the Rise and Fall of US Military Emissions.* Cambridge: MIT Press, 2022.
Crockett, Clayton. *Radical Political Theology.* Insurrections. New York: Columbia University Press, 2012.
Crossan, John. *Jesus: God and Empire.* 1st ed. San Francisco: HarperSanFrancisco, 2007.
———. *A Revolutionary Biography.* San Francisco: HarperSanFrancisco, 1995.
Crutzen, Paul, and Edward Stoermer. "The 'Anthropocene.'" *IGB Global Change Newsletter* 41 (2000) 17–18.

Cunsolo, Ashlee, and Karen Landman, eds. *Mourning Nature: Hope at the Heart of Ecological Loss and Grief.* Montreal: McGill-Queen's University Press, 2017.

Cunsolo, Ashlee, and Neville Ellis. "Ecological Grief as a Mental Health Response to Climate Change–Related Loss." *Nature Climate Change* 8 (2018) 275–81.

Cunsolo, Ashlee, et al. "Ecological Grief and Anxiety: The Start of a Healthy Response to Climate Change?" *The Lancet Planetary Health* 4.7 (2020) 261–63.

Cupitt, Don. *Ethics in the Last Days of Humanity.* Salem, OR: Polebridge, 2016.

———. *Radical Theology.* Santa Rosa, CA: Polebridge, 2006.

Cushman, Phillip. *Constructing the Self, Constructing America.* Boston: De Capo, 1995.

Cvetkovich, Ann. *Depression: A Public Feeling.* Durham, NC: Duke University Press, 2012.

Danner, Mark. *Stripping the Body Bare: Politics, Violence, War.* New York: Nation Books, 2009.

Dardot, Pierre, and Christian Laval. *The New Way of the World: On Neoliberal Society.* Translated by Gregory Elliott. London: Verso, 2013.

Davenport, Coral. "Pentagon Signals Security Risks of Climate Change," *New York Times,* October 13, 2014, http://www.nytimes.com/2014/10/14/us/pentagon-says-global-warming-presents-immediate-security-threat.html?_r=1/.

Debord, Guy. *The Society of the Spectacle.* Translated by Donald Nicholson-Smith. New York: Zone Books, 1994.

De La Torre, Miguel. *Embracing Hopelessness.* Minneapolis: Fortress, 2017.

De St. Croix, G. E. M. *Christian Persecution, Martyrdom, and Orthodoxy.* Edited by Michael Whitby and Joseph Streeter. Oxford: Oxford University Press. 2006.

Deleuze, Gilles, and Félix Guattari. *Anti-Oedipus: Capitalism and Schizophrenia.* Translated from the French by Robert Hurley et al. Minneapolis: University of Minnesota Press, 2003.

———. *A Thousand Plateaus: Capitalism and Schizophrenia.* Translation and foreword by Brian Massumi. Minneapolis: University of Minnesota Press, 1987.

Deloria, Vine. *God Is Red.* 3rd ed. Golden, CO: Fulcrum, 2003.

Derrida, Jacques. *The Animal That Therefore I Am.* Edited by Marie-Louise Mallet. Translated by David Wills. Perspectives in Continental Philosophy. New York: Fordham University Press, 2008.

Dickinson, Colby. "The Absence of Gender." In *Agamben's Coming Philosophy: Finding a New Use for Theology,* edited by Colby Dickinson and Adam Kotsko, 167–82. London: Rowman & Littlefield, 2015.

Doerner, Klaus. *Madmen and the Bourgeoisie.* Translated by Joachim Neugroschel and Jean Steinberg. Oxford: Blackwell, 1981.

Dostoevsky, Fyodor. *The Brothers Karamazov.* Translated by Constance Garnett. New York: Lowell, 2009.

Dufour, Dany-Robert. *The Art of Shrinking Heads: On the New Servitude of the Liberated in the Age of Total Capitalism.* Translated by David Macey. Cambridge: Polity, 2008.

Duménil, Girard, and Dominique Lévy. *The Crisis of Neoliberalism.* Cambridge: Harvard University Press, 2011.

Eagleton, Terry. *After Theory.* New York: Basic Books, 2003.

———. *Critical Revolutionaries.* New Haven: Yale University Press, 2022.

———. *Tragedy.* New Haven: Yale University Press, 2020.

———. *Why Marx Was Right.* New Haven: Yale University Press, 2018.

Egan, Kerry. "'No Love Is Ever Wasted.'" Modern Love. *New York Times*, March 16, 2023. https://www.nytimes.com/2023/03/10/style/modern-love-no-love-is-ever-wasted.html/.
Emerson, Ralph Waldo. *Nature and Selected Essays*. Edited with an introduction by Larzer Ziff. Penguin Classics. New York: Penguin, 2003.
Engster, Daniel. *The Heart of Justice: Care Ethics and Political Theory*. Oxford: Oxford University Press, 2007.
Erdoes, Richard, and Alphonso Ortiz, eds. *American Indian Myths and Legends*. Pantheon Fairy Tale & Folklore Library. New York: Pantheon, 1984.
Erikson, Erik. *Childhood and Society*. New York: Norton, 1950.
Fanon, Frantz. *Black Skin, White Masks*. 1952. Reprint, translated by Richard Philcox. With a foreword by Anthony Appiah. New York: Grove, 2008.
Farley, Edward. *Deep Symbols*. Valley Forge, PA: Trinity, 1996.
———. "Sin." In *Dictionary of Pastoral Care and Counseling*, edited by Rodney J. Hunter et al., 1173–76. Expanded ed. with CD-ROM. Nashville: Abingdon, 2005
Fergusson, Niall. *Colossus: The Rise and Fall of the American Empire*. New York: Penguin, 2004.
Feuerbach, Ludwig. *The Essence of Christianity*. Translated by George Eliot. Reprint, Great Books in Philosophy. New York: Prometheus, 1989.
Fingarette, Herbert. *Self-Deception*. 1969. Reprint, Berkeley: University of California Press, 2000.
Fish, Carl Russell. *The Path of Empire: A Chronicle of the United States as a World Power*. 1919. Reprint, Toronto: Glasgow Brook, 1978.
Ford, Richard Q. *Jesus' Parables Speak to Power and Greed*. Westar Studies. Eugene, OR: Cascade, 2022.
Foster, John Bellamy. *The Return of Nature*. New York: Monthly Review Press, 2020.
Frank, Thomas. *One Market under God: Extreme Capitalism, Market Populism, and the End of Economic Democracy*. New York: Anchor, 2000.
Fraser, Nancy. *Cannibal Capitalism*. London: Verso, 2022.
Fraser, Nancy, and Axel Honneth. *Redistribution or Recognition?* Translated by Joel Golb et al. London: Verso, 2003.
Friedman, Milton. *Capitalism and Freedom*. With the assistance of Rose D. Friedman. With a new foreword by Binyamin Appelbaum. Chicago: University of Chicago Press, 2020.
Freud, Sigmund. *Civilization and Its Discontents*. Edited and translated by James Strachey. In *The Standard Edition* 21:64–148. 24 vols. 1963. Reprint, London: Hogarth, 1999. First published in 1930.
———. *The Future of an Illusion*. Edited and translated by James Strachey. In *The Standard Edition* 21:5–58. 24 vols. 1963. Reprint, London: Hogarth, 1999. First published in 1927.
———. *General Theory of Neurosis*. Edited and translated by James Strachey. In *The Standard Edition*, 16:234–63. 24 vols. 1968. Reprint, London: Hogarth, 1999. First published in 1917.
———. *Totem and Taboo*. Edited and translated by James Strachey. In *The Standard Edition*, 12:vii–162. 24 vols. 1950. Reprint, London: Hogarth, 1999. First published in 1913.
Fromm, Erich. *The Dogma of Christ*. New York: Holt, Rinehart and Winston, 1963.
Fulbright, J. William. *The Arrogance of Power*. New York: Random House, 1966.

Gabbard, Glen O. *Psychodynamic Psychiatry in Clinical Practice*. 2nd ed. Washington, DC: American Psychiatric Press, 1994.

Gardner, Lloyd, and Marilyn Young, eds. *The New American Empire: A 21st Century Teach-In on US Foreign Policy*. New York: New Press, 2005.

Gardner, Stephen M. *A Perfect Moral Storm: The Ethical Tragedy of Climate Change*. Environmental Ethics and Science Policy. New York: Oxford University Press, 2011.

Gauthier, David J. *Martin Heidegger, Emmanuel Levinas, and the Politics of Dwelling*. Lanham, MD: Lexington, 2011.

Gellner, Ernst. *Nations and Nationalism*. 2nd printing. Ithaca: Cornell University Press, 1983.

George, Andrew R., trans. *The Epic of Gilgamesh*. Penguin Classics. London: Penguin, 2003.

———. Introduction. In *The Epic of Gilgamesh*, edited by Andrew R. George, xiii–liv. Penguin Classics. London: Penguin, 2003.

Gilman, Sander L. *Difference and Pathology*. Ithaca: Cornell University Press, 1985.

———. *Disease and Representation*. Ithaca: Cornell University Press, 1988.

———. *Picturing Health and Illness*. Baltimore: Johns Hopkins University Press, 1995.

Girard, René. *Violence and the Sacred*. Baltimore: Johns Hopkins University Press, 1972.

Giroux, Henry A. *Disposable Youth: Racialized Memories, and the Culture of Cruelty*. Framing 21st Century Social Issues. New York: Routledge, 2012.

Go, Julian. *Patterns of Empire: The British and American Empires, 1688 to the Present*. Cambridge: Cambridge University Press, 2012.

Goodall, Jane. *In the Shadow of Man*. Rev. ed. 1st Mariner Books ed. New York: Houghton Mifflin Harcourt, 2010.

Graham, Larry Kent. *Care of Persons, Care of Worlds: A Psychosystems Approach to Pastoral Care and Counseling*. Nashville: Abingdon, 1992.

Gray, John. *False Dawn: The Delusions of Global Capitalism*. New York: New Press, 2000.

Grayling, A. C. *The History of Philosophy*. New York: Penguin, 2019.

Grosby, Steven. *Nationalism: A Very Short Introduction*. Very Short Introductions 134. Oxford: Oxford University Press, 2005.

Groys, Boris. *Philosophy of Care*. London: Verso, 2022.

Guess, Raymond. *Changing the Subject: Philosophy from Socrates to Adorno*. Cambridge: Harvard University Press, 2017.

Gutiérrez, Gustavo. *A Theology of Liberation*. Maryknoll, NY: Orbis, 1985.

Hall, Douglas John. *Thinking the Faith*. 1st Fortress Press ed. Minneapolis: Fortress, 1991.

Hall, Stuart. *Cultural Studies 1983*. Stuart Hall, Selected Writings. Durham, NC: Duke University Press, 2016.

———, ed. *Representation: Cultural Representations and Signifying Practices*. Culture, Media, and Identities. London: Sage, 1997.

Hamilton, Clive, et al., comps. *The Anthropocene and the Global Environmental Crisis*. London: Routledge, 2015.

Hamington, Maurice. *Embodied Care*. Urbana: University of Illinois Press, 2004.

Hamington, Maurice, and Richard Flower, eds. *Care Ethics in the Age of Precarity*. Minneapolis: University of Minnesota Press, 2021.

Hardt, Michael, and Antonio Negri. *Empire*. Cambridge: Harvard University Press, 2000.

Harman, Chris. *A People's History of the World*. New ed. London: Verso, 2017.
Hartwich, Wolf-Daniel, et al. Afterword. In *The Political Theology of Paul*, by Jacob Taubes, 115–42. Edited by Aleida Assmann et al. Translated by Dana Hollander. Cultural Memory in the Present. Stanford: Stanford University Press, 2004.
Harvey, David. *A Brief History of Neoliberalism*. London: Oxford University Press, 2007.
———. *The Enigma of Capital and the Crisis of Capitalism*. Oxford: Oxford University Press, 2010.
Hayek, F. A. *The Road to Serfdom: Text and Documents*. Edited by Bruce Caldwell. Definitive ed. The Collected Works of F. A. Hayek 2. Chicago: University of Chicago Press, 2007.
Held, Virginia. *The Ethics of Care: Personal, Political, and Global*. Oxford: Oxford University Press, 2006.
Helsel, Phillip Browning. "Loving the World: Place Attachment and Environment in Pastoral Theology." *Journal of Pastoral Theology* 28.1 (2018) 22–33.
———. *Pastoral Power beyond Psychology's Marginalization*. New Approaches to Religion and Power. New York: Palgrave Macmillan, 2015.
Henriksen, Jan-Olav. "Hope: A Theological Exploration." *Studia Theologica—A Nordic Journal of Theology* 73.2 (2019) 117–33.
Hendricks, Obery M., Jr. *The Universe Bends toward Justice*. Maryknoll, NY: Orbis, 2011.
Herring, George C. *From Colony To Superpower: U.S. Foreign Relations since 1776*. The Oxford History of the United States. Oxford: Oxford University Press, 2008.
Hinds, Jay Paul. *A Gift Grows in the Ghetto*. Louisville: Westminster John Knox, 2022
Hochschild, Arlie Russell. *The Managed Heart: Commercialization of Human Feeling*. Updated ed., with a new preface. Berkeley: University of California Press, 2012.
Hoggett, Paul, ed. *Climate Psychology: On Indifference to Disaster*. Studies in the Psychosocial. Cham, Switzerland: Palgrave Macmillan, 2019.
———. "Governance and Social Anxieties." *Organizational and Social Dynamics* 13.1 (2013) 69–78.
Holifield, E. Brooks. *A History of Pastoral Care in America*. 1983. Reprint, Eugene, OR: Wipf & Stock, 2005.
Horsley, Richard A. *Covenant Economics: A Biblical Vision of Justice for All*. Louisville: Westminster John Knox, 2009.
———. *Jesus and Empire*. Minneapolis: Fortress, 2003.
———. *Jesus and the Powers: Conflict, Covenant, and the Hope of the Poor*. Minneapolis: Fortress, 2011.
———. *You Shall Not Bow Down and Serve Them*. Eugene, OR: Cascade, 2021.
Howard-Brook, Wes. *"Come Out My People!" God's Call Out of Empire in the Bible and Beyond*. Maryknoll, NY: Orbis, 2010.
Hudis, Peter. *Marx's Concept of the Alternative to Capitalism*. Chicago: Haymarket, 2013.
Hughes, Richard T. *Christian America and the Kingdom of God*. Urbana: University of Illinois Press, 2009.
Ikenberry, G. John. "America's Imperial Ambition." *Foreign Affairs* (2002) 44–60.
Illouz, Eva. *Cold Intimacies: The Making of Emotional Capitalism*. New York: Polity, 2007.
Intergovernmental Panel on Climate Change. *The Sixth Assessment Report*. Website. https://www.ipcc.ch/assessment-report/ar6/.

———. *Intergovernmental Panel on Climate Change 2023*. Website. https://www.ipcc.ch/?__cf_chl_tk=B6kJ9fhVaHc4ZD_Jky3zL1c8Hpry3Iboqelkltm_Lho-1679382216-0-gaNycGzNCWU/.
Isenberg, Nancy. *White Trash*. New York: Viking, 2016.
Jodelet, Denise. *Madness and Social Representation*. Translated by Tim Pownall. Sacramento: University of California Press, 1991.
Johnson, Chalmers. *Blowback*. New York: Owl, 1999.
———. *Dismantling the Empire*. New York: Metropolitan, 2010.
———. *Sorrows of Empire*. 1st Owl Books ed. New York: Holt, 2005.
Jones, Daniel Stedman. *Masters of the Universe*. Princeton: Princeton University Press, 2012.
Kamal, Baher. "Revealed: Rich Countries Miserably Fall Below Their Climate Promises, Further Indebt the Poor." *Inter Press Service*, November 4, 2022. https://www.ipsnews.net/2022/11/revealed-rich-countries-miserably-fall-climate-promises-indebt-poor/.
Kaplan, Amy. *The Anarchy of Empire in the Making of U.S. Culture*. Convergences. Cambridge: Harvard University Press, 2002.
Kassouf, Susan. "Psychoanalysis and Climate Change." *American Imago* 74.2 (2017) 141–71.
Kaur, Valerie. *See No Stranger: A Memoir and Manifesto of Revolutionary Love*. New York: One World, 2020.
Keller, Catherine. *Political Theology of the Earth*. Insurrections. New York: Columbia University Press, 2018.
Kendi, Ibram X., and Jason Reynolds. *Stamped from the Beginning. The Definitive History of Racist Ideas in America*. 2nd printing. New York: Bold Type, 2023.
Kerven, Rosiland. *Native American Myths: Collected 1636–1919*. Sharperton Morpeth, UK: Talking Stone, 2018.
Kestenberg, Judith, and Joan Weinstein. "Transitional Objects and Body Image Formation." In *Between Reality and Fantasy*, edited by Simon Grolnick and Leonard Barkin, 75–96. Northvale, NJ: Aronson, 1988.
King, Michael. "Greenspan: Crisis Prompted Re-examination of Economic Beliefs." *Newsmax Money* (website), October 23, 2013. https://www.newsmax.com/Finance/Economy/Greenspan-crisis-financial-bubbles/2013/10/23/ID/532650/.
Kinzer, Steven. *Overthrow: America's Century of Regime Change from Hawaii to Iraq*. New York: Times, 2006.
Kirsch, Adam. *The Revolt against Humanity: Imagining a Future without Us*. New York: Columbia Global Reports, 2023.
Kierkegaard, Søren. *Concluding Unscientific Postscript to the Philosophical Fragments*. Edited and translated with introduction and notes by Howard V. Hong and Edna H. Hong. 2 vols. Kierkegaard's Writings 12. Princeton: Princeton University Press, 1992.
Kishik, David. *The Power of Life: Agamben and the Coming Politics*. Stanford: Stanford University Press, 2012.
Klein, Naomi. *The Shock Doctrine*. New York: Holt, 2007.
———. *This Changes Everything*. New York: Simon & Schuster, 2014.
Kohn, Eduardo. *How Forests Think*. Berkeley: University of California Press, 2013.
Kolbert, Elizabeth. *The Sixth Extinction: An Unnatural History*. New York: Holt, 2014.

Kompridis, Nikolas. "Nonhuman Agency and Human Normativity." In *Nature and Value*, edited by Akeel Bilgrami, 240–60. New York: Columbia University Press, 2020.

Korsgaard, Christine M. *Fellow Creatures: Our Obligations to Other Animals*. Oxford: Oxford University Press, 2020.

Kovel, Joel. *The Radical Spirit*. London: Free Association Books, 1988.

———. *White Racism, a Psychohistory*. New York: Pantheon, 1970.

Krauthammer, Charles. "The Unipolar Era. In *The Imperial Tense*, edited by Andrew J. Bacevich, 47–65. Chicago: Dee, 2003.

LaMothe, Ryan. *Care of Souls, Care of Polis: Toward a Political Pastoral Theology*. Eugene, OR: Cascade, 2017.

———. "The Least of These: Political-Economic Dimensions of Roman Catholic Pastoral Theology." *Journal of Pastoral Theology* 28.2 (2018) 59–77. doi: 10.1080/10649867.2018.1513714/.

———. *Pastoral Care and the Anthropocene Age*. Emerging Perspectives in Pastoral Theology. Lanham, MD: Lexington, 2022.

———. "Pastoral Theology and the Problem of Political Violence," *Journal of Pastoral Theology* (2021) 1–20. doi: 10.1080/10649867.2021.2005287/.

———. "Patriotism: An Imaginary Love." In *Intricacies of Patriotism*, edited by Maciej Hulas and Stanislaw Fel, 81–104. Frankfurt: Lang, 2015.

———. *A Radical Political Theology for the Anthropocene*. Eugene, OR: Cascade, 2021.

———. "Raising Amos: Diagnosing Social-Political Pathologies as a Spiritual Practice." *Pastoral Psychology* (2022) 623–38. doi: 10.1007/s11089-22-01022-22/.

Layton, Lynn. *Toward a Social Psychoanalysis*. Edited by Marianna Leavy-Sperounis. Relational Perspectives. London: Routledge, 2020.

Lane, Melissa. *The Birth of Politics: Eight Greek and Roman Political Ideas and Why They Matter*. Princeton: Princeton University Press, 2014.

Latour, Bruno. *Facing Gaia: Eight Lectures on Climate Change*. Translated by Catherine Porter. Cambridge: Polity, 2017.

———. *We Have Never Been Modern*. Translated by Catherine Porter. Cambridge: Harvard University Press, 1993.

Laymon, Kiese. *Heavy: An American Memoir*. First Scribner trade paperback ed. New York: Scribner, 2019.

Lear, Jonathan. *Radical Hope: Ethics in the Face of Cultural Devastation*. Cambridge: Harvard University Press, 2006.

Leroi, Armand Marie. *The Lagoon: How Aristotle Invented Science*. With translations from the Greek by Simon MacPherson and original illustrations by David Koutsogiannopoulos. New York: Viking, 2014.

Levinas, Emmanuel. *Totality and Infinity*. Translated by Alphonso Lingis. Duquesne Studies. Philosophical Series 24. Pittsburgh: Duquesne University Press, 1969.

Lieven, Anatol. *Climate Change and the Nation State*. New York: Oxford, 2021.

London, Jack. *Call of the Wild*. In *The Unabridged Jack London*, edited by Lawrence Teacher and Richard E. Nicholls, 759–832. Philadelphia: Running, 1981.

Lopez, Barry. *Embrace Fearlessly the Burning World*. New York: Random House, 2022.

Lukács, Georg. *History and Class Consciousness*. Translated by Rodney Livingstone. Cambridge: MIT Press, 1968.

Lundestad, Geir. *The American "Empire" and Other Studies of US Foreign Policy in a Comparative Perspective*. Oxford: Oxford University Press, 1990.

MacDonald, G. Jeffery. *Thieves in the Temple: The Christian Church and the Selling of the American Soul*. New York: Basic Books, 2010.
Macmurray, John. *Persons in Relation*. Gifford Lectures 1954. 1961. Reprint, Atlantic Highlands, NJ: Humanities, 1991.
Macy, Joanna. "Working through Environmental Despair." In *Ecopsychology: Restoring the Earth, Healing the Mind*, edited by Theodore Roszak et al., 240–69. San Francisco: Sierra Club Books, 1995.
Mander, Jerry. *The Capitalism Papers: Fatal Flaws in an Obsolete System*. Berkeley: Counterpoint, 2012.
Mann, Bonnie. *Sovereign Masculinity: Gender Lessons from the War on Terror*. Studies in Feminist Philosophy. New York: Oxford University Press, 2014.
Mann, Geoff. *Disassembly Required*. Edinburgh: AK, 2013.
Mantena, Karuna. "Showdown for Nonviolence: The Theory and Practice of Nonviolent Politics." In *To Shape the New World*, edited by Tommie Shelby and Brandon M. Terry, 78–104. Cambridge: Belknap, 2018.
Margalit, Avishai. *The Decent Society*. Cambridge: Harvard University Press, 1996.
Mason, Mike. *Turbulent Empires*. Montreal: McGill-Queen's University Press.
Mattei, Clara E. *The Capital Order: How Economists Invented Austerity and Paved the Way for Fascism*. Chicago: University of Chicago Press, 2022.
McCarroll, Pamela R. "Listening for the Cries of the Earth: Practical Theology in the Anthropocene." *International Journal of Practical Theology* 24.1 (2020) 29–46.
McCormack, Pamela. *The Ahuman Manifesto: Activism for the End of the Anthropocene*. New York: Bloomsbury Academic, 2020.
McDonald, G. Jeffery. *Thieves in the Temple*. New York: Basic Books, 2010.
McDougall, John. *Jesus Was an Airborne Ranger: Find Your Purpose Following the Warrior Christ*. Colorado Springs: Multnomah, 2015.
McKinnon, Catriona. *Climate Change and Political Theory*. Cambridge: Polity, 2022.
Meares, Russell. *Intimacy and Alienation*. London: Routledge, 2001.
Meijer, Eva. *Animal Languages*. Translated by Laura Watkinson. Cambridge: MIT Press, 2020.
―――. *When Animals Speak: Toward an Interspecies Democracy*. Animals in Contact. New York: New York University Press, 2019.
Merry, Robert W. *Sands of Empire: Missionary Zeal, American Foreign Policy, and the Hazards of Global Ambition*. New York: Simon & Schuster, 2010.
Milbank, John. "Sovereignty, Empire, Capital, and Terror." In *The Imperial Tense*, edited by Andrew J. Bacevich, 159–71. Chicago: Dee, 2003.
Miller, Lulu. *Why Fish Don't Exist: A Story of Loss, Love, and the Hidden Order of Life*. Illustrations by Kate Samworth. New York: Simon & Schuster Paperbacks, 2021.
Miller, Sarah Clark. "Neoliberalism, Precarity, and the Crisis of Care." In *Care Ethics and the Age of Precarity*, edited by Maurice Hamington and Michael Flower, 48–67. Minneapolis: University of Minnesota Press, 2021.
Miller-McLemore, Bonnie. "Climate Violence and Earth Justice." *Religions* 13 (2022) 1–16. Also publishing in *International Journal of Practical Theology* 26 (2022) 329–66.
Mills, Charles W. *Black Rights/White Wrongs: The Critique of Racial Liberalism*. Oxford: Oxford University Press, 2017.
―――. *The Racial Contract*. Ithaca, NY: Cornell University Press, 1997.
Moltmann, Jürgen. *The Gospel of Liberation*. Translated by H. Wayne Pipkin. Waco, TX: Word, 1973.

———. *The Living God and the Fullness of Life*. Translated by Margaret Kohl. Louisville: Westminster John Knox, 2015.

Moore, Jason W. "Name the System! Anthropocene & the Capitalocene Alternative." *Jason W. Moore* (blog), October 9, 2016. https://jasonwmoore.wordpress.com/2016/10/09/name-the-system-anthropocenes-the-capitalocene-alternative/.

Murdoch, Iris. *The Sovereignty of the Good*. Routledge Classics. London: Routledge, 2001.

National Aeronautics and Space Administration (NASA). *Global Climate Change 2023*. Website. https://climate.nasa.gov/.

Newell, Peter, and Matthew Paterson. *Climate Capitalism: Global Warming and the Transformation of the Global Economy*. Cambridge: Cambridge University Press, 2010.

Newman, Saul. *Political Theology: A Critical Introduction*. London: Polity, 2019.

Niebuhr, H. Richard. *Faith on Earth*. Edited by Richard R. Niebuhr New Haven: Yale University Press, 1989.

Niebuhr, Reinhold. *The Irony of American History*. University of Chicago Press ed. Chicago: University of Chicago Press, 2008.

North, David. "America's Drive for World Domination." In *The Imperial Tense*, edited by Andrew J. Bacevich, 66–80. Chicago: Dee, 2003.

Northcott, Michael. "On Going Gently into the Anthropocene." In *Religion in the Anthropocene*, edited by Celia Deane Drummond et al., 19–34. Eugene, OR: Cascade, 2017.

Novak, Michael. *The Spirit of Democratic Capitalism*. New York: Simon & Schuster, 1982.

———. *Toward a Theology of the Corporation*. Rev. ed. Studies in Religion, Philosophy, and Public Policy. Washington, DC: AEI Press, 1990.

Nussbaum, Martha C. *Justice for Animals*. New York: Simon & Schuster, 2022.

Oakman, Douglas E. *The Radical Jesus, the Bible, and the Great Transformation*. Matrix: The Bible in Mediterranean Context 12. Eugene, OR: Cascade, 2021.

Oliner, Pearl M., and Samuel P. Oliner. *Toward a Caring Society*. Westport, CT: Praeger, 1995.

Oliver, Mary. *Devotions: The Selected Poems of Mary Oliver*. New York: Penguin, 2020.

Orange, Donna M. *Climate Crisis, Psychoanalysis, and Radical Ethics*. London: Routledge, 2017.

Pannenberg, Wolfart. *Theology and the Kingdom of God*. Philadelphia: Westminster, 1969.

Patterson, Orlando. *Slavery and Social Death*. Cambridge: Harvard University Press, 1982.

Peirce, Charles. *Peirce on Signs*. Edited by James Hoopes. Chapel Hill: University of North Carolina Press, 1991.

Pihkala, Panu. "Eco-Anxiety and Environmental Education." *Sustainability* 12.23 (2020) 10149. https:// doi.org/10.3390/su122310149/.

———. "Religious Communities and Climate Emotions: Encountering Climate Grief, Guilt, and Anger." In *Brooding over Creation: Affective Ecologies, Religion, and Theology*, edited by Jacob Erickson. London: Bloomsbury, forthcoming.

———. "Toward a Taxonomy of Climate Emotions." *Frontiers in Climate* 3 (2022) 738154. https://doi.org/10.3389/fclim/.

Piketty, Thomas. *Capital and Ideology*. Translated by Arthur Goldhammer. Cambridge: Harvard University Press, 2020.

———. *Capital in the Twenty-First Century*. Translated by Arthur Goldhammer. Cambridge: Belknap, 2014.

———. *Time for Socialism: Dispatches from a World on Fire, 2016–2021*. Translation from the original French by Kristin Couper. New Haven: Yale University Press, 2021.

Pistor, Katharina. *The Code of Capital: How the Law Creates Wealth and Inequality*. Princeton: Princeton University Press, 2019.

Pollock, Anne. *Sickening: Anti-Black Racism and Health Disparities in the United States*. Minneapolis: University of Minnesota Press, 2021.

Polkinghorne, Donald. *Methodology for the Human Sciences*. SUNY Series in Transpersonal and Humanistic Psychology. Albany: SUNY Press, 1983.

Popper, Karl. *The Open Society and Its Enemies*. With an introduction by Vaclav Havel. London: Routledge, 2002.

Porter, Roy, ed. *The Faber Book of Madness*. London: Faber & Faber, 1991.

———. *A Social History of Madness*. New York: Dutton, 1989.

Posner, Eric A., and Eric Glen Weyl. *Radical Markets: Uprooting Capitalism and Democracy for a Just Society*. New paperback ed. Princeton: University of Princeton Press, 2019.

Prozorov, Sergei. *Agamben and Politics: A Critical Introduction*. Thinking Politics. Edinburgh: Edinburgh University Press, 2014.

Pruyser, Paul W. *The Play of the Imagination: Towards a Psychoanalysis of Culture*. New York: International Universities Press, 1983.

Pulcini, Elena. "Global Vulnerability: Why Take Care of Future Generations?" In *Care Ethics and the Age of Precarity* edited by Maurice Hamington and Michael Flower, 120–43. Minneapolis: University of Minnesota Press.

Puryear, Stephen. "Schopenhauer on the Rights of Animals." *European Journal of Philosophy* 25 (2017) 250–69.

Ramsay, Nancy J. "Compassionate Resistance: An Ethic for Pastoral Care and Counseling." *Journal of Pastoral Care* 52 (1999) 217–26.

Reich, Robert B. *Saving Capitalism: For the Many, Not the Few*. New York: Random House, 2016.

———. *Supercapitalism: The Transformation of Business, Democracy, and Everyday Life*. New York: Vintage, 2007.

Reuther, Rosemary Radford. *Sexism and God Talk*. Boston: Beacon, 1983.

Rhodes, Edward. "Onward Liberal Soldiers? The Crusading Logic of Bush's Grand Strategy and What Is Wrong with It. In *The New American Empire*, edited by Lloyd Gardner and Marilyn Young, 227–52. New York: New Press, 2003.

Ricardo, David. *The Principles of Political Economy and Taxation*. Mineola, NY: Dover, 2004.

Rieger, Joerg. *Christ and Empire: From Paul to Postcolonial Times*. Minneapolis: Fortress, 2007.

———. *No Rising Tide: Theology, Economics, and the Future*. Minneapolis: Fortress, 2009.

Robbins, Jeffery. *Radical Democracy and Political Theology*. Insurrections. New York: Columbia University Press, 2011.

Robinson, Cedric. *Black Marxism: The Making of the Black Radical Tradition*. Chapel Hill: University of North Carolina Press, 1983.

Robinson, Fiona. *The Ethics of Care: A Feminist Approach to Human Security*. Global Ethics and Politics. Philadelphia: Temple University Press, 2011.

———. *Globalizing Care: Ethics, Feminist Theory, and International Relations*. Feminist Theory and Politics. Boulder, CO: Westview, 1999.

Rogers-Vaughn, Bruce. "Blessed Are Those Who Mourn: Depression as Political Resistance." *Pastoral Psychology* 63 (2014) 503–22.

———. *Caring for Souls in a Neoliberal Age*. New York: Palgrave Macmillan, 2016.

Rouse, W. H. D., trans. *The Great Dialogues of Plato*. A Mentor Book. New York: New American Library, 1956.

Rousseau, Jean-Jacques. *Discourse on the Origin of Inequality*. Translated by G. D. H. Cole. Primary Resources in International Affairs. Zurich: ETH Zurich, International Relations and Security Network, n.d. https://www.files.ethz.ch/isn/125494/5019_Rousseau_Discourse_on_the_Origin_of_Inequality.pdf/.

Rowley, Genny Carin. "Intersystemic Care: How Religious Environmental Praxis Expands the Pastoral Theological Norm of Justice." *Journal of Pastoral Theology* 25.2 (2015) 107–21.

———. "Practicing Hope: Congregational Environmentalism as Intersystemic Care." PhD diss., Brite Divinity School, 2013.

Rumscheidt, Barbara. *No Room for Grace: Pastoral Theology and Dehumanization in the Global Economy*. 1998. Reprint, Eugene, OR: Wipf & Stock, 2012.

Ryan, Alan. *On Politics: A History of Political Thought from Herodotus to the Present*. 2 vols. New York: Norton, 2012.

Ryn, Claes G. *America the Virtuous*. London New Brunswick, NJ: Transaction, 2003.

Said, Edward W. *Culture and Imperialism*. 1st Vintage ed. New York: Vintage, 1994.

———. *Orientalism*. 1st Vintage Books ed. New York: Vintage, 1979.

Sales, Ruby. "Where Does It Hurt?" Interview by Krista Tippett, *On Being with Krista Tippett*, NPR, September 15, 2020. Audio. https://onbeing.org/programs/ruby-sales-where-does-it-hurt/.

Samuels, Andrew. *The Political Psyche*. Routledge Mental Health Classic Editions. New York: Routledge, 2015.

Sandel, Michael J. *What Money Can't Buy: The Moral Limits of Markets*. New York: Farrar, Straus and Giroux, 2012.

Schafer, Roy. *Aspects of Internalization*. New York: International Universities Press, 1990.

Scheerer, Robert, dir. "True Q." *Star Trek: The Next Generation*, season 6 episode 6. Written by Gene Roddenberry et al. Starring Patrick Stewart et al. Originally aired on October 24, 1992. Available on Paramount Plus or for rent on Amazon Prime Video.

Schell, Jonathan. "The Human Shadow." In *Nature and Value*, edited by Akeel Bilgrami, 13–24. New York: Columbia University Press, 2020.

———. "Nature and Value." In *Nature and Value*, edited by Akeel Bilgrami, 1–12. New York: Columbia University Press, 2020.

Schmidt, Hans. *Maverick Marine: General Smedley D. Butler and the Contradictions of American Military History*. Lexington: University Press of Kentucky, 1987.

Schmitt, Carl. *Political Theology: Four Chapters on the Concept of Sovereignty*. Translated by George Schwab. University of Chicago Press ed. Chicago: University of Chicago Press, 2005.

Schüssler Fiorenza, Elisabeth. *Discipleship of Equals: A Critical Ekklesia-ology of Liberation*. New York: Crossroad, 1988.

Scull, Andrew. *Madness in Civilization*. Princeton: Princeton University Press, 2015.
Searles, Harold F. *The Nonhuman Environment, in Normal Development and Schizophrenia*. Monograph Series on Schizophrenia 5. New York: International Universities Press, 1960.
Segundo, Jon Luis. *The Liberation of Theology*. Translated by John Drury. Maryknoll, NY: Orbis, 1976.
Sevenhuijsen, Selma. *Citizenship and the Ethics of Care*. Translated from Dutch by Liz Savage. London: Routledge, 1998.
Shelby, Tommie, and Brandon M. Terry, eds. *To Shape a New World: Essays on the Political Philosophy of Martin Luther King Jr*. Cambridge: Belknap, 2018.
Silva, Jennifer M. *Coming Up Short: Working-Class Adulthood in the Age of Uncertainty*. New York: Oxford University Press, 2013.
Singer, Peter. *Animal Liberation*. London: Harper Collins, 1975.
Skinner, Quentin. "A Genealogy of the Modern State." *Proceedings of the British Academy* 162 (2008) 325–70.
Slobodian, Quinn. *Globalists: The End of Empire and the Birth of Neoliberalism*. 1st Harvard University Press paperback ed. Cambridge: Harvard University Press, 2020.
Smith, Adam. *The Wealth of Nations*. Edited, with notes and marginal summary, by Edwin Cannan. With an introduction by Alan B. Krueger. Bantam Classic ed. New York: Bantam Classic, 2003.
Smith, Anthony D. *Nationalism: Theory, Ideology, History*. 2nd ed. Key Concepts. Cambridge: Polity, 2010.
Sorabji, Richard. *Emotion and Peace of Mind: From Stoic Agitation to Christian Temptation*. Gifford Lectures. Oxford: Oxford University Press, 2003.
Stern, Daniel N. *The Interpersonal World of the Infant*. New York: Basic Books, 1985.
Stern, Donnel B. *Unformulated Experience*. Relational Perspectives 8. Hillsdale, NJ: Analytic, 1997.
Stone, Oliver, and Peter J. Kuznick. *The Untold History of the United States*. New York: Gallery, 2012.
Sunstein, Cass R. "The Rights of Animals." *University of Chicago Law Review* 70.1 (2003) 387–401.
Tanner, Kathryn. *Christianity and the New Spirit of Capitalism*. New Haven: Yale University Press, 2021.
Tanner, Norman. *The Church in the Later Middle Ages*. New York: I.B. Tauris, 2008.
Taubes, Jacob. *The Political Theology of Paul*. Edited by Aleida Assmann et al. Translated by Dana Hollander. Cultural Memory in the Present. Stanford: Stanford University Press, 2004.
Taylor, Charles. *Modern Social Imaginaries*. Public Planet Books. Durham, NC: Duke University Press, 2003.
———. *A Secular Age*. Cambridge: Belknap, 2007.
Taylor, Steven. "Anxiety Disorders, Climate Change, and the Challenges Ahead: Introduction to the Special Issue." *Journal of Anxiety Disorders* 76 (2020) 102313.
Teilhard de Chardin, Pierre. *The Divine Milieu*. 1st Perennial classics ed. New York: Perennial Classics, 2001.
Tonner, Philip. *Dwelling: Heidegger, Archaeology, Morality*. Routledge Studies in Archaeology. London: Routledge, 2018.
Tonstad. Linn Marie. *Queer Theology: Beyond Apologetics*. Cascade Companions. Eugene, OR: Cascade, 2018.

Tronto, Joan C. *Caring Democracy: Markets, Equality, and Justice.* New York: New York University Press, 2013.
———. *Moral Boundaries: A Political Argument for an Ethic of Care.* New York: Routledge, 1993.
Ugilt, Rasmus. *Giorgio Agamben: Political Philosophy.* N.p.: Humanities-E-books, 2014.
Ussher, Jane M. *The Madness of Women.* Women and Psychology. London: Routledge, 2011.
Valencia, Sayak. *Gore Capitalism.* Translated by John Pluecker. Semiotext(e) Intervention Series 24. South Pasadena, CA: Semiotext(e), 2018.
Van Alstyne, Robert Warren. *The Rising American Empire.* Oxford: Oxford University Press, 1960.
Villarosa, Linda. *Under the Skin: The Hidden Toll of Racism on American Lives and the Health of Our Nation.* New York: Doubleday, 2022.
Vogt, Markus. "Human Ecology as a Key Discipline of Environmental Ethics." In *Religion in the Anthropocene*, edited by Celia Deane-Drummond et al., 235–52. Eugene, OR: Cascade, 2017.
Wagner, Gernot, and Martin L. Weitzman. *Climate Shock: The Economic Consequences of a Hotter Planet.* Princeton: Princeton University Press, 2015.
Walker, Martin. "An Empire Unlike Any Other." In *The Imperial Tense*, edited by Andrew J. Bacevich, 134–45. Chicago: Dee, 2003.
Wallace-Wells, David. *The Uninhabitable Earth.* New York: Dugan, 2020.
Watts, Alan. *The Way of Zen.* New York: Vintage, 1957.
Weber, Max. *The Protestant Ethic and the Spirit of Capitalism.* Translated by Talcott Parsons. With an introduction by Anthony Giddens. London: Routledge. 1992.
Weintrobe, Sally, ed. *Engaging with Climate Change.* The New Library of Psychoanalysis. London: Routledge, 2013.
———. *The Psychological Roots of the Climate Crisis.* Psychoanalytic Horizons. London: Bloomsbury, 2021.
Wells, Samuel. *A Nazareth Manifesto: Being with God.* Chichester, UK: Wiley Blackwell, 2015.
West, Cornel. *Democracy Matters: Winning the Fight against Imperialism.* New York: Penguin, 2004.
Whitehead, Alfred North. *The Concept of Nature.* Tarner Lectures 1919. Cambridge: Cambridge University Press, 1964.
———. *Process and Reality.* Edited by David Ray Griffin and Donald W. Sherburne. Corrected ed. Gifford Lectures 1927–1928. New York: Free Press, 1978,
Whitehead Jason C. *Redeeming Fear: A Constructive Theology for Living into Hope.* Minneapolis: Fortress, 2013.
Wilkerson, Isabel. *Caste: The Origins of Our Discontents.* New York: Random House, 2020.
Wilson, Edward O. *The Future of Life.* New York: Abacus, 2005.
Winnicott, D. W. *Playing and Reality.* London: Routledge, 1971.
———. "Transitional Objects and Transitional Phenomena—A Study of the First Not-Me Possession." *International Journal of Psychoanalysis* 34.2 (1953) 89–97.
Wolff, Richard D. *Democracy at Work: A Cure for Capitalism.* Chicago: Haymarket, 2012.
———. *Occupy the Economy: Challenging Capitalism.* Open Media Series. San Francisco: City Lights, 2012.

Wolff, Richard D., and Stephen A. Resnick. *Contending Economic Theories*. Cambridge: MIT Press, 2012.

———. *Economics: Marxian versus Neoclassical*. Baltimore: Johns Hopkins University Press, 1987.

Wolin, Sheldon S. *Politics and Vision*. Princeton Classics ed., Expanded ed. Princeton Classics. Princeton: Princeton University Press, 2016.

Wood, David. *Reoccupy Earth: Notes toward an Other Beginning*. Groundworks: Ecological Issues in Philosophy and Theology. New York: Fordham University Press, 2019.

Wood, Ellen Meiksins. *The Origin of Capitalism: A Longer View*. New, revised and expanded ed. London: Verso, 2017.

X, Malcolm. *The Autobiography of Malcolm X*. With the assistance of Alex Haley. New York: Ballantine, 1964.

Young, Marilyn B. "Imperial Language." In *The New American Empire*, edited by Lloyd Gardner and Marilyn Young, 32–49. New York: New Press, 2005.

Young-Bruehl, Elisabeth. *Why Arendt Matters*. Why X Matters. New Haven: Yale University Press, 2006.

Zaretsky, Robert. *The Subversive Simone Weil: A Life in Five Ideas*. Chicago: Chicago University Press, 2021.

Zawisza, Rafael. "Between Adamite Dreams and Original Sin." In *""Faith in the World": Post-Secular Readings of Hannah Arendt*, edited by Rafael Zawisza and Ludger Hagedorn, 87–110. Frankfurt: Campus, 2021.

Zawisza, Rafael, and Hagedorn, Ludger. "Faith in the World or: The Philosophical Contraband of a Hidden Spiritual Tradition." In *"Faith in the World": Post-Secular Readings of Hannah Arendt*, edited by Rafael Zawisza and Ludger Hagedorn, 11–36. Frankfurt: Campus, 2021.

Zawisza, Rafael, and Ludger Hagedorn, eds. *"Faith in the World": Post-Secular Readings of Hannah Arendt*. Frankfurt: Campus, 2021.

Zeddies, Timothy J. "Behind, Beneath, Above, and Beyond: The Historical Unconscious." *Journal of the American Academy of Psychoanalysis* 30 (2002) 211–22.

Zinn, Howard. *A People's History of the United States: 1492–Present*. New York: HaperPerennial, 2003.

———. *The Twentieth Century: A People's History*. Rev. and updated ed. New York: HarperPerennial, 1998.

Žižek, Slavoj. "From Democracy to Divine Violence." In *Democracy in What State?*, by Giorgio Agamben et al., 100–127. New Directions. New York: Columbia University Press, 2012.

Zúñiga, Didier. *Pluralist Politics, Relational Worlds: Vulnerability and Care of the Earth*. Toronto: University of Toronto Press, 2023.

Subject Index

Abrahamic scriptures, 27–28, 90n22, 114, 115
Abrahamic traditions, 4, 6, 27n57, 126, 129–30
actuality, 150n31
African American population, 17, 23, 36, 42, 53, 155, 155n48
afterlife, 146n21
Agamben, Giorgio, 31, 32, 42, 84n182, 89, 90, 156, 162, 167
agrarian reforms, in England, 69
Alexander the Great, 60
alienation
    epistemological alienation, 123–24
    existential alienation, 9–10
    from the Ideal Forms, 134–35
    indigenous people's experiences, 115
    intrapsychic alienation, 103, 105, 125–26
    in Judeo-Christian scripture, 127–29
    in literature, 13nn66–67, 130–35
    Merriam-Webster definition, 116
    mystification as source of, 115–16, 134
    from nature, 123
    ontological alienation, 116
    overview, 113–15
    philosophical explanations for, 113–14, 126
    sin and, 114, 115, 134, 134n85
    spiritual remedy for, 114, 115
    term usage, 116
    theological explanations for, 113–14
Alkidamas, 93
alleviation, term usage, 113–15
altruism, 66
American imperialism, 50
American Revolution, 44–45
Americans, exceptionalism of, 4
anarchic care, 143n10, 144, 150
anarchy, 27n58, 144n13
Anderson, Benedict, 56–57
annihilation anxiety, 104
Anthropocene Age
    stories and practices in, 29
    term usage, 2–3, 29n61
antihumanist responses, 3–4n15
anxiety
    annihilation anxiety, 104
    climate change effects, 14–15
    intolerable anxiety, 104
    Murdoch on, 13
    stifles imagination, 177
apparatus, term usage, 4n19
Arendt, Hannah, 40n100, 56–57, 57n38, 86
Aristotle
    on actuality, 150n31
    era of, 42
    hierarchical taxonomy screens, 13
    on other species, 45n115, 82–83, 90–91

Aristotle (cont.)
   political philosophy, 120
   on potentiality, 150n31
   on slavery, 36, 93
   on sovereignty, 26–27, 30
   on women, 17, 54n23, 124
Ash, Gabriel, 67
Assmann, Aleida, 166–67
Assmann, Jan, 166–67
atomized society, 57
Auestad, Lene, 53n22
Augustine of Hippo, Saint, 127, 148

Bacon, Francis, 82–83
Barber, William, II, 157
"bare life" concept, 32–33, 149n30
"Bartleby, the Scrivener" (Melville), 156
Becker, Gary, 78
Beecher, Catherine, 18, 61
Being, Truth and, 100–101, 100n50
Benn, Tony, 75
Bentham, Jeremy, 88
Berkowitz, Roger, 151n35
Beveridge, Albert J., 18, 61
Black, Daniel, 94
Bodin, Jean, 30
Bollas, Christopher, 150–53, 157, 161
Boot, Max, 65–66
Breton Woods (financial conference), 64, 72
The Brothers Karamazov (Dostoevsky), 170–71
Brown, Wendy, 30, 32, 41, 60
Buddha, 149
Bush, George W., 61, 66

Calhoun, John C., 62
Call of the Wild (London), 107n68, 130–34
Calvin and Hobbes (cartoon), 108, 159–60
Camus, Albert, 87
capitalism
   Capitalocene Era, 2–3n9
   emersion of, 50, 69–72
   extreme capitalism, as religion, 75–76, 76n139
   Fraser on, 14n13, 45n114
   industrial capitalism, 68n92, 70–72
   laissez-faire, 70n105, 72
   laissez-faire capitalism, 70n105, 72
   LaMothe on, 14n13, 45n114
   market societies, 5
   Marx on, 71
   means of production, 71
   mercantile capitalism, 68n92, 70
   Moore on, 14n13
   Morris on, 3n10
   neoliberal capitalism, 68, 68n94, 70n105, 73–77, 77n146, 80
   origins of, 69–71
   to reduce greenhouse gas emissions, 138
   splitting/projection operations, 103, 103n59
   term usage, 68
   types of, 68–69
Capitalocene Era, 2–3n9, 80
Caputo, John, 167–68, 174
care
   anarchic care, 143n10, 144
   concept of, 143nn12–13
   intersystemic care, 143nn12–13
   parental care, 144–45, 150
care, concept of, 145
care theorists, 7
Carter, Jimmy, 74
Castro, Eduardo Viveiros de, 89
cave, allegory of, 116–19, 118n24
Chari, Anita, 74
children's literature, 107–8, 160
Christianity, 50, 61–62, 146n20
church life, analogy, 110
citizens' identification, 54
The City of God (Augustine), 127
city walls, 16
civil rights movement (1950's), 157
civilization
   continuity and discontinuity, 25–26
   developments characterizing, 15, 24–25
   functions of, 16–17
   indigenous persons. *see* indigenous people and traditions
   origin of, 24
   overview, 8

political thinkers on, 12
psychological dynamics, 22
term usage, 15
See also marriage, civilization and sovereignty
classes
in civilization, 22–23
Harman on, 35
hierarchies, 79
Popper on, 22n45
sovereignty and, 35–36
subjugation and, 37
tension between, 22–24
climate change
church life, analogy, 110
effects of, 3
extinct species, 142n8
greenhouse gas emissions, 67, 67n89
nationalism and, 59
"True Q" episode (Star Trek), 141–42
weak dissociation and, 137
climate deniers, 5
climate emergency, 5
Clinton, Bill, 61
The Coming (Black), 94
coming, term usage, 143n11
communication differences, 91
communism, emersion of, 72
communist revolutions, 39
Confessions (Augustine), 127–28
Copernicus, Nicolaus, 136–37
cosmological ordering of the universe, 56, 92
Cotton, John, 18
Cox, Harvey, 75
critical attitude, 8
critical race theory, 107
Crockett, Clayton, 85, 116
Crossan, John Dominic, 163–64
Crutzen, Paul, 138
Cupitt, Don, 164
Cvetkovich, Ann, 80

Dardot, Pierre, 73
Darwin, Charles, 136–37
De La Torre, Miguel, 176, 176n114, 177
Debord, Guy, 34

defiance, term usage, 140–41
Deleuze, Gilles, 79, 84n182
democracies, 41–42, 45
Derrida, Jacques, 89
DeSantis, Ron, 57–58
Diagnostic Statistical Manual (*DSM*), 113, 113n11
Discourse on the Origin of Inequality (Rousseau), 12
Dostoevsky, Fyodor, 170
Dufour, Dany-Robert, 79, 79n158

Eagleton, Terry, 75, 76
Eco Church Christian (United Kingdom), 178
ecological dead zones, 93n29
economics, term usage, 78
eco-remorse, 173–74n99
eco-sorrow, 2
Egan, Kerry, 161
Egyptian sovereignty, 41
Elliot, T. S., 80
Emerson, Ralph Waldo, 84n182
empathy, 104–5
Empire of Liberty (1780), 58
enclosure laws, 69
enslaved persons, 17
The Epic of Gilgamesh (George), 15
epistemological alienation, 123–24
estrangement, 111
European empires, 63
exceptionalism, 4, 54, 54n25, 65–66
existential alienation, 9–10
existential estrangement, 128–29
existential insignificance, 13
exodus story, 33, 33n85, 37, 105, 128
extreme capitalism, as religion, 75–76, 76n139

Farley, Edward, 174, 175
fear
climate change effects, 14
Murdoch on, 13
stifles imagination, 177
Federal Reserve, 74
Feuerbach, Ludwig, 91, 98, 103
Fingarette, Herbert, 104, 135
Ford, Gerald, 74

Ford, Richard, 43
Francis of Assisi, Saint, 88
Frank, Thomas, 75
Fraser, Nancy, 45n114
French people, exceptionalism of, 4
French Revolution (1789), 52
Freud, Sigmund
    on civilization, 12–13, 17, 21–22, 46
    developmental view of, 150
    on human narcissism, 136–37
    on humankind's origin, 42
    on nature, 19–20, 123
    on science, 83
Friedman, Milton, 73

Gauthier, David, 120–21
Gellner, Ernst, 57
George, Andrew, 15
Gilman, Sandor, 112
Girard, René, 42
Giroux, Henry, 79
Global Climate Change 2023 (website), 2n6
Global Ecovillage Network, 177
Go, Julian, 65n74
God
    estrangement from, 128
    imago dei, 92–93
    incarnation of, 92, 92n27, 103
    kingdom of, 92, 102
    law and justice, outside of, 90n22
    nonsovereignty of, 167–68, 168n89
    sovereignty of, 33–35, 33n85, 34nn87–88
    superiority (omnipotence, omniscience), 35
Goldman, Emma, 149
governing authorities, 6–7
Greek philosophers, 93
Greek physicians, 112
Green Churches Network, 177
Grosby, Steven, 51–52, 55, 57
gross domestic product (GDP), 71
Groys, Boris, 53n20
Guattari, Felix, 79, 84n182
Gulliver's Travels (Swift), 165

Hall, Douglas John, 66
Hall, Stuart, 17
Hardt, Michael, 67
Harman, Chris, 16, 22, 35
Hartwich, Wolf-Daniel, 166–67
Harvey, David, 73n119
Hebrew scriptures, 25, 33–34, 37
    See also Judeo-Christian scripture
Hegel, Georg, 120
Heidegger, Martin, 100, 120–22
hell, notion of, 92n28
Hellenistic Empire, 61
Henriksen, Jan-Olav, 174, 176
heresy, 147–48
hierarchical valuations, 78–79, 91, 91n24, 124–25
hierarchical-binary valuation, 118
historical unconscious, 107–8, 124–25
history books, 107
Hobbes, Thomas, 11–12, 13, 19, 20, 21, 39, 42, 52, 71
Hochschild, Arlie, 79
homelessness, 120–27
homo economicus, 78
homo oeconomicus, 75
hope, in the anthropocene, 173–79
Horsley, Richard, 25, 43, 164, 177
Hudis, Peter, 71
human beings
    as altricial creatures, 149–50
    care for living beings, 163n65
    Freud on, 19n33
human exceptionalism, 4
humiliation, class system use of, 36–37, 36n92

Ideal Forms (Plato), 117–18, 122, 125–26, 134
Illouz, Eva, 79
imagination, loss of, 151n33
imago dei, 92–93
imperialism, 50, 60–68
imperialistic ambitions, 62–63
impermanence, term usage, 10
impotentiality, 144, 150n31, 156–57
Indian Ocean tsunami (2004), 66
Indians (Native Americans). *See* indigenous people and traditions

indigenous people and traditions
   alienation experiences, 115
   civilization and, 21
   epistemologies, 159n60
   ethnic cleansing of, 41–42, 84
   historical consciousness, 107–8
   natural rights of, 18
   state violence against, 53
   stories and rituals, 24, 35
   on Truth, 100
   U.S. imperial ambitions, 62
industrial capitalism, 68n92, 70–72
inflexible narration, 104
injustice, other species and, 90
inoperativity, 167
inoperativity, term usage, 143nn9–10
instrumental epistemologies, 38–39
Interfaith Center for Sustainable Development, 177
Intergovernmental Panel on Climate Change (website), 2n6
International Monetary Fund (IMF), 64, 72, 73, 74
interspecific perspectivism, 151
intersystemic care, term usage, 143n10
intolerable anxiety, 104
intrapsychic alienation, 103, 105, 125–26
Iranian protesters, 52–53
Israelites
   exceptionalism of, 4
   leaders/leadership, 166
   sovereignty, 41
   suffering, 174
   theologies, 9, 28, 33–37, 33n85, 34n87
   traditions, 9
I-Thou experiences, 153–54, 153n44

Jackson, Andrew, 62
Jefferson, Thomas, 62
Jesus
   author's approach and use of, 145–49
   coming of radical Jesus, 162–73
   Deloria on, 146n20
   forgiveness, 170
   hope, in the anthropocene, 173–79
   parental care, 162
   as savior, 142
   vulnerability of, 169
Johnson, Chalmers, 61, 67
Judeo-Christian scripture, 33–35, 33n85, 37–38, 44, 111–16, 127–29, 164, 166–67, 167n84, 169–70
   See also Hebrew scriptures

Kaplan, Amy, 65
Kaur, Valerie, 177
Keller, Catherine, 175, 177
Keynesian economic, 72–73
Kierkegaard, Søren, 142
killing of life, 32–33
King, Martin Luther, Jr., 165
Klein, Naomi, 64
Knapp, Elizabeth, 112
Kohn, Eduardo, 159
Kojève, Alexander, 53n20
Kommune Niederkaufungen, Germany, 177
Krauthammer, Charles, 65n82

laissez-faire capitalism, 70n105, 72
Latour, Bruno, 89, 90, 96–97n45, 122–23
Laval, Christian, 73
Layton, Lynne, 107, 124
leaders/leadership, 26–37
Leroi, Armand Marie, 82
Levinas, Emmanuel, 120–22
liberal individualism, 57
Lieven, Anatol, 58–60
Linderman, Frank, 108–9
linguistic castration, 83–84
literature
   alienation in, 13nn66–67, 130–35
   as apparatus for ontological rift, 114
   children's literature, 107–8, 160
Locke, John, 71
London, Jack, 130–34
Longyearbyen, Norway, 178
Lopez, Barry, 177, 179
love
   forms of, 167
   unconditional, 133
Lukács, Georg, 78

202

Lumumba, Patrice, 149
Lundestad, 63

Macmurray, John, 154
magical thinking, 142
Mander, Jerry, 80
Manifest Destiny (1845), 58, 62
market societies. *See* capitalism
marriage, as metaphor, 14
marriage, civilization and sovereignty, 14–15
Marx, Karl, 22, 39, 50, 71, 78
"means of production," 71
medical profession, 112–13
Melville, Herman, 62, 156
mental diseases, 112
mercantile capitalism, 68n92, 70
military force/apparatuses, 34, 53, 59, 61–65, 65n74, 68
Miller, Lulu Clark, 83–84
Milton, John, 44
mimetic violence, 42–44
Moltmann, Jürgen, 175
monarch, 53
Monroe Doctrine (1823), 58, 62
Mont Pelerin Society, 73
Moore, Jason, 80–81
moralization, 105–6
Morris, William, 76–77
Mott, Lucretia, 149
multinaturalism, 150–51, 151n32
Murdoch, Iris, 13, 14
Mussolini, Benito, 62
mystification, 115–16, 134, 135–38

narcissism, 153n44
nation
    marginalization and oppression, 54n23
    other-than-human species exclusion, 54–55
    political violence and, 52–53
    post Enlightenment era, 56
    shared membership, 51–54
    sovereignty of, 53–55
    state versus, 52
    term usage, 51
national identity, 40–41, 65, 103

nationalism, 50, 51–60, 103
nation-states, 40, 41
native peoples. *See* indigenous people and traditions
nature
    alienation from, 123
    civilization and, 19–20, 20nn36–37, 96–97nn44–45, 96–99, 99n48, 133–34
    culture and, 122–23
    Freud on, 123
Nazis, Heidegger and, 121
necessity, term usage, 30n66
Negri, Antonio, 67
neoliberal capitalism, 68, 68n94, 70n105, 73–77, 77n146, 80
Neolithic revolution, 16, 24
    See also pre-Neolithic era
Nestorius, Archbishop of Constantinople, 148
Newell, Peter, 81
Newman, Saul, 32, 44
nihilism, term usage, 140
nihilistic responses, 3–4n15
nonsentient species, 106, 106n63
normative unconscious, 107
Northcott, Michael, 138
Novak, Michael, 77–78
Nussbaum, Martha C., 88

Oakman, Douglas, 164–65, 165n76, 177
Oedipal myth, 44
Ohm's law, 82
ontological alienation, 116
ontological rift
    attributes, 87, 89–101
    overview, 86–89
    psychosocial analysis of, 101–10
    sources, 89–101
    term usage, 80n166
origin stories/myths, 11–13, 102–3
ostensibly, term usage, 37n95
other species, killing of, 146n22
Othered human beings, 20–21, 89–90n18
Othered species, 21

Palestinian sovereignty, 41

SUBJECT INDEX

Pannenberg, Wolfart, 129, 174
Paradise Lost (Milton), 44
parental care, 144–45, 150, 155, 161–62
parent-infant interaction, 151–53
Parks, Rosa, 149
pastoral psychotherapist, role of, 8, 8n29
pastoral theologians, role of, 8
Paterson, Matthew, 81
patriarchal sovereignty, 12
Patterson, Orlando, 33
Peirce, Charles Sanders, 123
perspectivism, 100, 150–51, 151n32
philosophical explanations, for
    alienation, 113–14, 126
philosophical traditions, 86–87
Pistor, Katharina, 69
Plato
    Becoming, Realm of, 118
    Being, Realm of, 118
    cave, allegory of, 116–19, 123, 125
    on class, 124
    era of, 42
    hierarchical-binary valuation, 118
    humans/animals, gap between, 90
    Ideal Forms, 117–18, 122, 125–26, 134
    philosophical anthropology, 117–18
    political philosophy, 118–20
    Republic, 13, 116
    on sovereignty, 26–27, 44, 87
Plenty Coups, Crow chief, 108–9, 114
plurality, term usage, 7n24
Poiseuille's law, 82
political agency, 41–42
political belonging, without sovereignty, 166–67
political order, 12–13
political violence, 32–33, 33n85, 42–44, 52–53, 57–58
political-economic transgressors, 164–65
Poor People's Campaign (2018), 157
Popper, Karl, 13, 22
posthuman world, 173–74n99
potentiality, 150n31
power, political bodies and, 11
pre-Neolithic era, 24–25, 55
    See also Neolithic revolution

primitive peoples, 15–17, 21, 121
production, means of, 71
projection
    splitting and, 102–4
    term usage, 102
property, institution of, 70n105
Prozorov, Sergei, 31
Pruyser, Paul, 158
psychosocial analysis, of ontological rift, 101–10
psychosocial development, 144–45, 150–51
psychosocial dynamics and functions, 9, 22, 135–38
Puritan population, 17–18

racism, 36, 155–56
radical, term usage, 144
rationalization, 105–6
Reagan, Ronald, 61, 73–74, 73n119
reification, term usage, 78
religious practices/rituals, 10
remorse, lack of, 105
Republic (Plato), 13
rhizomes, as metaphor, 48–49
Rhodes, Edward, 64
Ricardo, David, 69
Robbins, Jeffery, 167–68
Roman citizens, exceptionalism of, 4
Roman Empire, 60
Rousseau, Jean-Jacques, 12, 12n5, 14, 21–22, 41, 76
Russia/Ukraine special operations, 57, 58

Said, Edward, 17
Sales, Ruby, 155–57
salvation, alienation, as spiritual remedy for, 114, 115, 171–72
Schell, Jonathan, 46, 99
Schiff, Adam, 44
Schmitt, Carl, 30–31, 32, 56
Schopenhauer, Arthur, 88
sciences, 50, 82–84
scriptures. *See* Abrahamic scriptures; Hebrew scriptures; Judeo-Christian scripture
Scull, Andrew, 111
Searles, Harold, F., 83n178

self-deception, 104, 135, 135n88
self-empathy, 105
sentient species, 91, 106
Shotoku Taishi, 149
Silva, Jennifer, 79
simplification, 66, 66n82
sin
    alienation and, 114, 115, 134, 134n85
    concept of, 129
    original sin, 48, 171–72, 171n97
Singer, Peter, 88
singularity, term usage, 7n24
slavery
    enslaved persons, 17
    of humans, 33, 36, 93–95
    Jesus in the form of, 170
Smith, Adam, 69, 71
social death, term usage, 33
social imaginary, term usage, 68n91
socialism, 3n10, 72
societal psyche, term usage, 65n76
Socrates, 44, 116–17, 119, 120, 147
soul, 20–21, 91–93
sovereignty
    "bare life" concept, 32–33, 149n30
    epistemologies, 8–9, 27–29
    of God, 33–35, 33n85, 34nn87–88
    Greek roots of, 27
    indispensable features, 30
    instrumental epistemologies, 38–39
    Merriam-Webster definition, 29, 29n62
    metaphors for, 48–51
    necessity of, 26–27, 27n58
    notable theorists on, 30–33
    ontological rift, 87
    original sin of, 48, 171–72
    other species and, 45–46, 88
    over territory, 41
    overview, 8, 45, 46–47, 85
    paradox of, 31
    as patriarchal, 32n74
    political agency, 41–42, 144–45n14
    political belonging and, 166–67
    political violence, 32–33, 33n85, 42–44
    secular dimensions, 32
    state of exception, 31–34
    subjugation and, 37
    types of, 1–14
    See also marriage, civilization, and sovereignty
Soviet Union, 52
splitting
    projection and, 102–4
    term usage, 102
Star Trek: The Next Generation (television series), 141–42
state, term usage, 52–54
Stern, Donnel, 104, 135–36, 138
Stoke's law, 82
suffering, 105–6, 111–12, 129
superiority, illusion of, 97–98
Swift, Jonathan, 165
symbolic-semiotic organizations, transition to, 157–60, 162

Taubes, Jacob, 162, 166–67
Teilhard de Chardin, Pierre, 88
territorial societies, 51
Thatcher, Margaret, 73n119, 75
theocratic nations, 55–56
Theodosius II, Emperor, 148
Theoharis, Liz, 157
theological explanations for alienation, 113–14
Tillich, Paul, 175
Tocqueville, Alexis de, 54n25
Tonner, Phillip, 120, 121
Totem and Taboo (Freud), 12
traditions, term usage, 113n12
transitional phenomena, 157–60, 162
Treaty of Westphalia (1648), 39, 55
tree, as metaphor, 48–49
tribalism, in political divisions, 18–19
Truth, as superior to belief, 118
Truth, Being and, 100–101, 100n50
Truth, Sojourner, 149
Tutu, Desmond, 149

Ukraine/Russia special operations, 57, 58, 68
unbridgeable chasm, 88
uncivilized people, 16–17
United Nations, 2n6

United States
 Central Intelligence Agency (CIA), 2n6
 exercising state violence, 53
 imperial ambitions, 60–64
 military bases in foreign countries, 64
 Pentagon, 2n6
 sovereignty and, 39–41
 violence against other nations, 58
"unthought knowns" concept, 151–55, 153n44, 161

vision, possession of, 177
Volcker, Paul, 74
Voltaire, 76
vulnerability, 168

Waal, Frans de, 83
Wagner, Gernot, 81, 138
Walter Lippmann Colloquium, 73
Washington, George, 62, 107
Waterson, Bill, 159
weak dissociation, 104–5, 135–38
weakness, connotation of, 168–69, 168n92
weapons, use of, 60
Weber, Max, 70
wedding, metaphor of, 29

Weitzman, Martin L., 138
Weitzman, Matthew, 81
Western civilization, term usage, 8
Western philosophies, 4, 6, 114, 142–43
White Fang (London), 107n68
Whitehead, Alfred North, 87, 90, 96m44, 99–100, 116
Whitehead, Jason, 175
Willard, Samuel, 112
Wilson, Woodrow, 61
Winnicott, Donald W., 150, 157–58, 160, 162
Winthrop, John, 18
The Wizard of Oz (movie), 137, 138–39
Wollstonecraft, Mary, 149
women
 medical diagnoses, 112
 political agency of, 17, 54n23, 107, 120n32, 124
 in political theologies and philosophies, 17n23, 110
 reasoning capabilities, 124
Wood, Ellen Meiksins, 69–70, 72
World Bank, 64, 72

Xenophanes (philosopher), 98, 145

Zawisza, Rafael, 148
Zeddies, Timothy J., 107, 124

Name Index

Agamben, Giorgio, 4n18, 4n19, 12n8, 14n12, 27n57, 30, 30n66, 32, 33nn81–82, 41, 42nn104–105, 76n139, 84n182, 89, 89n13, 90, 140n2, 143n9, 145n14, 149n30, 150n31, 154, 156n49, 162, 167, 167nn87–88
Ágoston, Csilla, 3n12
Alexander the Great, 60
Alkidamas (philosopher), 93
Altman, Neil, 102n56
Anderson, Benedict, 56–57, 56nn29–35
Arendt, Hannah, 14–15n13, 40n100, 43n111, 56–57, 57nn36–38, 86, 144n14, 147n23, 151n35, 168n89, 169n93, 171n97
Aristotle, 13, 27n57, 29n60, 30, 45n115, 54n23, 82–83, 90, 120n32, 124, 150n31
Ash, Gabriel, 67, 67n87
Assmann, Aleida, 166–67
Assmann, Jan, 166–67
Auestad, Lene, 53n22
Augustine of Hippo, Saint, 124n55, 127–28, 127nn61–62, 128n63, 148

Bacevich, Andrew J., 40n101, 61n56, 62n58, 64n71, 65n75
Bacon, Francis, 82–83
Baptist, Edward E., 77n148, 90n18, 93n31

Barber, William, II, 157
Barker, Ernest, 36n91, 45n115, 90n23, 90nn19–21, 93nn32–33
Barnett, Joshua Trey, 3n12
Barry, John M., 18n27
Becker, Gary, 78, 78n154
Beecher, Catherine, 18, 61
Bell, Daniel, 70n105
Benatar, David, 4n15, 173–74n99
Benn, Tony, 75, 75n138
Bentham, Jeremy, 6n22, 88
Berkowitz, Roger, 151n35
Beveridge, Albert J., 18, 61
Bielek-Robson, Agata, 147n23
Birch, Kean, 68n93, 74n126
Black, Danial, 94, 94nn36–41, 95n42
Bodin, Jean, 30, 30n63
Bollas, Christopher, 150–53, 151nn36–37, 152nn38–39, 152nn41–42, 157, 161
Boorstin, Daniel, 98n46
Boot, Max, 65–66
Brown, Wendy, 4n20, 16n20, 30, 30nn65–66, 31n71, 32, 32nn75–76, 41, 41n102, 42n106, 51n5, 55n28, 60n49, 140n1
Bubeck, Diemut Elisabet, 6n23, 143n12
Buber, Martin, 153n44
Buddha, 149
Bush, George W., 61, 66
Butler, Smedley, 63–64

NAME INDEX

Calhoun, John C., 62
Camus, Albert, 87, 87n5
Caputo, John, 167–68, 168n91, 174, 174n102
Carrette, Jeremy R., 75n138, 76n140
Carter, Jimmy, 74
Casey, Edward S., 127n60
Castro, Eduardo Viveiros de, 38n97, 87n4, 89, 89n16, 94n34, 100n51, 124n55, 151n32, 151n34, 159n60
Chari, Anita, 70n105, 74, 74n125, 75nn133–134, 78n152
Chatzidakis, Andreas, 6n23, 143n12
Chomsky, Noam, 40n101, 62n59
Clinebell, Howard, 3n13
Clinton, Bill, 61
Coates, Ta-Nehisi, 155n48
Colebrook, Claire, 150n31
Comtesse, Hannah, 2n5
Cone, James H., 145n18, 164n69
Copernicus, Nicolaus, 136–37
Cotton, John, 18
Couldry, Nick, 75n131
Cox, Harvey, 75, 75n136, 145n16
Crandon, Tara, 3n12
Crawford, Neta C., 68n90
Crockett, Clayton, 3, 3n14, 4, 83, 85n184, 116, 116n16, 138n96
Crossan, John Dominic, 145n18, 163–64, 163n66, 170n94
Crutzen, Paul, 2, 29n61, 138
Cunsolo, Ashlee, 2n5
Cupitt, Don, 97n45, 98, 145n18, 164, 164n74, 164nn67–68
Cushman, Phillip, 113n10
Cvetkovich, Ann, 80, 80n164

Danner, Mark, 90n18
Dardot, Pierre, 73, 73nn115–116, 75n133
Darwin, Charles, 136–37
Davenport, Coral, 2n6
De La Torre, Miguel, 176, 176nn111–114, 176nn116–117, 177
De St. Croix, G. E. M., 148nn27–28
Debord, Guy, 34, 34n86, 79n158, 98n46, 103n58

Deleuze, Gilles, 48, 49n4, 79, 79n159, 84n182
Deloria, Vine, 1n4, 24nn53, 95n43, 115n15, 146n20, 172n98
Derrida, Jacques, 89, 89n14
DeSantis, Ron, 57–58
Dickinson, Colby, 89n12
Doerner, Klaus, 112n7
Dostoevsky, Fyodor, 170, 170n95, 171n96
Dufour, Dany-Robert, 38n96, 77n148, 79, 79n161
Duménil, Girard,, 68n95, 75n131

Eagleton, Terry, 48nn1–2, 50n7, 75, 75n135, 76, 76nn141–143, 80n168
Eckhart, Meister, 98
Egan, Kerry, 151n32, 161, 161n63
Elliot, T. S., 48n2, 80
Ellis, Neville, 2n5
Emerson, Ralph Waldo, 84n182
Engels, Friedrich, 20n37, 22nn45, 69n96
Engster, Daniel, 6n23, 143n12
Erdoes, Richard, 24nn53, 35n89, 95n43, 115n15, 172n98
Erikson, Erik, 152n43

Fanon, Frantz, 8n29
Farley, Edward, 128n64, 174, 174n103, 175
Fergusson, Niall, 50n6, 62nn60–61, 67n84
Feuerbach, Ludwig, 91, 91nn25–26, 92n27, 98, 103, 103n57
Fingarette, Herbert, 104, 104n60, 135, 135nn86–88
Flower, Michael, 77n146, 143n12
Ford, Gerald, 74
Ford, Richard Q, 43, 43nn108–109
Foster, John Bellamy, 3n10, 20n37, 69n96, 77nn144–145, 80n167
Foucault, Léon, 4n19
Francis of Assisi, Saint, 6n22, 88
Frank, Thomas, 38n96, 75, 75n137
Fraser, Nancy, 14n13, 38n96, 45n114, 77n148

NAME INDEX

Freud, Sigmund, 12, 12n6–17, 13, 17n22, 19–20, 19nn33–35, 21–23, 22nn41–42, 41, 83n177, 98, 118n24, 123nn52–53, 136–37, 136n92, 137n93, 150
Friedman, Milton, 73, 73n121, 77
Fulbright, J. William, 65n79

Gabbard, Glen, 102nn54–55
Gardner, Lloyd, 9n30, 49n5
Gauthier, David, 120–21, 120nn34–35, 121nn39–40, 121nn43–47, 122n48
Gellner, Ernst, 51nn12–13, 52n16, 52n18, 57, 57n39
George, Andrew R., 15, 15n17
Gilman, Sandor, 112, 112n9
Girard, René, 42, 42n106
Giroux, Henry, 79, 80n163
Go, Julian, 65n74
Goldman, Emma, 149
Goodall, Jane, 84n183
Gray, John, 75n132
Grayling, A. C., 12n4, 21n39, 27n58, 82n176, 98n47, 118nn26–27, 120n33, 145n15
Greenspan, Alan, 70n106
Grosby, Steven, 51–52, 51n14, 51nn9–11, 52n17, 54n24, 55, 55n27, 57, 57nn41–42
Groys, Boris, 6n23, 53n20
Guattari, Felix, 48, 49n4, 79, 79n159, 84n182
Guess, Raymond, 121n41
Guevara, Che, 165
Gutiérrez, Gustavo, 145n18, 164n69

Hagedorn, Ludger, 140n4
Hall, Douglas John, 66
Hall, Stuart, 16, 17n25, 66n83, 130n66
Hamilton, Clive, 29n61
Hamington, Maurice, 6n23, 77n146, 143n12
Hardt, Michael, 67, 67n88
Harman, Chris, 16nn18–19, 22–23, 22nn46, 35, 35n90
Hartwich, Wolf-Daniel, 166–67, 166nn78–83, 167nn85–86

Harvey, David, 68n93, 73n119, 73nn118–119, 75n131
Hayek, F. A., 71n111, 73n121, 77
Hegel, Georg, 120
Heidegger, Martin, 100, 120–22
Held, Virginia, 6n23, 143n12
Helsel, Phillip Browning, 3n13, 6n23, 144n12
Hendricks, Obery M., 71n110
Henriksen, Jan-Olav, 174, 174n105, 176, 176n115
Herod, King (biblical figure), 128
Herring, George C., 18n31
Hinds, Jay Paul, 155n48
Hobbes, Thomas, 11–12, 13, 19, 20, 21, 23, 27n58, 30, 39, 41, 52, 71, 144n13
Hochschild, Arlie, 79, 79n161
Hoggett, Paul, 3n13
Holifield, E. Brooks, 112nn4–5
Honneth, Axel, 38n96
Horkheimer, Max, 7–8
Horsley, Richard A., 25n54, 43, 43n107, 44n113, 145n18, 164, 164nn69–71, 177
Howard-Brook, Wes, 164n69
Hudis, Peter, 71, 71n108
Hughes, Richard T., 61n50

Ikenberry, G. John, 65n80
Illouz, Eva, 79
Isenberg, Nancy, 23, 23nn49, 36n93

Jackson, Andrew, 62
Jaspers, Karl, 32n79
Jefferson, Thomas, 62
Jeffords, Clayton, 27n59
Jodelet, Denise, 112n8
Johnson, Chalmers, 18n30, 40n101, 61, 61n55, 61nn52–53, 64n70, 66n86, 67, 67n86
Jones, Daniel Stedman, 72n114, 73n120, 74n124

Kamal, Baher, 59n45
Kaplan, Amy, 18n29, 61n51, 65, 65n77
Kassouf, Susan, 83n178
Kaur, Valerie, 140n3, 177, 177n120

NAME INDEX

Keller, Catherine, 3n13, 175, 175nn108–110, 177
Kendi, Ibram X., 23, 23nn51
Kerven, Rosiland, 24nn53, 35n89, 95n43, 115n15, 172n98
Kestenberg, Judith, 157n54
Keynes, John Maynard, 71n110
Kierkegaard, Søren, 142, 142n7
King, Martin Luther, Jr., 118n24, 165
King, Michael, 75n138, 76n140
Kinzer, Steven, 40n101, 63n63
Kirsch, Adam, 4n15, 173–74n99
Kishik, David, 11nn1–2, 111n2, 144–45n14
Klein, Naomi, 2n7, 38n96, 40n101, 64, 64n69, 73n118
Knapp, Elizabeth, 112
Kohn, Eduardo, 87n4, 101n52, 107n67, 124n55, 159, 159n61
Kojève, Alexander, 53n20
Kolbert, Elizabeth, 2n7
Kompridis, Nikolas, 89n17
Korsgaard, Christine M., 146n22, 161n64
Kovel, Joel, 86n2, 102n56, 111n1, 113n10
Krauthammer, Charles, 66n82
Krippner, Greta, 70n105
Kuznick, Peter J., 18n31, 70n104

Laius, King (biblical figure), 128
LaMothe, Ryan, 2n6, 2n7, 6n23, 8n28, 15n16, 43n110, 57n40, 76n139, 144n12, 157n51, 174n100
Landman, Karen, 2n5
Lane, Melissa, 93nn30–31
Latour, Bruno, 80n166, 83n179, 86n1, 87n6, 89, 89n15, 90, 96–97n45, 122–23, 122nn50–51
Laval, Christian, 73, 73nn115–116, 75n133
Laymon, Kiese, 155n48
Layton, Lynne, 107, 107n65, 124, 124n56
Lear, Jonathan, 108n69, 109n70, 114n13
Leroi, Armand Marie, 82, 82n174
Levinas, Emmanuel, 120–22, 122n49
Lévy, Dominique, 68n95, 75n131

Lieven, Anatol, 58–60, 58n43, 60nn47–48
Linderman, Frank, 108–9
Locke, John, 71
London, Jack, 107n68, 130–34, 130n68, 131nn69–73, 132nn74–80, 133nn81–84
Lopez, Barry, 177, 177nn118–119, 179, 179n125
Lukács, Georg, 78, 78n151, 78n153
Lumumba, Patrice, 149
Lundestad, Geir, 61n54, 63, 63nn65–66

MacDonald, G. Jeffery, 76n140, 145n16
Macmurray, John, 154, 154nn45–46, 155n47
Macy, Joanna, 2n5
Mander, Jerry, 80, 80n165
Mann, Bonnie, 32n74
Mann, Geoff, 73n122
Mantena, Karuna, 157n52
Margalit, Avishai, 36n92
Marx, Karl, 20n37, 22, 39, 50, 71, 78
Mason, Mike, 67n89
Mattei, Clara E., 69n102
Maxwell, Jason, 150n31
McCarroll, Pamela R., 3, 3n13, 4n17
McCormack, Pamela, 4n15, 173–74n99
McDougall, John, 145n17
McKinnon, Catriona, 85n184, 115n14
Meares, Russell, 125n59
Meijer, Eva, 101n52
Melville, Herman, 62, 154
Merry, Robert W., 61n50
Milbank, John, 67n85
Miller, Lulu Clark, 83–84
Miller, Sarah Clark, 77n146, 83n180
Miller-McLemore, Bonnie, 3n13, 4n16, 4n18
Mills, Charles, 23, 23nn50, 90n18
Milton, John, 44
Moltmann, Jürgen, 145n18, 164n69, 175, 175n107
Montaigne, Michel, de, 16n21
Moore, Jason, 2–3n9, 14n13, 67n89, 80, 80n169
Morris, William, 3n10, 69n96, 76–77
Mott, Lucretia, 149

NAME INDEX

Murdoch, Iris, 13, 13n10, 14
Musk, Elon, 3n11
Mussolini, Benito, 62

Negri, Antonio, 67, 67n88
Nestorius, Archbishop of
    Constantinople, 148
Newell, Peter, 81, 81n171
Newman, Saul, 32, 32nn77–78, 42n106,
    44, 44n112
Niebuhr, H. Richard, 39n98
Nietzsche, Friedrich, 118n24
North, David, 67n85
Northcott, Michael, 138, 138n95
Novak, Michael, 76n140, 77–78,
    77nn149–150, 145n16
Nussbaum, Martha C., 6n22, 84n183,
    88, 88n11, 115n14, 146n22,
    161n64

Oakman, Douglas, 164–65, 164nn72–
    73, 165n76, 177
Oliner, Pearl M., 6n23, 144n12
Oliner, Samuel P., 6n23, 144n12
Oliver, Mary, 141n5
Orange, Donna M., 3n13
Ortiz, Alphonso, 24nn53, 35n89, 95n43,
    115n15, 172n98

Pannenberg, Wolfart, 129, 129n65, 174,
    174n104
Parks, Rosa, 149
Paterson, Matthew, 81
Patterson, Orlando, 33n84, 90n18
Peirce, Charles Sanders, 123, 123n54
Peterson, Matthew, 81n171
Pihkala, Panu, 2n5
Piketty, Thomas, 77n147, 78, 82n172
Pistor, Katharina, 69, 69n102
Plato, 13, 25, 26–27n57, 87, 90, 116,
    118n24, 120n32, 123–25, 127
Plenty Coups, Crow chief, 108–9, 114
Plutarch (philosopher), 6n22
Polkinghorne, Donald, 82n173, 82n175
Pollock, Anne, 113n10
Popper, Karl, 13, 13n11, 22–23,
    22nn44–45
Porphyry of Tyre, 6n22

Porter, Roy, 112n8
Posner, Eric A.,, 82n172
Proudhon, Pierre-Joseph, 27n58, 144n13
Prozorov, Sergei, 30, 31n71, 31n73,
    32n80, 143n9, 149n30, 156n50
Pruyser, Paul, 158, 159n59
Pulcini, Elena, 13n9
Puryear, Stephen, 88n9

Ramsay, Nancy J., 6n23, 144n12
Reagan, Ronald, 61, 73–74, 73n119
Reich, Robert B., 64n69, 68n93
Resnick, Stephen A., 68n93, 71n109,
    73n117
Reuther, Rosemary Radford, 32n74,
    145n18, 164n69
Reynolds, Jason, 23nn51
Rhodes, Edward, 64, 64n73
Ricardo, David, 68n92, 69
Rieger, Joerg, 61n50, 74n128
Rizzuto, Ana-Maria, 98
Robbins, Jeffery, 167–68, 168n90
Robinson, Fiona, 6n23, 94n35, 144n12
Rogers-Vaughn, Bruce, 6n23, 80n164,
    144n12
Rouse, W.H.D., 117nn19–23, 118n25,
    118n28, 119nn30–31, 147n24
Rousseau, Jean-Jacques, 12, 12n5, 17,
    21–22, 27n58, 41, 76
Rowley, Genny, 143n10
Rumscheidt, Barbara, 6n23, 144n12
Ryan, Alan, 12n3, 21n40, 27n58,
    41n103, 118n29
Ryn, Claes G., 61n57

Said, Edward, 16, 17n24, 130n66
Sales, Ruby, 155–57, 155n48
Samuels, Andrew, 65n76
Sandel, Michael J., 74n129, 78nn155–156
Schafer, Roy, 107n64
Scheerer, Robert, 141n6
Schell, Jonathan, 46, 46n116, 99, 99n48
Schiff, Adam, 44–45
Schmitt, Carl, 4, 30–31, 30n64, 32, 51,
    56, 63n67, 64n68
Schopenhauer, Arthur, 6n22, 88
Schüssler Fiorenza, Elizabeth, 145n18
Scull, Andrew, 111, 111n3, 112n6

Searles, Harold F., 83n178
Sedgewick, Henry, 6n22
Segundo, Jon Luis, 145n18, 164n69
Sevenhuijsen, Selma, 6n23, 144n12
Shelby, Tommie, 165n75
Shotoku Taishi, 149
Silva, Jennifer, 79, 79n157, 79n160
Singer, Peter, 6n22, 84n183, 88, 88n10, 146n22, 161n64
Skinner, Quentin, 31n67, 31nn68–70, 39n99
Slobodian, Quinn, 73n123
Smith, Adam, 68n92, 69, 71
Smith, Anthony D., 51n15
Socrates, 44, 116, 117, 118n24, 119, 120, 127, 147
Sorabji, Richard, 125n58
Spinoza, Baruch, 144n14
Stern, Donnel, 104, 104nn61–62, 135–36, 135n89, 136nn90–91, 138, 152n40
Stoermer, Edward, 2, 29n61
Stone, Oliver, 18n31, 70n104
Sunstein, Cass R., 88n8
Swift, Jonathan, 165

Tanner, Kathryn, 76n139, 76n140, 148nn25–26
Taubes, Jacob, 162, 166–67, 166n77
Taylor, Charles, 25, 25n56, 68n91
Taylor, Steven, 2n5
Teilhard de Chardin, Pierre, 6n22, 88, 88n7
Terry, Brandon M., 165n75
Thatcher, Margaret, 73n119, 75
Theodosius II, Emperor, 148
Theoharis, Liz, 157
Tillich, Paul, 175
Tiresias (Greek mythology), 118n24
Tocqueville, Alexis de, 54n25
Tonner, Phillip, 120, 120n38, 121n42
Tonstad, Linn Marie, 146n19
Tronto, Joan C., 6n23, 144n12
Trump, Donald, 18n32
Truth, Sojourner, 149
Tutu, Desmond, 149

Ugilt, Rasmus, 33n83, 150n31

Ussher, Jane M., 112n8

Valencia, Sayak, 38n96, 77n148
Van Alstyne, Robert Warren, 63n64
Villarosa, Linda, 113n10
Viveiros de Castro, Eduardo, 151n32
Vogt, Markus, 120n36
Volcker, Paul, 74
Voltaire, François-Marie Arouet, 76

Waal, Frans de, 83
Wagner, Gernot, 81, 81n170, 138, 138n94
Walker, Martin, 65n78
Wallace-Wells, David, 6n22, 22nn43
Waterson, Bill, 159
Watts, Alan, 99n48
Weber, Max, 25, 25n55, 70, 70n103, 76n139
Weil, Simone, 1n3
Weinstein, Joan, 157n54
Weintrobe, Sally, 3n13
Weitzman, Martin L., 138, 138n94
Weitzman, Matthew, 81, 81n170
Wells, Samuel, 20n38
West, Cornel, 61n57
Weyl, Eric Glen, 82n172
Whitehead, Alfred North, 26–27n57, 87, 87n3, 90, 96n44, 99–100, 100n49, 116, 116n18, 174n101, 175n106
Whitehead, Jason, 175
Wilkerson, Isabel, 22nn47, 23, 23nn48, 53n19, 90n18
Willard, Samuel, 112
Wilson, Edward O., 2n7, 22nn43, 142n8
Wilson, Woodrow, 61
Winnicott, Donald W., 150, 157–59, 157n53, 157n55, 158nn56–58, 160n62, 162
Winthrop, John, 18
Wolff, Richard D., 38n96, 68n93, 69n96, 71n109, 73n117
Wolin, Sheldon, 1n2, 7, 7nn25–26, 8n27
Wollstonecraft, Mary, 149
Wood, David, 120n37
Wood, Ellen Meiksins, 69–70, 69nn97–101, 71n107, 72, 120n37

Xenophanes (philosopher), 98

Young, Marilyn B., 3n13, 64n72
Young-Bruehl, Elisabeth, 16n21

Zaretsky, Zaretsky, 1n1
Zawisza, Rafael, 140n4, 144n14, 145n14, 148, 148n29, 168n89, 171n96

Zeddies, Timothy J., 107, 107n66, 124, 124n57
Zinn, Howard, 17n26, 18n28, 53n19, 53n21, 62n62, 72n112
Žižek, Slavoj, 23nn52
Zúñiga, Didier, 6n23, 124n55

www.ingramcontent.com/pod-product-compliance
Lightning Source LLC
Chambersburg PA
CBHW031358230426
43670CB00006B/583